MORNING *by* MORNING

for Graduates

CHARLES SPURGEON

HENDRICKSON
PUBLISHERS

Morning by Morning

© Hendrickson Publishers Marketing, LLC
P. O. Box 3473
Peabody, Massachusetts 01961–3473

ISBN 978-1-59856-685-7

First Hendrickson edition published in 1998

First printing paperback edition — April 2011

Printed in China

Publisher's Preface

Charles Haddon Spurgeon
(1834–1892)

How earnestly do I wish that my life may be spent
in lighting one soul after another with the sacred flame of eternal life!
—Charles Haddon Spurgeon

Charles Haddon Spurgeon was first and foremost a preacher. It's said that over a his lifetime—some 40 years in the pulpit—he preached to over ten million people. Preaching was his passion, and it was something at which he excelled. But it was not the theatrics or the audiences or the fame that compelled this man called "the Prince of Preachers." It was the Gospel, the message of Scripture that Jesus Christ died and rose again to redeem each and every one of us.

Spurgeon, however, did not consider the Gospel merely a fire escape. His was not simply a Sunday message. *Morning by Morning* is evidence that for Charles Spurgeon, every day was to be committed to Jesus Christ and to a fresh experience of God's provision and blessing. He once wrote about Scripture, "I would rather lay my soul asoak in half a dozen verses all day than rinse my hand in several chapters."

The daily habit of spending time with God is both an ancient tradition and a spiritual absolute. After all, the only way lives truly change is through disciplines like Scripture reading and prayer. To be like Christ, to be righteous, to be godly, we must spend time with the Holy.

Daily prayer is a gift from the Early Church. Throughout the Scripture, set times of worship—first through sacrifice and prayer, later through Scripture reading and prayer—were the standard for Israel and later, the Early Church, which after all was made up of Jewish believers.

The practice of praying at fixed hours was passed down from the Apostles, and finally formalized in the fifth century by Saint Benedict. He developed his

Rule for monastics, which established a schedule of hours, or eight times over the day when member would stop and spend time praying. What began with the recitation of the Psalms and other songs from Scripture, ultimately grew to include hymns, spiritual readings from the Church fathers and others, and other prayers.

Today, most Christian traditions encourage the habit of daily prayer and Bible reading, be it through something as formal as the Daily Office or the Liturgy of the Hours, or a program as straight-forward as a through-the-Bible-in-one-year reading plan. And most of us are very familiar and comfortable with the one-reading-per-day format as part of out daily quiet time with God. We enjoy a wealth of options today: writers like Eugene Peterson, Max Lucado, and C. S. Lewis; and traditional volumes, like Oswald Chambers' *My Utmost for His Highest*, Mrs. Cowman's *Streams in the Desert*, or *Daily Light on the Daily Path*. And of course, we can't forget subscription resources like *Our Daily Bread*.

But what is so familiar to us was not common when Charles Spurgeon wrote this book. In fact, he pioneered this format that now feels so familiar. *Morning by Morning* was published in the 1860s, and offered a new way to meet God daily. In this book, Spurgeon gave people daily what had been available only on Sundays: guidance, encouragement, inspiration, wisdom, and personal companionship into the Presence of God.

The original title for this book was *Morning by Morning; or, Daily Readings for the Family or the Closet*, referring of course, to Jesus' instructions in his Sermon on the Mount:

> But thou, when thou prayest, enter into thy closet, and when thou hast shut thy door, pray to thy Father which is in secret; and thy Father which seeth in secret shall reward thee openly. (Matt 6:6, KJV)

The word "closet" is a clue. This edition uses Spurgeon's original text, King James language and all. For many, Elizabethan English poses no difficulties; for others it makes reading a bit of a challenge. Take that challenge! Begin each day in the company of this great man who was passionate for Jesus Christ. Accept his invitation to join him, morning by morning, and learn to say with the prophet Isaiah:

> *Morning by morning he wakens me*
> *and opens my understanding to his will.*

❦

January 1

They did eat of the fruit of the land of Canaan that year.
—Joshua 5:12

ISRAEL'S weary wanderings were all over, and the promised rest was attained. No more moving tents, fiery serpents, fierce Amalekites, and howling wildernesses: they came to the land which flowed with milk and honey, and they ate the old corn of the land. Perhaps this year, beloved Christian reader, this may be thy case or mine. Joyful is the prospect, and if faith be in active exercise, it will yield unalloyed delight. To be with Jesus in the rest which remaineth for the people of God, is a cheering hope indeed, and to expect this glory so soon is a double bliss. Unbelief shudders at the Jordan which still rolls between us and the goodly land, but let us rest assured that we have already experienced more ills than death at its worst can cause us. Let us banish every fearful thought, and rejoice with exceeding great joy, in the prospect that this year we shall begin to be "forever with the Lord."

A part of the host [of God's people] will this year tarry on earth, to do service for their Lord. If this should fall to our lot, there is no reason why the New Year's text should not still be true. "We who have believed do enter into rest." The Holy Spirit is the earnest of our inheritance; he give us "glory begun below." In heaven they are secure, and so are we preserved in Christ Jesus; there they triumph over their enemies, and we have victories too. Celestial spirits enjoy communion with their Lord, and this is not denied to us; they rest in his love, and we have perfect peace in him: they hymn his praise, and it is our privilege to bless him too. We will this year gather celestial fruits on earthly ground, where faith and hope have made the desert like the garden of the Lord. Man did eat angels' food of old, and why not now? O for grace to feed on Jesus, and so to eat of the fruit of the land of Canaan this year!

JANUARY 2

Continue in prayer.
—Colossians 4:2

IT is interesting to remark how large a portion of Sacred Writ is occupied with the subject of prayer, either in furnishing examples, enforcing precepts, or pronouncing promises. We scarcely open the Bible before we read, "Then began men to call upon the name of the Lord;" and just as we are about to close the volume, the "Amen" of an earnest supplication meets our ear. Instances are plentiful. Here we find a wrestling Jacob—there a Daniel who prayed three times a day—and a David who with all his heart called upon his God. On the mountain we see Elias; in the dungeon Paul and Silas. We have multitudes of commands, and myriads of promises. What does this teach us, but the sacred importance and necessity of prayer? We may be certain that whatever God has made prominent in his Word, he intended to be conspicuous in our lives. If he has said much about prayer, it is because he knows we have much need of it. So deep are our necessities, that until we are in heaven we must not cease to pray. Dost thou want nothing? Then, I fear thou dost not know thy poverty. Hast thou no mercy to ask of God? Then, may the Lord's mercy show thee thy misery! A prayerless soul is a Christless soul. Prayer is the lisping of the believing infant, the shout of the fighting believer, the requiem of the dying saint falling asleep in Jesus. It is the breath, the watchword, the comfort, the strength, the honor of a Christian. If thou be a child of God, thou wilt seek thy Father's face, and live in thy Father's love. Pray that this year thou mayst be holy, humble, zealous, and patient; have closer communion with Christ, and enter oftener into the banqueting-house of his love. Pray that thou mayst be an example and a blessing unto others, and that thou mayst live more to the glory of thy Master. The motto for this year must be, "Continue in prayer."

JANUARY 3

I will give thee for a covenant of the people.
—Isaiah 49:8

JESUS Christ is himself the sum and substance of the covenant, and as one of its gifts he is the property of every believer. Believer, canst thou estimate what thou hast gotten in Christ? "In him dwelleth all the fullness of the Godhead bodily." Consider that word "God" and its infinity, and then meditate upon "perfect man" and all his beauty; for all that Christ, as God and man, ever had, or can have, is thine—out of pure free favor, passed over to thee to be thine entailed property forever. Our blessed Jesus, as God, is omniscient, omnipresent, omnipotent. Will it not console you to know that all these great and glorious attributes are altogether yours? Has he power? That power is yours to support and strengthen you, to overcome your enemies, and to preserve you even to the end. Has he love? Well, there is not a drop of love in his heart which is not yours; you may dive into the immense ocean of his love, and you may say of it all, "It is mine." Hath he justice? It may seem a stern attribute, but even that is yours, for he will by his justice see to it that all which is promised to you in the covenant of grace shall be most certainly secured to you. And all that he has as *perfect man* is yours. As a perfect man, the Father's delight was upon him. He stood accepted by the Most High. O believer, God's acceptance of Christ is thine acceptance; for knowest thou not that the love which the Father set on a perfect Christ, he sets on thee *now*? For all that Christ did is thine. That perfect righteousness which Jesus wrought out, when through his stainless life he kept the law and made it honorable, is thine, and is imputed to thee. Christ is in the covenant.

> My God, I am thine—what a comfort divine!
> What a blessing to know that the Savior is mine!
> In the heavenly Lamb thrice happy I am,
> And my heart, it doth dance at the sound of his name.

JANUARY 4

*Grow in grace, and in the knowledge
of our Lord and Savior Jesus Christ.*
—2 Peter 3:18

ROW in grace"—not in one grace only, but in *all* grace. Grow in that root-grace, *faith*. Believe the promises more firmly than you have done. Let faith increase in fullness, constancy, simplicity. Grow also in *love*. Ask that your love may become extended, more intense, more practical, influencing every thought, word, and deed. Grow likewise in *humility*. Seek to lie very low, and know more of your own nothingness. As you grow *downward* in humility, seek also to grow *upward*—having nearer approaches to God in prayer and more intimate fellowship with Jesus. May God the Holy Spirit enable you to "grow in the knowledge of our Lord and Savior." He who grows not in the knowledge of Jesus, refuses to be blessed. To know him is "life eternal," and to advance in the knowledge of him is to increase in happiness. He who does not long to know more of Christ, knows nothing of him yet. Whoever hath sipped this wine will thirst for more, for although Christ doth satisfy, yet it is such a satisfaction, that the appetite is not cloyed, but whetted. If you know the love of Jesus—as the hart panteth for the water-brooks, so will you pant after deeper droughts of his love. If you do not desire to know him better, then you love him not, for love always cries, "Nearer, nearer." Absence from Christ is hell; but the presence of Jesus is heaven. Rest not then content without an increasing acquaintance with Jesus. Seek to know more of him in his divine nature, in his human relationship, in his finished work, in his death, in his resurrection, in his present glorious intercession, and in his future royal advent. Abide hard by the Cross, and search the mystery of his wounds. An increase of love to Jesus, and a more perfect apprehension of his love to us is one of the best tests of growth in grace.

January 5

And God saw the light, that it was good:
and God divided the light from the darkness.
—Genesis 1:4

LIGHT might well be good since it sprang from that fiat of goodness, "Let there be light." We who enjoy it should be more grateful for it than we are, and see more of God in it and by it. Light *physical* is said by Solomon to be sweet, but *gospel* light is infinitely more precious, for it reveals eternal things, and ministers to our immortal natures. When the Holy Spirit gives us *spiritual* light, and opens our eyes to behold the glory of God in the face of Jesus Christ, we behold sin in its true colors, and ourselves in our real position; we see the Most Holy God as he reveals himself, the plan of mercy as he propounds it, and the world to come as the Word describes it. Spiritual light has many beams and prismatic colors, but whether they be knowledge, joy, holiness, or life, all are divinely good. If the light received be thus good, what must the *essential* light be, and how glorious must be the place where he reveals himself! O Lord, since light is so good, give us more of it, and more of thyself, the true light.

No sooner is there a good thing in the world, than *a division is necessary.* Light and darkness have no communion; God has divided them, let us not confound them. Sons of light must not have fellowship with deeds, doctrines, or deceits of darkness. The children of the day must be sober, honest, and bold in their Lord's work, leaving the works of darkness to those who shall dwell in it forever. Our Churches should by discipline divide the light from the darkness, and we should by our distinct separation from the world do the same. In judgment, in action, in hearing, in teaching, in association, we must discern between the precious and the vile, and maintain the great distinction which the Lord made upon the world's first day. O Lord Jesus, be thou our light throughout the whole of this day, for thy light is the light of men.

JANUARY 6

Casting all your care upon him; for he careth for you.
—1 Peter 5:7

IT is a happy way of soothing sorrow when we can feel—"HE careth for *me*." Christian! do not dishonor religion by always wearing a brow of care; come, cast your burden upon your Lord. You are staggering beneath a weight which your Father would not feel. What seems to you a crushing burden, would be to him but as the small dust of the balance. Nothing is so sweet as to

> Lie passive in God's hands,
> And know no will but his.

O child of suffering, be thou patient; God has not passed thee over in his providence. He who is the feeder of sparrows, will also furnish *you* with what you need. Sit not down in despair; hope on, hope ever. Take up the arms of faith against a sea of trouble, and your opposition shall yet end your distresses. *There is* One who careth for you. His eye is fixed on you, his heart beats with pity for your woe, and his hand omnipotent shall yet bring you the needed help. The darkest cloud shall scatter itself in showers of mercy. The blackest gloom shall give place to the morning. He, if thou art one of his family, will bind up thy wounds, and heal thy broken heart. Doubt not his grace because of thy tribulation, but believe that he loveth thee as much in seasons of trouble as in times of happiness. What a serene and quiet life might you lead if you would leave providing to the God of providence! With a little oil in the cruse, and a handful of meal in the barrel, Elijah outlived the famine, and you will do the same. If God cares for you, why need you care too? Can you trust him for your soul, and not for your body? He has never refused to bear your burdens, he has never fainted under their weight. Come, then, soul! have done with fretful care, and leave all thy concerns in the hand of a gracious God.

January 7

For me to live is Christ
—Philippians 1:21

THE believer did not always live to Christ. He began to do so when God the Holy Spirit convinced him of sin, and when by grace he was brought to see the dying Savior making a propitiation for his guilt. From the moment of the new and celestial birth the man begins to live to Christ. Jesus is to believers the one pearl of great price, for whom we are willing to part with all that we have. He has so completely won our heart, that it beats alone for him; to his glory we would live, and in defense of his gospel we would die; he is the pattern of our life, and the model after which we would sculpture our character. Paul's words mean more than most men think; they imply that the *aim and end of his life was Christ*—nay, his life itself was Jesus. In the words of an ancient saint, he did eat, and drink, and sleep eternal life. Jesus was his very breath, the soul of his soul, the heart of his heart, the life of his life. Can you say, as a professing Christian, that you live up to this idea? Can you honestly say that for you to live is Christ? Your business—are you doing it *for Christ?* Is it not done for self-aggrandizement and for family advantage? Do you ask, "Is that a mean reason?" For the *Christian* it is. He professes to live for Christ; how can he live for another object without committing a spiritual adultery? Many there are who carry out this principle in some measure; but who is there that dare say that he hath lived wholly for Christ as the apostle did? Yet, this alone is the true life of a Christian—its source, its sustenance, its fashion, its end, all gathered up in one word—*Christ Jesus.* Lord, accept me; I here present myself, praying to live only in thee and to thee. Let me be as the bullock which stands between the plough and the altar, to work or to be sacrificed; and let my motto be, "Ready for either."

JANUARY 8

The iniquity of the holy things.
—Exodus 28:38

WHAT a veil is lifted up by these words, and what a disclosure is made! It will be humbling and profitable for us to pause awhile and see this sad sight. The iniquities of our public worship, its hypocrisy, formality, lukewarmness, irreverence, wandering of heart and forgetfulness of God, what a full measure have we there! Our work for the Lord, its emulation, selfishness, carelessness, slackness, unbelief, what a mass of defilement is there! Our private devotions, their laxity, coldness, neglect, sleepiness, and vanity, what a mountain of dead earth is there! If we looked more carefully we should find this iniquity to be far greater than appears at first sight. Dr. Payson, writing to his brother, says,

> My parish, as well as my heart, very much resembles the garden of the sluggard; and what is worse, I find that very many of my desires for the melioration of both, proceed either from pride or vanity or indolence. I look at the weeds which overspread my garden, and breathe out an earnest wish that they were eradicated. But why? What prompts the wish? It may be that I may walk out and say to myself, "In what fine order is my garden kept!' This is *pride.* Or, it may be that my neighbors may look over the wall and say, "How finely your garden flourishes!" This is *vanity.* Or I may wish for the destruction of the weeds, because I am weary of pulling them up. This is *indolence.*

So that even our desires after holiness may be polluted by ill motives. Under the greenest sods worms hide themselves; we need not look long to discover them. How cheering is the thought, that when the High Priest bore the iniquity of the holy things he wore upon his brow the words, *"Holiness to the Lord:"* and even so while Jesus bears our sin, he presents before his Father's face not our unholiness, but his own holiness. O for grace to view our great High Priest by the eye of faith!

January 9

I will be their God.
—Jeremiah 31:33

HRISTIAN! here is all thou canst require. To make thee happy thou wantest something that shall satisfy thee; and is not this enough? If thou canst pour this promise into thy cup, wilt thou not say, with David, "My cup runneth over; I have more than heart can wish"? When this is fulfilled, *"I am thy God,"* art thou not possessor of all things? Desire is insatiable as death, but he who filleth all in all can fill it. The capacity of our wishes who can measure? but the immeasurable wealth of God can more than overflow it. I ask thee if thou art not complete when God is thine? Dost thou want anything but God? Is not his all-sufficiency enough to satisfy thee if all else should fail? But thou wantest more than quiet satisfaction; thou desirest *rapturous delight.* Come, soul, here is music fit for heaven in this thy portion, for God is the Maker of Heaven. Not all the music blown from sweet instruments, or drawn from living strings, can yield such melody as this sweet promise, "I will be their God." Here is a deep sea of bliss, a shoreless ocean of delight; come, bathe thy spirit in it; swim an age, and thou shalt find no shore; dive throughout eternity, and thou shalt find no bottom. "I will be their God." If this do not make thine eyes sparkle, and thy heart beat high with bliss, then assuredly thy soul is not in a healthy state. But thou wantest more than present delights—thou cravest something concerning which thou mayest exercise *hope;* and what more canst thou hope for than the fulfillment of this great promise, "I will be their God"? This is the masterpiece of all the promises; its enjoyment makes a heaven below, and will make a heaven above. Dwell in the light of thy Lord, and let thy soul be always ravished with his love. Get out the marrow and fatness which this portion yields thee. Live up to thy privileges, and rejoice with unspeakable joy.

JANUARY 10

There is laid up for me a crown of righteousness.
—2 Timothy 4:8

OUBTING one! thou hast often said, "I fear I shall never enter heaven." Fear not! all the people of God shall enter there. I love the quaint saying of a dying man, who exclaimed,

> I have no fear of going home; I have sent all before me;
> God's finger is on the latch of my door, and I am ready for
> him to enter.

"But," said one, "are you not afraid lest you should miss your inheritance?" "Nay," said he,

> . . . nay; there is one crown in heaven which the angel Gabriel could not
> wear, it will fit no head but mine. There is one throne in heaven which
> Paul the apostle could not fill; it was made for me, and I shall have it.

O Christian, what a joyous thought! Thy portion is secure; "there remaineth a rest." "But cannot I forfeit it?" No, it is entailed. If I be a child of God I shall not lose it. It is mine as securely as if I were there. Come with me, believer, and let us sit upon the top of Nebo, and view the goodly land, even Canaan. Seest thou that little river of death glistening in the sunlight, and across it dost thou see the pinnacles of the eternal city? Dost thou mark the pleasant country, and all its joyous inhabitants? Know, then, that if thou could'st fly across thou wouldst see written upon one of its many mansions, "This remaineth for such a one; preserved for him only. He shall be caught up to dwell forever with God." Poor doubting one, see the fair inheritance; it is thine. If thou believest in the Lord Jesus, if thou hast repented of sin, if thou hast been renewed in heart, thou art one of the Lord's people, and there is a place reserved for thee, a crown laid up for thee, a harp specially provided for thee. No one else shall have thy portion, it is reserved in heaven for thee, and thou shalt have it ere long, for there shall be no vacant thrones in glory when all the chosen are gathered in.

JANUARY 11

These have no root.
—Luke 8:13

Y soul, examine thyself this morning by the light of this text. Thou hast received the word with joy; thy feelings have been stirred and a lively impression has been made; but, remember, that to receive the word in the ear is one thing, and to receive Jesus into thy very soul is quite another; superficial feeling is often joined to inward hardness of heart, and a lively impression of the word is not always a lasting one. In the parable, the seed in one case fell upon ground having a rocky bottom, covered over with a thin layer of earth; when the seed began to take root, its downward growth was hindered by the hard stone and therefore it spent its strength in pushing its green shoot aloft as high as it could, but having no inward moisture derived from root nourishment, it withered away. Is this my case? Have I been making a fair show in the flesh without having a corresponding inner life? Good growth takes place upwards and downwards at the same time. Am I rooted in sincere fidelity and love to Jesus? If my heart remains unsoftened and unfertilized by grace, the good seed may germinate for a season, but it must ultimately wither, for it cannot flourish on a rocky, unbroken, unsanctified heart. Let me dread a godliness as rapid in growth and as wanting in endurance as Jonah's gourd; let me count the cost of being a follower of Jesus, above all let me feel the energy of his Holy Spirit, and then I shall possess an abiding and enduring seed in my soul. If my mind remains as obdurate as it was by nature, the sun of trial will scorch, and my hard heart will help to cast the heat the more terribly upon the ill-covered seed, and my religion will soon die, and my despair will be terrible; therefore, O heavenly Sower, plough me first, and then cast the truth into me, and let me yield thee a bounteous harvest.

JANUARY 12

Ye are Christ's.
—1 Corinthians 3:23

"YE *are* Christ's." You are his by donation, for the Father gave you to the Son; his by his bloody purchase, for he counted down the price for your redemption; his by dedication, for you have consecrated yourself to him; his by relation, for you are named by his name, and made one of his brethren and joint-heirs. Labor practically to show the world that you are the servant, the friend, the bride of Jesus. When tempted to sin, reply, "I cannot do this great wickedness, for I am Christ's." Immortal principles forbid the friend of Christ to sin. When wealth is before you to be won by sin, say that you are Christ's, and touch it not. Are you exposed to difficulties and dangers? Stand fast in the evil day, remembering that you are Christ's. Are you placed where others are sitting down idly, doing nothing? Rise to the work with all your powers; and when the sweat stands upon your brow, and you are tempted to loiter, cry,

> No, I cannot stop, for I am Christ's. If I were not purchased by blood, I might be like Issachar, crouching between two burdens; but I am Christ's, and cannot loiter.

When the siren song of pleasure would tempt you from the path of right, reply, "Thy music cannot charm me; I am Christ's." When the cause of God invites thee, give thyself to it; when the poor require thee, give thy goods and thyself away, for thou art Christ's. Never belie thy profession. Be thou ever one of those whose manners are Christian, whose speech is like the Nazarene, whose conduct and conversation are so redolent of heaven, that all who see you may know that you are the Savior's, recognizing in you his features of love and his countenance of holiness. "I am a Roman!" was of old a reason for integrity; far more, then, let it be your argument for holiness, "I am Christ's!"

JANUARY 13

Jehoshaphat made ships of Tharshish
to go to Ophir for gold: but they went not;
for the ships were broken at Ezion-geber.
—1 Kings 22:48

OLOMON'S ships had returned in safety, but Jehoshaphat's vessels never reached the land of gold. Providence prospers one, and frustrates the desires of another, in the same business and at the same spot, yet the Great Ruler is as good and wise at one time as another. May we have grace today, in the remembrance of this text, to bless the Lord for ships broken at Ezion-geber, as well as for vessels freighted with temporal blessings; let us not envy the more successful, nor murmur at our losses as though we were singularly and specially tried. Like Jehoshaphat, we may be precious in the Lord's sight, although our schemes end in disappointment.

The secret cause of Jehoshaphat's loss is well worthy of notice, for it is the root of very much of the suffering of the Lord's people; it was his alliance with a sinful family, his fellowship with sinners. In 2 Chron. 20:37, we are told that the Lord sent a prophet to declare, "Because thou hast joined thyself with Ahaziah, the Lord hath broken thy works." This was a fatherly chastisement, which appears to have been blest to him; for in the verse which succeeds our morning's text we find him refusing to allow his servants to sail in the same vessels with those of the wicked king. Would to God that Jehoshaphat's experience might be a warning to the rest of the Lord's people, to avoid being unequally yoked together with unbelievers! A life of misery is usually the lot of those who are united in marriage, or in any other way of their own choosing, with the men of the world. O for such love to Jesus that, like him, we may be holy, harmless, undefiled, and separate from sinners; for if it be not so with us, we may expect to hear it often said, "The Lord hath broken thy works."

JANUARY 14

Mighty to save.
—Isaiah 63:1

Y the words "to save" we understand the whole of the great work of salvation, from the first holy desire onward to complete parro; indeed, here is all mercy in one word. Christ is not only "mighty to save" those who repent, but he is able to make men repent. He will carry those to heaven who believe; but he is, moreover, mighty to give men new hearts and to work faith in them. He is mighty to make the man who hates holiness love it, and to constrain the despiser of his name to bend the knee before him. Nay, this is not all the meaning, for the divine power is equally seen in the after-work. The life of a believer is a series of miracles wrought by "the Mighty God." The bush burns, but is not consumed. He is mighty to keep his people holy after he has made them so, and to preserve them in his fear and love until he consummates their spiritual existence in heaven. Christ's might doth not lie in making a believer and then leaving him to shift for himself; but he who begins the good work carries it on; he who imparts the first germ of life in the dead soul, prolongs the divine existence, and strengthens it until it bursts asunder every bond of sin, and the soul leaps from earth, perfected in glory. Believer, here is encouragement. Art thou praying for some beloved one? Oh, give not up thy prayers, for Christ is "mighty to save." You are powerless to reclaim the rebel, but your Lord is Almighty. Lay hold on that mighty arm, and rouse it to put forth its strength. Does your own case trouble you? Fear not, for his strength is sufficient for you. Whether to begin with others, or to carry on the work in you, Jesus is "mighty to save;" the best proof of which lies in the fact that he has saved *you.* What a thousand mercies that you have not found him mighty to destroy!

JANUARY 15

Do as thou hast said.
—2 Samuel 7:25

OD'S promises were never meant to be thrown aside as waste paper; he intended that they should be used. God's gold is not miser's money, but is minted to be traded with. Nothing pleases our Lord better than to see his promises put in circulation; he loves to see his children bring them up to him, and say, "Lord, do as thou hast said." We glorify God when we plead his promises. Do you think that God will be any the poorer for giving you the riches he has promised? Do you dream that he will be any the less holy for giving holiness to you? Do you imagine he will be any the less pure for washing you from your sins? He has said:

> "Come now, and let us reason together," saith the Lord: "though your sins be as scarlet, they shall be as white as snow; though they be red like crimson, they shall be as wool."

Faith lays hold upon the promise of pardon, and it does not delay, saying, "This is a precious promise, I wonder if it be true?" but it goes straight to the throne with it, and pleads, "Lord, here is the promise, 'Do as thou hast said.'" Our Lord replies, "Be it unto thee even as thou wilt." When a Christian grasps a promise, if he do not take it to God, he dishonors him; but when he hastens to the throne of grace, and cries, "Lord, I have nothing to recommend me but this, 'Thou hast said it;'" then his desire shall be granted. Our heavenly Banker delights to cash his own notes. Never let the promise rust. Draw the word of promise out of its scabbard, and use it with holy violence. Think not that God will be troubled by your importunately reminding him of his promises. He loves to hear the loud outcries of needy souls. It is his delight to bestow favors. He is more ready to hear than you are to ask. The sun is not weary of shining, nor the fountain of flowing. It is God's nature to keep his promises; therefore go at once to the throne with "Do as thou hast said."

JANUARY 16

I will help thee, saith the Lord.
—Isaiah 41:14

HIS morning let us hear the Lord Jesus speak to each one of us: "I will *help* thee."

It is but a small thing for me, thy God, to *help* thee. Consider what I have done already. What! not help thee? Why, I bought thee with my blood. What! not help thee? I have died for thee; and if I have done the greater, will I not do the less? *Help* thee! It is the least thing I will ever do for thee; I *have* done more, and *will* do more. Before the world began I chose thee. I made the covenant for thee. I laid aside my glory and became a man for thee; I gave up my life for thee; and if I did all this, I will surely help thee now. In helping thee, I am giving thee what I have bought for thee already. If thou hadst need of a thousand times as much help, I would give it thee; thou requirest little compared with what I am ready to give. 'Tis much for thee to need, but it is nothing for me to bestow. "*Help* thee?" Fear not! If there were an ant at the door of thy granary asking for help, it would not ruin thee to give him a handful of thy wheat; and thou art nothing but a tiny insect at the door of my all-sufficiency. "I will help thee."

O my soul, is not this enough? Dost thou need more strength than the omnipotence of the United Trinity? Dost thou want more wisdom than exists in the Father, more love than displays itself in the Son, or more power than is manifest in the influences of the Spirit? Bring hither thine empty pitcher! Surely this well will fill it. Haste, gather up thy wants, and bring them here—thine emptiness, thy woes, thy needs. Behold, this river of God is full for thy supply; what canst thou desire beside? Go forth, my soul, in this thy might. The Eternal God is thine helper!

Fear not, I am with thee, oh, be not dismay'd!
I, I am thy God, and will still give thee aid.

JANUARY 17

And I looked, and, lo, a Lamb stood on the mount Sion.
—Revelation 14:1

THE apostle John was privileged to look within the gates of heaven, and in describing what he saw, he begins by saying, "I looked, and, lo, a Lamb!" This teaches us that the chief object of contemplation in the heavenly state is "the Lamb of God, which taketh away the sins of the world." Nothing else attracted the apostle's attention so much as the person of that Divine Being, who hath redeemed us by his blood. He is the theme of the songs of all glorified spirits and holy angels. Christian, here is joy for thee; thou hast looked, and thou hast seen the Lamb. Through thy tears thine eyes have seen the Lamb of God taking away thy sins. Rejoice, then. In a little while, when thine eyes shall have been wiped from tears, thou wilt see the same Lamb *exalted on his throne.* It is the joy of thy heart to hold daily fellowship with Jesus; thou shalt have the same joy to a higher degree in heaven; thou shalt enjoy the constant vision of his presence; thou shalt dwell with him forever. "I looked, and, lo, a Lamb!" Why, that Lamb is heaven itself; for as good Rutherford says, "Heaven and Christ are the same thing;" to be with Christ is to be in heaven, and to be in heaven is to be with Christ. That prisoner of the Lord very sweetly writes in one of his glowing letters—

> O my Lord Jesus Christ, if I could be in heaven without thee, it would be a hell; and if I could be in hell, and have thee still, it would be a heaven to me, for thou art all the heaven I want.

It is true, is it not, Christian? Does not thy soul say so?

> *Not all the harps above*
> *Can make a heavenly place,*
> *If God his residence remove,*
> *Or but conceal his face.*

All thou needest to make thee blessed, supremely blessed, is "to be with Christ."

JANUARY 18

There remaineth therefore a rest to the people of God.
—Hebrews 4:9

OW different will be the state of the believer in heaven from what it is here! Here he is born to toil and suffer weariness, but in the land of the immortal, fatigue is never known. Anxious to serve his Master, he finds his strength unequal to his zeal: his constant cry is, "Help me to serve thee, O my God." If he be thoroughly active, he will have much Labor; not too much for his will, but more than enough for his power, so that he will cry out, "I am not wearied *of* the Labor, but I am wearied *in it*." Ah! Christian, the hot day of weariness lasts not forever; the sun is nearing the horizon; it shall rise again with a brighter day than thou hast ever seen upon a land where they serve God day and night, and yet rest from their labors. *Here*, rest is but partial, *there*, it is *perfect*. *Here*, the Christian is always unsettled; he feels that he has not yet attained. *There*, all are at rest; they have attained the summit of the mountain; they have ascended to the bosom of their God. Higher they cannot go. Ah, toil-worn laborer, only think when thou shalt rest forever! Canst thou conceive it? It is a rest *eternal*; a rest that "remaineth." Here, my best joys bear "mortal" on their brow; my fair flowers fade; my dainty cups are drained to dregs; my sweetest birds fall before Death's arrows; my most pleasant days are shadowed into nights; and the flood-tides of my bliss subside into ebbs of sorrow; but *there*, everything is immortal; the harp abides unrusted, the crown unwithered, the eye undimmed, the voice unfaltering, the heart unwavering, and the immortal being is wholly absorbed in infinite delight. Happy day! happy! when mortality shall be swallowed up of life, and the Eternal Sabbath shall begin.

January 19

I sought him, but I found him not.
—Song of Solomon 3:1

ELL me where you lost the company of Christ, and I will tell you the most likely place to find him. Have you lost Christ in the closet by restraining prayer? Then it is there you must seek and find him. Did you lose Christ by sin? You will find Christ in no other way but by the giving up of the sin, and seeking by the Holy Spirit to mortify the member in which the lust doth dwell. Did you lose Christ by neglecting the Scriptures? You must find Christ in the Scriptures. It is a true proverb, "Look for a thing where you dropped it, it is there." So look for Christ where you lost him, for he has not gone away. But it is hard work to go back for Christ. Bunyan tells us, the pilgrim found the piece of the road back to the Arbor of Ease, where he lost his roll, the hardest he had ever traveled. Twenty miles onward is easier than to go one mile back for the lost evidence. Take care, then, when you find your Master, to cling close to him. But how is it you have lost him? One would have thought you would never have parted with such a precious friend, whose presence is so sweet, whose words are so comforting, and whose company is so dear to you! How is it that you did not watch him every moment for fear of losing sight of him? Yet, since you have let him go, what a mercy that you are seeking him, even though you mournfully groan, "O that I knew where I might find him!" Go on seeking , for it is dangerous to be without thy Lord. Without Christ you are like a sheep without its shepherd; like a tree without water at its roots; like a sere leaf in the tempest—not bound to the tree of life. With thine whole heart seek him, and he will be found of thee: only give thyself thoroughly up to the search, and verily, thou shalt yet discover him to thy joy and gladness.

JANUARY 20

Abel was a keeper of sheep.
—Genesis 4:2

S a shepherd, Abel *sanctified his work to the glory of God, and offered a sacrifice of blood upon his altar, and the Lord had respect unto Abel and his offering.* This early type of our Lord is exceedingly clear and distinct. Like the first streak of light which tinges the east at sunrise, it does not reveal everything, but it clearly manifests the great fact that the sun is coming. As we see Abel, a shepherd and yet a priest, offering a sacrifice of sweet smell unto God, we discern our Lord, who brings before his Father a sacrifice to which Jehovah ever hath respect. Abel was hated by his brother—hated without a cause; and even so was the Savior: the natural and carnal man hated the accepted man in whom the Spirit of grace was found, and rested not until his blood had been shed. Abel fell, and sprinkled his altar and sacrifice with his own blood, and therein sets forth the Lord Jesus slain by the enmity of man while serving as a priest before the Lord. "The good Shepherd layeth down his life for the sheep." Let us weep over him as we view him slain by the hatred of mankind, staining the horns of his altar with his own blood. *Abel's blood speaketh.* "The Lord said unto Cain, 'The voice of thy brother's blood crieth unto me from the ground.'" The blood of Jesus hath a mighty tongue, and the import of its prevailing cry is not vengeance but mercy. It is precious beyond all preciousness to stand at the altar of our good Shepherd! to see him bleeding there as the slaughtered priest, and then to hear his blood speaking peace to all his flock, peace in our conscience, peace between Jew and Gentile, peace between man and his offended Maker, peace all down the ages of eternity for blood-washed men. Abel is the first shepherd in order of time, but our hearts shall ever place Jesus first in order of excellence. Thou great Keeper of the sheep, we the people of thy pasture bless thee with our whole hearts when we see thee slain for us.

JANUARY 21

And so all Israel shall be saved.
—Romans 11:26

WHEN Moses sang at the Red Sea, it was his joy to know that *all* Israel[ites] were safe. Not a drop of spray fell from that solid wall until the last of God's Israel had safely planted his foot on the other side the flood. That done, immediately the floods dissolved into their proper place again, but not till then. Part of that song was, "Thou in thy mercy hast led forth the people which thou hast redeemed." In the last time, when the elect shall sing the song of Moses, the servant of God, and of the Lamb, it shall be the boast of Jesus, "Of all whom thou hast given me, I have lost none." In heaven there shall not be a vacant throne.

> For all the chosen race
> Shall meet around the throne,
> Shall bless the conduct of his grace,
> And make his glories known.

As many as God hath chosen, as many as Christ hath redeemed, as many as the Spirit hath called, as many as believe in Jesus, shall safely cross the dividing sea. We are not all safely landed yet:

> Part of the host have crossed the flood,
> And part are crossing now.

The vanguard of the army has already reached the shore. We are marching through the depths; we are at this day following hard after our Leader into the heart of the sea. Let us be of good cheer: the rear-guard shall soon be where the vanguard already is; the last of the chosen ones shall soon have crossed the sea, and then shall be heard the song of triumph, when all are secure. But oh! if one were absent—oh! if one of his chosen family should be cast away—it would make an everlasting discord in the song of the redeemed, and cut the strings of the harps of paradise, so that music could never be extorted from them.

JANUARY 22

Son of man, what is the vine tree, more than any tree,
or than a branch which is among the trees of the forest?
—Ezekiel 15:2

THESE words are for the humbling of God's people; they are called God's vine, but what are they by nature more than others? They, by God's goodness, have become fruitful, having been planted in a good soil; the Lord hath trained them upon the walls of the sanctuary, and they bring forth fruit to his glory; but what are they without their God? What are they without the continual influence of the Spirit, begetting fruitfulness in them? O believer, learn to reject pride, seeing that thou hast no ground for it. Whatever thou art, thou hast nothing to make thee proud. The more thou hast, the more thou art in debt to God; and thou shouldst not be proud of that which renders thee a debtor. Consider thine origin; look back to what thou wast. Consider what thou wouldst have been but for divine grace. Look upon thyself as thou art now. Doth not thy conscience reproach thee? Do not thy thousand wanderings stand before thee, and tell thee that thou art unworthy to be called his son? And if he hath made thee anything, art thou not taught thereby that it is grace which hath made thee to differ? Great believer, thou wouldst have been a great sinner if God had not made thee to differ. O thou who art valiant for truth, thou wouldst have been as valiant for error if grace had not laid hold upon thee. Therefore, be not proud, though thou hast a large estate—a wide domain of grace, thou hadst not once a single thing to call thine own except thy sin and misery. Oh! strange infatuation, that thou, who hast borrowed everything, shouldst think of exalting thyself; a poor dependent pensioner upon the bounty of thy Savior, one who hath a life which dies without fresh streams of life from Jesus, and yet proud! Fie on thee, O silly heart!

JANUARY 23

I have exalted one chosen out of the people.
—Psalm 89:19

HY was Christ chosen out of the people? Speak, my heart, for heart-thoughts are best. Was it not that he might be able to be *our brother*, in the blest tie of kindred blood? Oh, what relationship there is between Christ and the believer! The believer can say,

> I have a Brother in heaven; I may be poor, but I have a Brother who is rich, and is a King, and will he suffer me to want while he is on his throne? Oh, no! He loves me; he is my Brother.

Believer, wear this blessed thought, like a necklace of diamonds, around the neck of thy memory; put it, as a golden ring, on the finger of recollection, and use it as the King's own seal, stamping the petitions of thy faith with confidence of success. He is a brother born for adversity, treat him as such.

Christ was also chosen out of the people that he might know our wants and sympathize with us. "He was tempted in all points like as we are, yet without sin." In all our sorrows we have his sympathy. Temptation, pain, disappointment, weakness, weariness, poverty—he knows them all, for he has felt all. Remember this, Christian, and let it comfort thee. However difficult and painful thy road, it is marked by the footsteps of thy Savior; and even when thou reachest the dark valley of the shadow of death, and the deep waters of the swelling Jordan, thou wilt find his footprints there. In all places whithersoever we go, he has been our forerunner; each burden we have to carry, has once been laid on the shoulders of Immanuel.

> His way was much rougher and darker than mine;
> Did Christ, my Lord, suffer, and shall I repine?

Take courage! Royal feet have left a blood-red track upon the road, and consecrated the thorny path forever.

JANUARY 24

Surely he shall deliver thee from the snare of the fowler.
—Psalm 91:3

OD delivers his people from the snare of the fowler in two senses. *From,* and *out of.* First, he delivers them *from* the snare—does not let them enter it; and secondly, if they should be caught therein, he delivers them *out of* it. The first promise is the most precious to some; the second is the best to others.

"He shall deliver thee *from* the snare." How? Trouble is often the means whereby God delivers us. God knows that our backsliding will soon end in our destruction, and he in mercy sends the rod. We say, "Lord, why is this?" not knowing that our trouble has been the means of delivering us from far greater evil. Many have been thus saved from ruin by their sorrows and their crosses; these have frightened the birds from the net. At other times, God keeps his people *from* the snare of the fowler by giving them great spiritual strength, so that when they are tempted to do evil they say, "How can I do this great wickedness, and sin against God?" But what a blessed thing it is that if the believer shall, in an evil hour, come into the net, yet God will bring him *out* of it! O backslider, be cast down, but do not despair. Wanderer though thou hast been, hear what thy Redeemer saith—"Return, O backsliding children; I will have mercy upon you." But you say you cannot return, for you are a captive. Then listen to the promise—"Surely he shall deliver thee out of the snare of the fowler." Thou shalt yet be brought out of all evil into which thou hast fallen, and though thou shalt never cease to repent of thy ways, yet he that hath loved thee will not cast thee away; he will receive thee, and give thee joy and gladness, that the bones which he has broken may rejoice. No bird of paradise shall die in the fowler's net.

January 25

I will mention the lovingkindnesses of the Lord,
and the praises of the Lord,
according to all that the Lord hath bestowed on us.
—Isaiah 63:7

AND canst *thou* not do this? Are there no mercies which thou *hast experienced*? What though thou art gloomy now, canst thou forget that blessed hour when Jesus met thee, and said, "Come unto me"? Canst thou not remember that rapturous moment when he snapped thy fetters, dashed thy chains to the earth, and said, "I came to break thy bonds and set thee free"? Or if the love of thine espousals be forgotten, there must surely be some precious milestone along the road of life not quite grown over with moss, on which thou canst read a happy memorial of his mercy towards thee? What, didst thou never have a sickness like that which thou art suffering now, and did he not restore thee? Wert thou never poor before, and did he not supply thy wants? Wast thou never in straits before, and did he not deliver thee? Arise, go to the river of thine experience, and pull up a few bulrushes, and plait them into an ark, wherein thine infant-faith may float safely on the stream. Forget not what thy God has done for thee; turn over the book of thy remembrance, and consider the days of old. Canst thou not remember the hill Mizar? Did the Lord never meet with thee at Hermon? Hast thou never climbed the Delectable Mountains? Hast thou never been helped in time of need? Nay, I know thou hast. Go back, then, a little way to the choice mercies of yesterday, and though all may be dark *now*, light up the lamps of the past, they shall glitter through the darkness, and thou shalt trust in the Lord till the day break and the shadows flee away. "Remember, O Lord, thy tender mercies and thy lovingkindnesses, for they have been ever of old."

JANUARY 26

Your heavenly Father.
—Matthew 6:26

OD'S people are doubly his children, they are his offspring by creation, and they are his sons by adoption in Christ. Hence they are privileged to call him, "Our Father which art in heaven." Father! Oh, what precious word is that. Here is *authority:* "If I be a Father, where is mine honor?" If ye be sons, where is your obedience? Here is *affection* mingled with authority; an authority which does not provoke rebellion; an obedience demanded which is most cheerfully rendered—which would not be withheld even if it might. The obedience which God's children yield to him must be *loving* obedience. Do not go about the service of God as slaves to their taskmaster's toil, but run in the way of his commands because it is your *Father's* way. Yield your bodies as instruments of righteousness, because righteousness is your Father's will, and *his* will should be the will of his child. *Father!*—Here is a kingly attribute so sweetly veiled in love, that the King's crown is forgotten in the King's face, and his scepter becomes, not a rod of iron, but a silver scepter of mercy—the scepter indeed seems to be forgotten in the tender hand of him who wields it. Father!—Here is honor and love. How great is a Father's love to his children! That which friendship cannot do, and mere benevolence will not attempt, a father's heart and hand must do for his sons. They are his offspring, he must bless them; they are his children, he must show himself strong in their defense. If an earthly father watches over his children with unceasing love and care, how much more does our heavenly Father? Abba, Father! He who can say this, hath uttered better music than cherubim or seraphim can reach. There is heaven in the depth of that word—Father! There is all I can ask; all my necessities can demand; all my wishes can desire. I have all in all to all eternity when I can say, "Father."

January 27

And of his fullness have all we received.
—John 1:16

THESE words tell us that there is a fullness in Christ. There is a fullness of essential Deity, for "in him dwelleth all the fullness of the Godhead." There is a fullness of perfect manhood, for in him, bodily, that Godhead was revealed. There is a fullness of atoning efficacy in his blood, for "the blood of Jesus Christ, his Son, cleanseth us from all sin." There is a fullness of justifying righteousness in his life, for "there is therefore now no condemnation to them that are in Christ Jesus." There is a fullness of divine prevalence in his plea, for "He is able to save to the uttermost them that come unto God by him; seeing he ever liveth to make intercession for them." There is a fullness of victory in his death, for through death he destroyed him that had the power of death, that is the devil. There is a fullness of efficacy in his resurrection from the dead, for by it "we are begotten again unto a lively hope." There is a fullness of triumph in his ascension, for "when he ascended up on high, he led captivity captive, and received gifts for men." There is a fullness of blessings of every sort and shape; a fullness of grace to pardon, of grace to regenerate, of grace to sanctify, of grace to preserve, and of grace to perfect. There is a fullness at all times; a fullness of comfort in affliction; a fullness of guidance in prosperity. A fullness of every divine attribute, of wisdom, of power, of love; a fullness which it were impossible to survey, much less to explore. "It pleased the Father that in him should *all* fullness dwell." Oh, what a fullness must this be of which *all* receive! Fullness, indeed, must there be when the stream is always flowing, and yet the well springs up as free, as rich, as full as ever. Come, believer, and get all thy need supplied; ask largely, and thou shalt receive largely, for this "fullness" is inexhaustible, and is treasured up where all the needy may reach it, even in Jesus, Immanuel—God with us.

JANUARY 28

Perfect in Christ Jesus.
—*Colossians* 1:28

O you not feel in your own soul that perfection is not in you? Does not every day teach you that? Every tear which trickles from your eye, weeps "imperfection;" every sigh which bursts from your heart, cries "imperfection;" every harsh word which proceeds from your lip, mutters "imperfection." You have too frequently had a view of your own heart to dream for a moment of any perfection *in yourself.* But amidst this sad consciousness of imperfection, here is comfort for you—you are "perfect *in Christ Jesus.*" In God's sight, you are "complete in him;" *even now* you are "accepted in the Beloved." But there is a second perfection, yet to be realized, which is sure to all the seed. Is it not delightful to look forward to the time when every stain of sin shall be removed from the believer, and he shall be presented faultless before the throne, without spot, or wrinkle, or any such thing? The Church of Christ then will be so pure, that not even the eye of Omniscience will see a spot or blemish in her; so holy and so glorious, that Hart did not go beyond the truth when he said —

> With my Savior's garments on,
> Holy as the Holy One.

Then shall we know, and taste, and feel the happiness of this vast but short sentence, "Complete in Christ." Not till then shall we fully comprehend the heights and depths of the salvation of Jesus. Doth not thy heart leap for joy at the thought of it? Black as thou art, thou shalt be white one day; filthy as thou art, thou shalt be clean. Oh, it is a marvelous salvation this! Christ takes a worm and transforms it into an angel; Christ takes a black and deformed thing and makes it clean and matchless in his glory, peerless in his beauty, and fit to be the companion of seraphs. O my soul, stand and admire this blessed truth of perfection in Christ.

January 29

The things which are not seen.
—2 Corinthians 4:18

IN our Christian pilgrimage it is well, for the most part, to be looking forward. Forward lies the crown, and onward is the goal. Whether it be for hope, for joy, for consolation, or for the inspiring of our love, the future must, after all, be the grand object of the eye of faith. Looking into the future we see sin cast out, the body of sin and death destroyed, the soul made perfect, and fit to be a partaker of the inheritance of the saints in light. Looking further yet, the believer's enlightened eye can see death's river passed, the gloomy stream forded, and the hills of light attained on which standeth the celestial city; he seeth himself enter within the pearly gates, hailed as more than conqueror, crowned by the hand of Christ, embraced in the arms of Jesus, glorified with him, and made to sit together with him on his throne, even as he has overcome and has sat down with the Father on his throne. The thought of this future may well relieve the darkness of the past and the gloom of the present. The joys of heaven will surely compensate for the sorrows of earth. Hush, my fears! this world is but a narrow span, and thou shalt soon have passed it. Hush, hush, my doubts! death is but a narrow stream, and thou shalt soon have forded it. Time, how short—eternity, how long! Death, how brief—immortality, how endless! Methinks I even now eat of Eshcol's clusters, and sip of the well which is within the gate. The road is so, so short! I shall soon be there.

> When the world my heart is rending
> With its heaviest storm of care,
> My glad thoughts to heaven ascending,
> Find a refuge from despair.
> Faith's bright vision shall sustain me
> Till life's pilgrimage is past;
> Fears may vex and troubles pain me,
> I shall reach my home at last.

JANUARY 30

*When thou hearest the sound of a going
in the tops of the mulberry trees, then thou shalt bestir thyself.*
—2 Samuel 5:24

HE members of Christ's Church should be very prayerful, always seeking the unction of the Holy One to rest upon their hearts, that the kingdom of Christ may come, and that his "will be done on earth, even as it is in heaven;" but there are times when God seems especially to favor Zion, such seasons ought to be to them like "the sound of a going in the tops of the mulberry trees." We ought then to be doubly prayerful, doubly earnest, wrestling more at the throne than we have been wont to do. Action should then be prompt and vigorous. The tide is flowing—now let us pull manfully for the shore. O for Pentecostal outpourings and Pentecostal labors. Christian, in *yourself* there are times "when thou hearest the sound of a going in the tops of the mulberry trees." You have a peculiar power in prayer; the Spirit of God gives you joy and gladness; the Scripture is open to you; the promises are applied; you walk in the light of God's countenance; you have peculiar freedom and liberty in devotion, and more closeness of communion with Christ than was your wont. Now, at such joyous periods when you hear the "sound of a going in the tops of the mulberry trees," is the time to bestir yourself; now is the time to get rid of any evil habit, while God the Spirit helpeth your infirmities. Spread your sail; but remember what you sometimes sing—

> I can only spread the sail;
> Thou! Thou! must breathe the auspicious gale.

Only be sure you have the sail up. Do not miss the gale for want of preparation for it. Seek help of God, that you may be more earnest in duty when made more strong in faith; that you may be more constant in prayer when you have more liberty at the throne; that you may be more holy in your conversation whilst you live more closely with Christ.

January 31

The Lord, our Righteousness.
—Jeremiah 23:6

IT will always give a Christian the greatest calm, quiet, ease, and peace, to think of the perfect righteousness of Christ. How often are the saints of God downcast and sad! I do not think they ought to be. I do not think they would if they could always see their perfection in Christ. There are some who are always talking about corruption, and the depravity of the heart, and the innate evil of the soul. This is quite true, but why not go a little further, and remember that we are "perfect in Christ Jesus." It is no wonder that those who are dwelling upon their own corruption should wear such downcast looks; but surely if we call to mind that "Christ is made unto us righteousness," we shall be of good cheer. What though distresses afflict me, though Satan assault me, though there may be many things to be experienced before I get to heaven, those are done for me in the covenant of divine grace; there is nothing wanting in my Lord, Christ hath done it all. On the cross he said, "It is finished!" and if it be finished, then am I complete in him, and can rejoice with joy unspeakable and full of glory,

> Not having mine own righteousness, which is of the law, but that which is through the faith of Christ, the righteousness which is of God by faith.

You will not find on this side [of] heaven a holier people than those who receive into their hearts the doctrine of Christ's righteousness. When the believer says, "I live on Christ alone; I rest on him solely for salvation; and I believe that, however unworthy, I am still saved in Jesus;" then there rises up as a motive of gratitude this thought—"Shall I not live to Christ? Shall I not love him and serve him, seeing that I am saved by his merits?" "The love of Christ constraineth us," "that they which live should not henceforth live unto themselves but unto him which died for them." If saved by imputed righteousness, we shall greatly value imparted righteousness.

FEBRUARY 1

They shall sing in the ways of the Lord.—Psalm 138:5

HE time when Christians begin to sing in the ways of the Lord is when they first lose their burden at the foot of the Cross. Not even the songs of the angels seem so sweet as the first song of rapture which gushes from the inmost soul of the forgiven child of God. You know how John Bunyan describes it. He says when poor Pilgrim lost his burden at the Cross, he gave three great leaps, and went on his way singing—

> Blest Cross! blest Sepulcher! blest rather be
> The Man that there was put to shame for me!

Believer, do you recollect the day when *your* fetters fell off? Do you remember the place when Jesus met you, and said,

> I have loved thee with an everlasting love; I have blotted out as a cloud thy transgressions, and as a thick cloud thy sins; they shall not be mentioned against thee any more forever.

Oh! what a sweet season is that when Jesus takes away the pain of sin. When the Lord first pardoned my sin, I was so joyous that I could scarce refrain from dancing. I thought on my road home from the house where I had been set at liberty, that I must tell the stones in the street the story of my deliverance. So full was my soul of joy, that I wanted to tell every snow-flake that was falling from heaven of the wondrous love of Jesus, who had blotted out the sins of one of the chief of rebels. But it is not only at the commencement of the Christian life that believers have reason for song; as long as they live they discover cause to sing in the ways of the Lord, and their experience of his constant lovingkindness leads them to say, "I will bless the Lord at all times: his praise shall continually be in my mouth." See to it, brother, that thou magnifiest the Lord *this day.*

> Long as we tread this desert land,
> New mercies shall new songs demand.

FEBRUARY 2

Without the shedding of blood, [there] is no remission.
—Hebrews 9:22

THIS is the voice of unalterable truth. In none of the Jewish ceremonies were sins, even typically, removed without blood-shedding. In no case, by no means can sin be pardoned without atonement. It is clear, then, that there is no hope for me out of Christ; for there is no other blood-shedding which is worth a thought as an atonement for sin. Am I, then, believing in him? Is the blood of his atonement truly applied to my soul? All men are on a level as to their need of him. If we be never so moral, generous, amiable, or patriotic, the rule will not be altered to make an exception for us. Sin will yield to nothing less potent than the blood of him whom God hath set forth as a propitiation. What a blessing that there is the one way of pardon! Why should we seek another?

Persons of merely formal religion cannot understand how we can rejoice that all our sins are forgiven us for Christ's sake. Their works, and prayers, and ceremonies, give them very poor comfort; and well may they be uneasy, for they are neglecting the one great salvation, and endeavoring to get remission without blood. My soul, sit down, and behold the justice of God as bound to punish sin; see that punishment all executed upon thy Lord Jesus, and fall down in humble joy, and kiss the dear feet of him whose blood has made atonement for thee. It is in vain when conscience is aroused to fly to feelings and evidences for comfort: this is a habit which we learned in the Egypt of our legal bondage. The only restorative for a guilty conscience is a sight of Jesus suffering on the cross. "The blood is the life thereof," says the Levitical law, and let us rest assured that it is the life of faith and joy and every other holy grace.

> Oh! how sweet to view the flowing
> Of my Savior's precious blood;
> With divine assurance knowing
> He has made my peace with God.

FEBRUARY 3

Therefore, brethren, we are debtors.
—Romans 8:12

S God's creatures, we are all debtors to him: to obey him with all our body, and soul, and strength. Having broken his commandments, as we all have, we are debtors to his justice, and we owe to him a vast amount which we are not able to pay. But of the *Christian* it can be said that he does not owe God's *justice* anything, for Christ has paid the debt his people owed; for this reason the believer owes the more to *love*. I am a debtor to God's grace and forgiving mercy; but I am no debtor to his justice, for he will never accuse me of a debt already paid. Christ said, "It is finished!" and by that he meant, that whatever his people owed was wiped away forever from the book of remembrance. Christ, to the uttermost, has satisfied divine justice; the account is settled; the handwriting is nailed to the cross; the receipt is given, and we are debtors to God's justice no longer. But then, because we are not debtors to our Lord in that sense, we become ten times more debtors to God than we should have been otherwise. Christian, pause and ponder for a moment. What a debtor thou art to divine *sovereignty!* How much thou owest to his disinterested love, for he gave his own Son that he might die for thee. Consider how much you owe to his forgiving *grace*, that after ten thousand affronts he loves you as infinitely as ever. Consider what you owe to his *power;* how he has raised you from your death in sin; how he has preserved your spiritual life; how he has kept you from falling; and how, though a thousand enemies have beset your path, you have been able to hold on your way. Consider what you owe to his *immutability*. Though you have changed a thousand times, he has not changed once. Thou art as deep in debt as thou canst be to every attribute of God. To God thou owest thyself, and all thou hast—yield thyself as a living sacrifice, it is but thy reasonable service.

FEBRUARY 4

The love of the Lord.
—Hosea 3:1

BELIEVER, *look back* through all thine experience, and think of the way whereby the Lord thy God has led thee in the wilderness, and how he hath fed and clothed thee every day—how he hath borne with thine ill manners—how he hath put up with all thy murmurings, and all thy longings after the flesh-pots of Egypt—how he has opened the rock to supply thee, and fed thee with manna that came down from heaven. Think of how his grace has been sufficient for thee in all thy troubles—how his blood has been a pardon to thee in all thy sins—how his rod and his staff have comforted thee. When thou hast thus looked back upon the love of the Lord, then let faith survey his love *in the future*, for remember that Christ's covenant and blood have something more in them than the *past. He* who has loved thee and pardoned thee, shall never cease to love and pardon. He is Alpha, and he shall be Omega also: he is first, and he shall be *last.* Therefore, bethink thee, when thou shalt pass through the valley of the shadow of death, thou needest fear no evil, for he is with thee. When thou shalt stand in the cold floods of Jordan, thou needest not fear, for death cannot separate thee from his love; and when thou shalt come into the mysteries of eternity thou needest not tremble,

> For I am persuaded, that neither death; nor life, nor angels, nor principalities, nor powers, nor things present, nor things to come, nor height, nor depth, nor any other creature, shall be able to separate us from the love of God, which is in Christ Jesus our Lord.

Now, soul, is not thy love refreshed? Does not this make thee love Jesus? Doth not a flight through illimitable plains of the ether of love inflame thy heart and compel thee to delight thyself in the Lord thy God? Surely as we meditate on "the love of the Lord," our hearts burn within us, and we long to love him more.

FEBRUARY 5

The Father sent the Son to be the Savior of the world.
—1 John 4:14

IT is a sweet thought that Jesus Christ did not come forth without his Father's permission, authority, consent, and assistance. He was sent of the Father, that he might be the Savior of men. We are too apt to forget that, while there are distinctions as to the *persons* in the Trinity, there are no distinctions of *honor*. We too frequently ascribe the honor of our salvation, or at least the depths of its benevolence, more to Jesus Christ than we do the Father. This is a very great mistake. What if Jesus came? Did not his Father send him? If he spake wondrously, did not his Father pour grace into his lips, that he might be an able minister of the new covenant? He who knoweth the Father, and the Son, and the Holy Ghost as he should know them, never setteth one before another in his love; he sees them at Bethlehem, at Gethsemane, and on Calvary, all equally engaged in the work of salvation. O Christian, hast thou put thy confidence in the Man Christ Jesus? Hast thou placed thy reliance solely on him? And art thou united with him? Then believe that thou art united unto the God of heaven. Since to the Man Christ Jesus thou art brother, and holdest closest fellowship, thou art linked thereby with God the Eternal, and "the Ancient of days" is thy Father and thy friend. Didst thou ever consider the depth of love in the heart of Jehovah, when God the Father equipped his Son for the great enterprise of mercy? If not, be this thy day's meditation. The *Father* sent him! Contemplate that subject. Think how Jesus works what the *Father* wills. In the wounds of the dying Savior see the love of the great I AM. Let every thought of Jesus be also connected with the Eternal, ever-blessed God, for "It pleased the Lord to bruise him; he hath put him to grief."

February 6

Praying always.
—Ephesians 6:18

HAT multitudes of prayers we have put up from the first moment when we learned to pray. Our first prayer was a prayer for ourselves; we asked that God would have mercy upon us, and blot out our sin. He heard us. But when he had blotted out our sins like a cloud, then we had more prayers for ourselves. We have had to pray for sanctifying grace, for constraining and restraining grace; we have been led to crave for a fresh assurance of faith, for the comfortable application of the promise, for deliverance in the hour of temptation, for help in the time of duty, and for succor in the day of trial. We have been compelled to go to God for our souls, as constant beggars asking for everything. Bear witness, children of God, you have never been able to get anything for your souls elsewhere. All the bread your soul has eaten has come down from heaven, and all the water of which it has drank has flowed from the living rock—Christ Jesus the Lord. Your soul has never grown rich in itself; it has always been a pensioner upon the daily bounty of God; and hence your prayers have ascended to heaven for a range of spiritual mercies all but infinite. Your wants were innumerable, and therefore the supplies have been infinitely great, and your prayers have been as varied as the mercies have been countless. Then have you not cause to say, "I love the Lord, because he hath heard the voice of my supplication"? For as your prayers have been many, so also have been God's answers to them. He has heard you in the day of trouble, has strengthened you, and helped you, even when you dishonored him by trembling and doubting at the mercy seat. Remember this, and let it fill your heart with gratitude to God, who has thus graciously heard your poor weak prayers. "Bless the Lord, O my soul, and forget not all his benefits."

FEBRUARY 7

Arise ye, and depart.
—Micah 2:10

HE hour is approaching when the message will come to us, as it comes to all—

Arise, and go forth from the home in which thou hast dwelt, from the city in which thou hast done thy business, from thy family, from thy friends. Arise, and take thy last journey.

And what know we of the journey? And what know we of the country to which we are bound? A little we have read thereof, and somewhat has been revealed to us by the Spirit; but how little do we know of the realms of the future! We know that there is a black and stormy river called "Death." God bids us cross it, promising to be with us. And, after death, what cometh? What wonder-world will open upon our astonished sight? What scene of glory will be unfolded to our view? No traveler has ever returned to tell. But we know enough of the heavenly land to make us welcome our summons thither with joy and gladness. The journey of death may be dark, but we may go forth on it fearlessly, knowing that God is with us as we walk through the gloomy valley, and therefore we need fear no evil. We shall be departing from all we have known and loved here, but we shall be going to our Father's house—to our Father's home, where Jesus is—to that royal "city which hath foundations, whose builder and maker is God." This shall be our *last* removal, to dwell forever with him we love, in the midst of his people, in the presence of God. Christian, meditate much on heaven, it will help thee to press on, and to forget the toil of the way. This vale of tears is but the pathway to the better country: this world of woe is but the stepping-stone to a world of bliss.

> Prepare us, Lord, by grace divine,
> For thy bright courts on high;
> Then bid our spirits rise, and join
> The chorus of the sky.

🌾

February 8

Thou shalt call his name Jesus.
—Matthew 1:21

HEN a person is dear, everything connected with him becomes dear for his sake. Thus, so precious is the person of the Lord Jesus in the estimation of all true believers, that everything about him they consider to be inestimable beyond all price. "All thy garments smell of myrrh, and aloes, and cassia," said David, as if the very vestments of the Savior were so sweetened by his person that he could not but love them. Certain it is, that there is not a spot where that hallowed foot hath trodden—there is not a word which those blessed lips have uttered—nor a thought which his loving Word has revealed—which is not to us precious beyond all price. And this is true of the *names* of Christ—they are all sweet in the believer's ear. Whether he be called the Husband of the Church, her Bridegroom, her Friend; whether he be styled the Lamb slain from the foundation of the world—the King, the Prophet, or the Priest—every title of our Master—Shiloh, Emmanuel, Wonderful, the Mighty Counselor—every name is like the honeycomb dropping with honey, and luscious are the drops that distil from it. But if there be one name sweeter than another in the believer's ear, it is the name of *Jesus.* Jesus! it is the name which moves the harps of heaven to melody. Jesus! the life of all our joys. If there be one name more charming, more precious than another, it is this name. It is woven into the very warp and woof of our psalmody. Many of our hymns begin with it, and scarcely any, that are good for anything, end without it. It is the sum total of all delights. It is the music with which the bells of heaven ring; a song in a word; an ocean for comprehension, although a drop for brevity; a matchless oratorio in two syllables; a gathering up of the hallelujahs of eternity in five letters.

> Jesus, I love thy charming name,
> 'Tis music to mine ear.

FEBRUARY 9

And David enquired of the Lord.
—2 Samuel 5:23

WHEN David made this enquiry he had just fought the Philistines, and gained a signal victory. The Philistines came up in great hosts, but, by the help of God, David had easily put them to flight. Note, however, that when they came a second time, David did not go up to fight them without enquiring of the Lord. Once he had been victorious, and he might have said, as many have in other cases,

> I shall be victorious again; I may rest quite sure that if I have conquered once I shall triumph yet again. Wherefore should I tarry to seek at the Lord's hands?

Not so, David. He had gained one battle by the strength of the Lord; he would not venture upon another until he had ensured the same. He enquired, "Shall I go up against them?" He waited until God's sign was given. Learn from David to take no step without God. Christian, if thou wouldst know the path of duty, take God for thy compass; if thou wouldst steer thy ship through the dark billows, put the tiller into the hand of the Almighty. Many a rock might be escaped, if we would let our Father take the helm; many a shoal or quicksand we might well avoid, if we would leave to his sovereign will to choose and to command. The Puritan said, "As sure as ever a Christian carves for himself, he'll cut his own fingers;" this is a great truth. Said another old divine, "he that goes before the cloud of God's providence goes on a fool's errand;" and so he does. We must mark God's providence leading us; and if providence tarries, tarry till providence comes. He who goes before providence, will be very glad to run back again. "I will instruct thee and teach thee in the way which thou shalt go," is God's promise to his people. Let us, then, take all our perplexities to him, and say, "Lord, what wilt thou have me to do?" Leave not thy chamber this morning without enquiring of the Lord.

February 10

I know how to abound.
—Philippians 4:12

THERE are many who know "how to be abased" who have not learned "how to abound." When they are set upon the top of a pinnacle their heads grow dizzy, and they are ready to fall. The Christian far oftener disgraces his profession in prosperity than in adversity. It is a dangerous thing to be prosperous. The crucible of adversity is a less severe trial to the Christian than the fining-pot of prosperity. Oh, what leanness of soul and neglect of spiritual things have been brought on through the very mercies and bounties of God! Yet this is not a matter of necessity, for the apostle tells us that he knew how to abound. When he had much he knew how to use it. Abundant grace enabled him to bear abundant prosperity. When he had a full sail he was loaded with much ballast, and so floated safely. It needs more than human skill to carry the brimming cup of mortal joy with a steady hand, yet Paul had learned that skill, for he declares, "In all things I am instructed both to be full and to be hungry." It is a divine lesson to know how to be full, for the Israelites were full once, but while the flesh was yet in their mouth, the wrath of God came upon them. Many have asked for mercies that they might satisfy their own hearts' lust. Fullness of bread has often made fullness of blood, and that has brought on wantonness of spirit. When we have much of God's providential mercies, it often happens that we have but little of God's grace, and little gratitude for the bounties we have received. We are full and we forget God: satisfied with earth, we are content to do without heaven. Rest assured it is harder to know how to be full than it is to know how to be hungry—so desperate is the tendency of human nature to pride and forgetfulness of God. Take care that you ask in your prayers that God would teach you "how to be full."

> Let not the gifts thy love bestows
> Estrange our hearts from thee.

FEBRUARY 11

And they took knowledge of them, that they had been with Jesus.
—Acts 4:13

Christian should be a striking likeness of Jesus Christ. You have read lives of Christ, beautifully and eloquently written, but the best life of Christ is his living biography, written out in the words and actions of his people. If we were what we profess to be, and what we should be, we should be pictures of Christ; yea, such striking likenesses of him, that the world would not have to hold us up by the hour together, and say, "Well, it seems somewhat of a likeness;" but they would, when they once beheld us, exclaim,

> He has been with Jesus; he has been taught of him; he is like him; he has caught the very idea of the holy Man of Nazareth, and he works it out in his life and every-day actions.

A Christian should be like Christ in his *boldness*. Never blush to own your religion; your profession will never disgrace you: take care you never disgrace *that*. Be like Jesus, very valiant for your God. Imitate him in your *loving* spirit; think kindly, speak kindly, and do kindly, that men may say of you, "He has been with Jesus." Imitate Jesus in his *holiness*. Was he zealous for his Master? So be you; ever go about doing good. Let not time be wasted: it is too precious. Was he self-denying, never looking to his own interest? Be the same. Was he devout? Be you fervent in your prayers. Had he deference to his Father's will? So submit yourselves to him. Was he patient? So learn to endure. And best of all, as the highest portraiture of Jesus, try to forgive your enemies, as he did; and let those sublime words of your Master, "Father, forgive them; for they know not what they do," always ring in your ears. Forgive, as you hope to be forgiven. Heap coals of fire on the head of your foe by your kindness to him. Good for evil, recollect, is godlike. Be godlike, then; and in all ways and by all means, so live that all may say of you, "He has been with Jesus."

February 12

For as the sufferings of Christ abound in us,
so our consolation also aboundeth by Christ.
—2 Corinthians 1:5

HERE is a blessed proportion. The Ruler of Providence bears a pair of scales—in this side he puts his people's trials, and in that he puts their consolations. When the scale of trial is nearly empty, you will always find the scale of consolation in nearly the same condition; and when the scale of trials is full, you will find the scale of consolation just as heavy. When the black clouds gather most, the light is the more brightly revealed to us. When the night lowers and the tempest is coming on, the Heavenly Captain is always closest to his crew. It is a blessed thing, that when we are most cast down, then it is that we are most lifted up by the consolations of the Spirit. One reason is, because *trials make more room for consolation.* Great hearts can only be made by great troubles. The spade of trouble digs the reservoir of comfort deeper, and makes more room for consolation. God comes into our heart—he finds it full—he begins to break our comforts and to make it empty; then there is more room for grace. The humbler a man lies, the more comfort he will always have, because he will be more fitted to receive it. Another reason why we are often most happy in our troubles, is this—*then we have the closest dealings with God.* When the barn is full, man can live without God: when the purse is bursting with gold, we try to do without so much prayer. But once take our *gourds* away, and we want our *God;* once cleanse the idols out of the house, then we are compelled to honor Jehovah. "Out of the depths have I cried unto thee, O Lord." There is no cry so good as that which comes from the bottom of the mountains; no prayer half so hearty as that which comes up from the depths of the soul, through deep trials and afflictions. Hence they bring us to God, and we are happier; for nearness to God is happiness. Come, troubled believer, fret not over your heavy troubles, for they are the heralds of weighty mercies.

FEBRUARY 13

Behold, what manner of love the Father hath bestowed upon us,
that we should be called the sons of God:
therefore the world knoweth us not, because it knew him not.
Beloved, now are we the sons of God.
—1 John 3:1–2

EHOLD, what manner of love the Father hath bestowed upon *us."* Consider who we were, and what *we* feel ourselves to be even now when corruption is powerful in us, and you will wonder at our adoption. Yet *we* are called *"the sons of God."* What a high relationship is that of a son, and what privileges it brings! What care and tenderness the son expects from his father, and what love the father feels towards the son! But all *that,* and more than *that,* we now have through Christ. As for the temporary drawback of suffering with the elder brother, this we accept as an honor: "Therefore the world knoweth us not, because it knew him not." We are content to be unknown with him in his humiliation, for we are to be exalted with him. *"Beloved, now are we the sons of God."* That is easy to read, but it is not so easy to feel. How is it with your heart this morning? Are you in the lowest depths of sorrow? Does corruption rise within your spirit, and grace seem like a poor spark trampled under foot? Does your faith almost fail you? Fear not, it is neither your graces nor feelings on which you are to live: you must live simply by faith on Christ. With all these things against us, *now*—in the very depths of our sorrow, wherever we may be—*now,* as much in the valley as on the mountain, "Beloved, *now* are we the sons of God." "Ah, but," you say, "see how I am arrayed! my graces are not bright; my righteousness does not shine with apparent glory." But read the next: *"It doth not yet appear what we shall be: but we know that, when he shall appear, we shall be like him."* The Holy Spirit shall purify our minds, and divine power shall refine our bodies, then shall *we see him as he is.*

February 14

*And his allowance was a continual allowance given him of the king,
a daily rate for every day, all the days of his life.*
—2 Kings 25:30

JEHOIACHIN was not sent away from the king's palace with a store to last him for months, but his provision was given him as a daily pension. Herein he well pictures the happy position of all the Lord's people. A daily portion is *all that a man really wants.* We do not need tomorrow's supplies; that day has not yet dawned, and its wants are as yet unborn. The thirst which we may suffer in the month of June does not need to be quenched in February, for we do not feel it yet; if we have enough for each day as the days arrive we shall never know want. Sufficient for the day is *all that we can enjoy.* We cannot eat or drink or wear more than the day's supply of food and raiment; the surplus gives us the care of storing it, and the anxiety of watching against a thief. One staff aids a traveler, but a bundle of staves is a heavy burden. Enough is not only as good as a feast, but is all that the veriest glutton can truly enjoy. This is *all that we should expect;* a craving for more than this is ungrateful. When our Father does not give us more, we should be content with his daily allowance. Jehoiachin's case is ours, we have a *sure* portion, a portion *given us of the king,* a *gracious* portion, and a *perpetual* portion. Here is surely ground for thankfulness.

Beloved Christian reader, in matters of grace *you need a daily supply.* You have no store of strength. Day by day must you seek help from above. It is a very sweet assurance that *a daily portion is provided for you.* In the word, through the ministry, by meditation, in prayer, and waiting upon God you shall receive renewed strength. In Jesus all needful things are laid up for you. Then *enjoy your continual allowance.* Never go hungry while the daily bread of grace is on the table of mercy.

FEBRUARY 15

To him be glory both now and forever.
—2 Peter 3:18

EAVEN will be full of the ceaseless praises of Jesus. Eternity! thine unnumbered years shall speed their everlasting course, but forever and forever, "to him be glory." Is he not a "Priest forever after the order of Melchisedek"? "To him be glory." Is he not king forever?—King of kings and Lord of lords, the everlasting Father? "To him be glory *forever.*" Never shall his praises cease. That which was bought with blood deserves to last while immortality endures. The glory of the cross must never be eclipsed; the luster of the grave and of the resurrection must never be dimmed. O Jesus! thou shalt be praised forever. Long as immortal spirits live—long as the Father's throne endures—forever, forever, unto thee shall be glory. Believer, you are anticipating the time when you shall join the saints above in ascribing all glory to Jesus; but are you glorifying him *now*? The apostle's words are, "To him be glory both now and forever." Will you not this day make it your prayer?

> Lord, help me to glorify thee; I am poor, help me to glorify thee by contentment; I am sick, help me to give thee honor by patience; I have talents, help me to extol thee by spending them for thee; I have time, Lord, help me to redeem it, that I may serve thee; I have a heart to feel, Lord, let that heart feel no love but thine, and glow with no flame but affection for thee; I have a head to think, Lord, help me to think *of* thee and *for* thee; thou hast put me in this world for something, Lord, show me what that is, and help me to work out my life-purpose: I cannot do much, but as the widow put in her two mites, which were all her living, so, Lord, I cast my time and eternity too into thy treasury; I am all thine; take me, and enable me to glorify thee *now*, in all that I say, in all that I do, and with all that I have.

February 16

I have learned, in whatever state I am, therewith to be content.
—Philippians 4:11

THESE words show us that contentment is not a natural propensity of man. "Ill weeds grow apace." Covetousness, discontent, and murmuring are as natural to man as thorns are to the soil. We need not sow thistles and brambles; they come up naturally enough, because they are indigenous to earth: and so, we need not teach men to complain; they complain fast enough without any education. But the precious things of the earth must be cultivated. If we would have wheat, we must plough and sow; if we want flowers, there must be the garden, and all the gardener's care. Now, contentment is one of the flowers of heaven, and if we would have it, it must be cultivated; it will not grow in us by nature; it is the new nature alone that can produce it, and even then we must be specially careful and watchful that we maintain and cultivate the grace which God has sown in us. Paul says, "I have *learned* . . . to be content;" as much as to say, he did not know how at one time. It cost him some pains to attain to the mystery of that great truth. No doubt he sometimes thought he had learned, and then broke down. And when at last he had attained unto it, and could say, "I have learned in whatsoever state I am, therewith to be content," he was an old, grey-headed man, upon the borders of the grave—a poor prisoner shut up in Nero's dungeon at Rome. We might well be willing to endure Paul's infirmities, and share the cold dungeon with him, if we too might by any means attain unto his good degree. Do not indulge the notion that you can be contented with *learning*, or learn without discipline. It is not a power that may be exercised naturally, but a science to be acquired gradually. We know this from experience. Brother, hush that murmur, natural though it be, and continue a diligent pupil in the College of Content.

FEBRUARY 17

Isaac dwelt by the well Lahai-roi.
—*Genesis 25:11*

HAGAR had once found deliverance there and Ishmael had drank from the water so graciously revealed by the God who liveth and seeth the sons of men; but this was a merely casual visit, such as worldlings pay to the Lord in times of need, when it serves their turn. They cry to him in trouble, but forsake him in prosperity. Isaac *dwelt* there, and made the well of the living and all-seeing God his constant source of supply. The usual tenor of a man's life, the *dwelling* of his soul, is the true test of his state. Perhaps the providential visitation experienced by Hagar struck Isaac's mind, and led him to revere the place; its mystical name endeared it to him; his frequent musings by its brim at eventide made him familiar with the well; his meeting Rebecca there had made his spirit feel at home near the spot; but best of all, the fact that he there enjoyed fellowship with the living God, had made him select that hallowed ground for his dwelling. Let us learn to live in the presence of the living God; let us pray the Holy Spirit that this day, and every other day, we may feel, "Thou God seest me." May the Lord Jehovah be as a well to us, delightful, comforting, unfailing, springing up unto eternal life. The bottle of the creature cracks and dries up, but the well of the Creator never fails; happy is he who dwells at the well, and so has abundant and constant supplies near at hand. The Lord has been a sure helper to others: his name is Shaddai, God All-sufficient; our hearts have often had most delightful intercourse with him; through him our soul has found her glorious Husband, the Lord Jesus; and in him this day we live, and move, and have our being; let us, then, dwell in closest fellowship with him. Glorious Lord, constrain us that we may never leave thee, but dwell by the well of the living God.

FEBRUARY 18

Shew me wherefore thou contendest with me.
—Job 10:2

PERHAPS, O tried soul, the Lord is doing this to develop thy graces. There are some of thy graces which would never be *discovered* if it were not for thy trials. Dost thou not know that thy faith never looks so grand in summer weather as it does in winter? Love is too often like a glow-worm, showing but little light except it be in the midst of surrounding darkness. Hope itself is like a star—not to be seen in the sunshine of prosperity, and only to be discovered in the night of adversity. Afflictions are often the black foils in which God doth set the jewels of his children's graces, to make them shine the better. It was but a little while ago that on thy knees thou wast saying, "Lord, I fear I have no faith: let me know that I have faith." Was not this really, though perhaps unconsciously, praying for trials?—for how canst thou know that thou hast faith until thy faith is exercised? Depend upon it, God often sends us trials that our graces may be discovered, and that we may be certified of their existence. Besides, it is not merely discovery, *real growth* in grace is the result of sanctified trials. God often takes away our comforts and our privileges in order to make us better Christians. He trains his soldiers, not in tents of ease and luxury, but by turning them out and using them to forced marches and hard service. He makes them ford through streams, and swim through rivers, and climb mountains, and walk many a long mile with heavy knapsacks of sorrow on their backs. Well, Christian, may not this account for the troubles through which thou art passing? Is not the Lord bringing out your graces, and making them grow? Is not this the reason why he is contending with you?

> Trials make the promise sweet;
> Trials give new life to prayer;
> Trials brig me to his feet,
> Lay me low, and keep me there.

FEBRUARY 19

Thus saith the Lord God; "I will yet for this be enquired of by the house of Israel, to do it for them."
—*Ezekiel 36:37*

PRAYER is the forerunner of mercy. Turn to sacred history, and you will find that scarcely ever did a great mercy come to this world unheralded by supplication. You have found this true in your own personal experience. God has given you many an unsolicited favor, but still great prayer has always been the prelude of great mercy with you. When you first found peace through the blood of the cross, you had been praying much, and earnestly interceding with God that he would remove your doubts, and deliver you from your distresses. Your assurance was the result of prayer. When at any time you have had high and rapturous joys, you have been obliged to look upon them as answers to your prayers. When you have had great deliverances out of sore troubles, and mighty helps in great dangers, you have been able to say, "I sought the Lord, and he heard me, and delivered me from all my fears." Prayer is always the preface to blessing. It goes before the blessing *as the blessing's shadow.* When the sunlight of God's mercies rises upon our necessities, it casts the shadow of prayer far down upon the plain. Or, to use another illustration, when God piles up a hill of mercies, he himself shines behind them, and he casts on our spirits the shadow of prayer, so that we may rest certain, if we are much in prayer, our pleadings are the shadows of mercy. Prayer is thus connected with the blessing *to show us the value of it.* If we had the blessings without asking for them, we should think them common things; but prayer makes our mercies more precious than diamonds. The things we ask for are precious, but we do not realize their preciousness until we have sought for them earnestly.

> Prayer makes the darken'd cloud withdraw;
> Prayer climbs the ladder Jacob saw;
> Gives exercise to faith and love;
> Brings every blessing from above.

FEBRUARY 20

God, that comforteth those that are cast down.
—2 Corinthians 7:6

ND who comforteth like him? Go to some poor, melancholy, distressed child of God; tell him sweet promises, and whisper in his ear choice words of comfort; he is like the deaf adder, he listens not to the voice of the charmer, charm he never so wisely. He is drinking gall and wormwood, and comfort him as you may, it will be only a note or two of mournful resignation that you will get from him; you will bring forth no psalms of praise, no hallelujahs, no joyful sonnets. But let *God* come to his child, let him lift up his countenance, and the mourner's eyes glisten with hope. Do you not hear him sing—

> 'Tis paradise, if thou art here;
> If thou depart, 'tis hell?

You could not have cheered him: but the Lord has done it; "He is the God of all comfort." There is no balm in Gilead, but there is balm in God. There is no physician among the creatures, but the Creator is *Jehovah Rophi*. It is marvelous how one sweet word of God will make whole songs for Christians. One word of God is like a piece of gold, and the Christian is the goldbeater, and can hammer that promise out for whole weeks. So, then, poor Christian, thou needest not sit down in despair. Go to the Comforter, and ask him to give thee consolation. Thou art a poor dry well. You have heard it said, that when a pump is dry, you must pour water down it first of all, and then you will get water, and so, Christian, when thou art dry, go to God, ask him to shed abroad his joy in thy heart, and then thy joy shall be full. Do not go to earthly acquaintances, for you will find them Job's comforters after all; but go first and foremost to thy "God, that comforteth those that are cast down," and you will soon say, "In the multitude of my thoughts within me thy comforts delight my soul."

FEBRUARY 21

He hath said.
—Hebrews 13:5

F we can only grasp these words by faith, we have an all-conquering weapon in our hand. What doubt will not be slain by this two-edged sword? What fear is there which shall not fall smitten with a deadly wound before this arrow from the bow of God's covenant? Will not the distresses of life and the pangs of death; will not the corruptions within, and the snares without; will not the trials from above, and the temptations from beneath, all seem but light afflictions, when we can hide ourselves beneath the bulwark of "he hath said"? Yes; whether for delight in our quietude, or for strength in our conflict, "he hath said" must be our daily resort. And this may teach us the extreme value of *searching* the Scriptures. There may be a promise in the Word which would exactly fit your case, but you may not know of it, and therefore you miss its comfort. You are like prisoners in a dungeon, and there may be one key in the bunch which would unlock the door, and you might be free; but if you will not look for it, you may remain a prisoner still, though liberty is so near at hand. There may be a potent medicine in the great pharmacopoeia of Scripture, and you may yet continue sick unless you will examine and search the Scriptures to discover what "he hath said." Should you not, besides reading the Bible, store your memories richly with the promises of God? You can recollect the sayings of great men; you treasure up the verses of renowned poets; ought you not to be profound in your knowledge of the words of God, so that you may be able to quote them readily when you would solve a difficulty, or overthrow a doubt? Since "he hath said" is the source of all wisdom, and the fountain of all comfort, let it dwell in you richly, as "A well of water, springing up unto everlasting life." So shall you grow healthy, strong, and happy in the divine life.

FEBRUARY 22

His bow abode in strength, and the arms of his hands were made strong by the hands of the mighty God of Jacob.
—*Genesis 49:24*

THAT strength which God gives to his Josephs is *real* strength; it is not a boasted velour, a fiction, a thing of which men talk, but which ends in smoke; it is true—*divine strength*. Why does Joseph stand against temptation? Because God gives him aid. There is naught that we can do without the power of God. All true strength comes from "the mighty God of Jacob." Notice in what a *blessedly familiar way* God gives this strength to Joseph—"The arms of his hands were made strong by the hands of the mighty God of Jacob." Thus God is represented as putting his hands on Joseph's hands, placing his arms on Joseph's arms. Like as a father teaches his children, so the Lord teaches them that fear him. He puts his arms upon them. Marvelous condescension! God Almighty, Eternal, Omnipotent, stoops from his throne and lays his hand upon the child's hand, stretching his arm upon the arm of Joseph, that he may be made strong! This strength was also covenant strength, for it is ascribed to "the mighty *God of Jacob*." Now, wherever you read of the God of Jacob in the Bible, you should remember the covenant with Jacob. Christians love to think of God's covenant. All the power, all the grace, all the blessings, all the mercies, all the comforts, all the things we have, flow to us from the wellhead, through the covenant. If there were no covenant, then we should fail indeed; for all grace proceeds from it, as light and heat from the sun. No angels ascend or descend, save upon that ladder which Jacob saw, at the top of which stood a covenant God. Christian, it may be that the archers have sorely grieved you, and shot at you, and wounded you, but still your bow abides in strength; be sure, then, to ascribe all the glory to Jacob's God.

February 23

I will never leave thee.
—Hebrews 13:5

NO promise is of private interpretation. Whatever God has said to any one saint, he has said to all. When he opens a well for one, it is that all may drink. When he openeth a granary-door to give out food, there may be some one starving man who is the occasion of its being opened, but all hungry saints may come and feed too. Whether he gave the word to Abraham or to Moses, matters not, O believer; he has given it to thee as one of the covenanted seed. There is not a high blessing too lofty for thee, nor a wide mercy too extensive for thee. Lift up now thine eyes to the north and to the south, to the east and to the west, for all this is thine. Climb to Pisgah's top, and view the utmost limit of the divine promise, for the land is all thine own. There is not a brook of living water of which thou mayst not drink. If the land floweth with milk and honey, eat the honey and drink the milk, for both are thine. Be thou bold to believe, for he hath said, "I will never leave *thee,* nor forsake *thee.*" In this promise, God gives to his people everything. "I will never leave thee." Then no attribute of God can cease to be engaged for us. Is he mighty? He will show himself strong on the behalf of them that trust him. Is he love? Then with lovingkindness will he have mercy upon us. Whatever attributes may compose the character of Deity, every one of them to its fullest extent shall be engaged on our side. To put everything in one, there is nothing you can want, there is nothing you can ask for, there is nothing you can need in time or in eternity, there is nothing living, nothing dying, there is nothing in this world, nothing in the next world, there is nothing now, nothing at the resurrection-morning, nothing in heaven which is not contained in this text—"I will never leave thee, nor forsake thee."

February 24

*I will cause the shower to come down in his season;
there shall be showers of blessing.
—Ezekiel 34:26*

HERE is *sovereign mercy*—"I will give them the shower in its season." Is it not sovereign, *divine* mercy?—for who can say, "I will give them showers," except God? There is only one voice which can speak to the clouds, and bid them beget the rain. Who sendeth down the rain upon the earth? Who scattereth the showers upon the green herb? Do not I, the Lord? So grace is the gift of God, and is not to be created by man. It is also *needed* grace. What would the ground do without showers? You may break the clods, you may sow your seeds, but what can you do without the rain? As absolutely needful is the divine blessing. In vain you labor, until God the plenteous shower bestows, and sends salvation down. Then, it is *plenteous grace.* "I will send them showers." It does not say, "I will send them drops," but "showers." So it is with grace. If God gives a blessing, he usually gives it in such a measure that there is not room enough to receive it. Plenteous grace! Ah! we want plenteous grace to keep us humble, to make us prayerful, to make us holy; plenteous grace to make us zealous, to preserve us through this life, and at last to land us in heaven. We cannot do without saturating showers of grace. Again, it is *seasonable grace.* "I will cause the shower to come down *in his season.*" What is thy season this morning? Is it the season of drought? Then that is the season for showers. Is it a season of great heaviness and black clouds? Then that is the season for showers. "As thy days so shall thy strength be." And here is a *varied* blessing. "I will give thee *showers* of blessing." The word is in the plural. All kinds of blessings God will send. All God's blessings go together, like links in a golden chain. If he gives converting grace, he will also give comforting grace. He will send "showers of blessing." Look up today, O parched plant, and open thy leaves and flowers for a heavenly watering.

FEBRUARY 25

The wrath to come.
—Matthew 3:7

IT is pleasant to pass over a country after a storm has spent itself; to smell the freshness of the herbs after the rain has passed away, and to note the drops while they glisten like purest diamonds in the sunlight. That is the position of a Christian. He is going through a land where the storm has spent itself upon his Savior's head, and if there be a few drops of sorrow falling, they distil from clouds of mercy, and Jesus cheers him by the assurance that they are not for his destruction. But how terrible it is to witness the approach of a tempest: to note the forewarnings of the storm; to mark the birds of heaven as they droop their wings; to see the cattle as they lay their heads low in terror; to discern the face of the sky as it groweth black, and look to the sun which shineth not, and the heavens which are angry and frowning! How terrible to await the dread advance of a hurricane—such as occurs, sometimes, in the tropics—to wait in terrible apprehension till the wind shall rush forth in fury, tearing up trees from their roots, forcing rocks from their pedestals, and hurling down all the dwelling-places of man! And yet, sinner, this is your present position. No hot drops have as yet fallen, but a shower of fire is coming. No terrible winds howl around you, but God's tempest is gathering its dread artillery. As yet the water-floods are dammed up by mercy, but the flood-gates shall soon be opened: the thunderbolts of God are yet in his storehouse, but lo! the tempest hastens, and how awful shall that moment be when God, robed in vengeance, shall march forth in fury! Where, where, where, O sinner, wilt thou hide thy head, or whither wilt thou flee? O that the hand of mercy may now lead you to Christ! He is freely set before you in the gospel: his riven side is the rock of shelter. Thou knowest thy need of him; believe in him, cast thyself upon him, and then the fury shall be overpast forever.

February 26

Salvation is of the Lord.
—Jonah 2:9

ALVATION is the work of God. It is he alone who quickens the soul "dead in trespasses and sins," and it is he also who maintains the soul in its spiritual life. He is both "Alpha and Omega." "Salvation is of the Lord." If I am prayerful, God makes me prayerful; if I have graces, they are God's gifts to me; if I hold on in a consistent life, it is because he upholds me with his hand. I do nothing whatever towards my own preservation, except what God himself first does in me. Whatever I have, all my goodness is of the Lord alone. Wherein I sin, that is my own; but wherein I act rightly, that is of God, wholly and completely. If I have repulsed a spiritual enemy, the Lord's strength nerved my arm. Do I live before men a consecrated life? It is not I, but Christ who liveth in me. Am I sanctified? I did not cleanse myself: God's Holy Spirit sanctifies me. Am I weaned from the world? I am weaned by *God's* chastisements sanctified to my good. Do I grow in knowledge? The great Instructor teaches me. All my jewels were fashioned by heavenly art. I find in God all that I want; but I find in myself nothing but sin and misery. "He only is my rock and my salvation." Do I feed on the Word? That Word would be no food for me unless the Lord made it food for my soul, and helped me to feed upon it. Do I live on the manna which comes down from heaven? What is that manna but Jesus Christ himself incarnate, whose body and whose blood I eat and drink? Am I continually receiving fresh increase of strength? Where do I gather my might? My help cometh from heaven's hills: without Jesus I can do nothing. As a branch cannot bring forth fruit except it abide in the vine, no more can I, except I abide in him. What Jonah learned in the great deep, let me learn this morning in my closet: "Salvation is of the Lord."

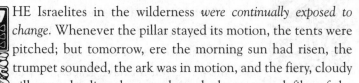

FEBRUARY 27

Thou hast made the Lord, which is my refuge,
even the Most High, thy habitation.
—Psalm 91:9

THE Israelites in the wilderness *were continually exposed to change*. Whenever the pillar stayed its motion, the tents were pitched; but tomorrow, ere the morning sun had risen, the trumpet sounded, the ark was in motion, and the fiery, cloudy pillar was leading the way through the narrow defiles of the mountain, up the hillside, or along the arid waste of the wilderness. They had scarcely time to rest a little before they heard the sound of "Away! this is not your rest; you must still be onward journeying towards Canaan!" They were never long in one place. Even wells and palm trees could not detain them. Yet they had an abiding home in their God, his cloudy pillar was their roof-tree, and its flame by night their household fire. They must go onward from place to place, continually changing, never having time to settle, and to say, "Now we are secure; in this place we shall dwell." "Yet," says Moses, "though we are always changing, Lord, thou hast been our dwelling-place throughout all generations." The Christian knows no change with regard to God. He may be rich today and poor tomorrow; he may be sickly today and well to-morrow; he may be in happiness today, tomorrow he may be distressed—but there is no change with regard to his relationship to God. If he loved me yesterday, he loves me today. My unmoving mansion of rest is my blessed Lord. Let prospects be blighted; let hopes be blasted; let joy be withered; let mildews destroy everything; I have lost nothing of what I have in God. He is "my strong habitation whereunto I can continually resort." I am a pilgrim in the world, but at home in my God. In the earth I wander, but in God I dwell in a quiet habitation.

FEBRUARY 28

My expectation is from him.
—Psalm 62:5

T is the believer's privilege to use this language. If he is look-ing for aught from the world, it is a poor "expectation" in-deed. But if he looks to God for the supply of his wants, whether in temporal or spiritual blessings, his "expectation" will not be a vain one. Constantly he may draw from the bank of faith, and get his need supplied out of the riches of God's lovingkindness. This I know, I had rather have God for my banker than all the Rothschilds. My Lord never fails to honor his promises; and when we bring them to his throne, he never sends them back unanswered. Therefore I will wait only at his door, for he ever opens it with the hand of munificent grace. At this hour I will try him anew. But we have "expectations" beyond this life. We shall die soon; and then our "expectation is from him." Do we not expect that when we lie upon the bed of sickness he will send angels to carry us to his bosom? We believe that when the pulse is faint, and the heart heaves heavily, some angelic messenger shall stand and look with loving eyes upon us, and whis-per, "Sister spirit, come away!" As we approach the heavenly gate, we expect to hear the welcome invitation, "Come, ye blessed of my Father, inherit the kingdom prepared for you from the foundation of the world." We are expect-ing harps of gold and crowns of glory; we are hoping soon to be amongst the multitude of shining ones before the throne; we are looking forward and longing for the time when we shall be like our glorious Lord—for "We shall see him as he is." Then if these be thine "expectations," O my soul, live for God; live with the desire and resolve to glorify him from whom cometh all thy supplies, and of whose grace in thy election, redemption, and calling, it is that thou hast any "expectation" of coming glory.

FEBRUARY 29

With lovingkindness have I drawn thee.—Jeremiah 31:3

THE thunders of the law and the terrors of judgment are all used to bring us to Christ; but the final victory is effected by lovingkindness. The prodigal set out to his father's house from a sense of need; but his father saw him a great way off, and ran to meet him; so that the last steps he took towards his father's house were with the kiss still warm upon his cheek, and the welcome still musical in his ears.

> Law and terrors do but harden
> All the while they work alone;
> But a sense of blood-bought pardon
> Will dissolve a heart of stone.

The Master came one night to the door, and knocked with the iron hand of the law; the door shook and trembled upon its hinges; but the man piled every piece of furniture which he could find against the door, for he said, "I will not admit the man." The Master turned away, but by-and-bye he came back, and with his own soft hand, using most that part where the nail had penetrated, he knocked again—oh, so softly and tenderly. This time the door did not shake, but, strange to say, it opened, and there upon his knees the once unwilling host was found rejoicing to receive his guest.

> Come in, come in; thou hast so knocked that my bowels are moved for thee. I could not think of thy pierced hand leaving its blood-mark on my door, and of thy going away houseless, "Thy head filled with dew, and thy locks with the drops of the night." I yield, I yield, thy love has won my heart.

So in every case: lovingkindness wins the day. What Moses with the tablets of stone could never do, Christ does with his pierced hand. Such is the doctrine of effectual calling. Do I understand it experimentally? Can I say, "he drew me, and I followed on, glad to confess the voice divine?" If so, may he continue to draw me, till at last I shall sit down at the marriage supper of the Lamb.

March 1

Awake, O north wind; and come, thou south; blow upon my garden,
that the spices thereof may flow out.
—*Song of Solomon 4:16*

NYTHING is better than the dead calm of indifference. Our souls may wisely desire the north wind of trouble if that alone can be sanctified to the drawing forth of the perfume of our graces. So long as it cannot be said, "The Lord was not in the wind," we will not shrink from the most wintry blast that ever blew upon plants of grace. Did not the spouse in this verse humbly submit herself to the reproofs of her Beloved; only entreating him to send forth his grace in some form, and making no stipulation as to the peculiar manner in which it should come? Did she not, like ourselves, become so utterly weary of deadness and unholy calm that she sighed for any visitation which would brace her to action? Yet she desires the warm south wind of comfort, too, the smiles of divine love, the joy of the Redeemer's presence; these are often mightily effectual to arouse our sluggish life. She desires either one or the other, or both; so that she may but be able to delight her Beloved with the spices of her garden. She cannot endure to be unprofitable, nor can we. How cheering a thought that Jesus can find comfort in our poor feeble graces. Can it be? It seems far too good to be true. Well may we court trial or even death itself if we shall thereby be aided to make glad Immanuel's heart. O that our heart were crushed to atoms if only by such bruising our sweet Lord Jesus could be glorified. Graces unexercised are as sweet perfumes slumbering in the cups of the flowers: the wisdom of the great Husbandman overrules diverse and opposite causes to produce the one desired result, and makes both affliction and consolation draw forth the grateful odors of faith, love, patience, hope, resignation, joy, and the other fair flowers of the garden. May we know by sweet experience, what this means.

MARCH 2

But all the Israelites went down to the Philistines,
to sharpen every man his share, and his coulter,
and his ax, and his mattock.
—1 Samuel 13:20

E are engaged in a great war with the Philistines of evil. Every weapon within our reach must be used. Preaching, teaching, praying, giving, all must be brought into action, and talents which have been thought too mean for service, must now be employed. Coulter, and axe, and mattock, may all be useful in slaying Philistines; rough tools may deal hard blows, and killing need not be elegantly done, so long as it is done effectually. Each moment of time, in season or out of season; each fragment of ability, educated or untutored; each opportunity, favorable or unfavorable, must be used, for our foes are many and our force but slender.

Most of our tools want sharpening; we need quickness of perception, tact, energy, promptness, in a word, complete adaptation for the Lord's work. Practical common sense is a very scarce thing among the conductors of Christian enterprises. We might learn from our enemies if we would, and so *make the Philistines sharpen our weapons.* This morning let us note enough to sharpen our zeal during this day by the aid of the Holy Spirit. See the energy of the Papists, how they compass sea and land to make one proselyte, are they to monopolize all the earnestness? Mark the heathen devotees, what tortures they endure in the service of their idols! are they alone to exhibit patience and self-sacrifice? Observe the prince of darkness, how persevering in his endeavors, how unabashed in his attempts, how daring in his plans, how thoughtful in his plots, how energetic in all! The devils are united as one man in their infamous rebellion, while we believers in Jesus are divided in our service of God, and scarcely ever work with unanimity. O that from Satan's infernal industry we may learn to go about like good Samaritans, seeking whom we may bless!

MARCH 3

I have chosen thee in the furnace of affliction.
—Isaiah 48:10

COMFORT thyself, tried believer, with this thought: God saith, "I have chosen thee in the furnace of affliction." Does not the word come like a soft shower, assuaging the fury of the flame? Yea, is it not an asbestos armor, against which the heat hath no power? Let affliction come—God has chosen me. Poverty, thou mayst stride in at my door, but God is in the house already, and he has chosen me. Sickness, thou mayst intrude, but I have a balsam ready—God has chosen me. Whatever befalls me in this vale of tears, I know that he has "chosen" me. If, believer, thou requirest still greater comfort, remember *that you have the Son of Man with you in the furnace.* In that silent chamber of yours, there sitteth by your side One whom thou hast not seen, but whom thou lovest; and ofttimes when thou knowest it not, he makes all thy bed in thy affliction, and smooths thy pillow for thee. Thou art in poverty; but in that lovely house of thine the Lord of life and glory is a frequent visitor. He loves to come into these desolate places, that he may visit thee. Thy friend sticks closely to thee. Thou canst not see him, but thou mayst feel the pressure of his hands. Dost thou not hear his voice? Even in the valley of the shadow of death he says, "Fear not, I am with thee; be not dismayed, for I am thy God." Remember that noble speech of Caesar: "Fear not, thou carriest Caesar and all his fortune." Fear not, Christian; Jesus is with thee. In all thy fiery trials, his presence is both thy comfort and safety. He will never leave one whom he has chosen for his own. "Fear not, for I am with thee," is his sure word of promise to his chosen ones in the "furnace of affliction." Wilt thou not, then, take fast hold of Christ, and say—

> Through floods and flames, if Jesus lead,
> I'll follow where he goes.

MARCH 4

My grace is sufficient for thee.
—2 Corinthians 12:9

 F none of God's saints were poor and tried, we should not know half so well the consolations of divine grace. When we find the wanderer who has not where to lay his head, who yet can say, "Still will I trust in the Lord;" when we see the pauper starving on bread and water, who still glories in Jesus; when we see the bereaved widow overwhelmed in affliction, and yet having faith in Christ, oh! what honor it reflects on the gospel. God's grace is illustrated and magnified in the poverty and trials of believers. Saints bear up under every discouragement, believing that all things work together for their good, and that out of apparent evils a real blessing shall ultimately spring—that their God will either work a deliverance for them speedily, or most assuredly support them in the trouble, as long as he is pleased to keep them in it. This patience of the saints proves the power of divine grace. There is a lighthouse out at sea: it is a calm night—I cannot tell whether the edifice is firm; the tempest must rage about it, and then I shall know whether it will stand. So with the Spirit's work: if it were not on many occasions surrounded with tempestuous waters, we should not know that it was true and strong; if the winds did not blow upon it, we should not know how firm and secure it was. The master-works of God are those men who stand in the midst of difficulties, steadfast, unmovable,—

> Calm mid the bewildering cry,
> Confident of victory.

He who would glorify his God must set his account upon meeting with many trials. No man can be illustrious before the Lord unless his conflicts be many. If then, yours be a much-tried path, rejoice in it, because you will the better show forth the all-sufficient grace of God. As for his failing you, never dream of it—hate the thought. The God who has been sufficient until now, should be trusted to the end.

MARCH 5

Let us not sleep, as do others.
—1 Thessalonians 5:6

THERE are many ways of promoting Christian wakefulness. Among the rest, let me strongly advise Christians to converse together concerning the ways of the Lord. Christian and Hopeful, as they journeyed towards the Celestial City, said to themselves, "To prevent drowsiness in this place, let us fall into good discourse." Christian enquired, "Brother, where shall we begin?" And Hopeful answered, "Where God began with us." Then Christian sang this song—

> When saints do sleepy grow, let them come hither,
> And hear how these two pilgrims talk together;
> Yea, let them learn of them, in any wise,
> Thus to keep open their drowsy slumb'ring eyes.
> Saints' fellowship, if it be managed well,
> Keeps them awake, and that in spite of hell.

Christians who isolate themselves and walk alone, are very liable to grow drowsy. Hold Christian company, and you will be kept wakeful by it, and refreshed and encouraged to make quicker progress in the road to heaven. But as you thus take "sweet counsel" with others in the ways of God, take care that the theme of your converse is the Lord Jesus. Let the eye of faith be constantly looking unto him; let your heart be full of him; let your lips speak of his worth. Friend, live near to the cross, and thou wilt not sleep. *Labor to impress thyself with a deep sense of the value of the place to which thou art going.* If thou rememberest that thou art going to heaven, thou wilt not sleep on the road. If thou thinkest that hell is behind thee, and the devil pursuing thee, thou wilt not loiter. Would the manslayer sleep with the avenger of blood behind him, and the city of refuge before him? Christian, wilt thou sleep whilst the pearly gates are open—the songs of angels waiting for thee to join them—a crown of gold ready for thy brow? Ah! no; in holy fellowship continue to watch and pray that ye enter not into temptation.

MARCH 6

Ye must be born again.
—John 3:7

REGENERATION is a subject which lies at the very basis of salvation, and we should be very diligent to take heed that we really are "born again," for there are many who fancy they are, who are not. Be assured that the name of a Christian is not the nature of a Christian; and that being born in a Christian land, and being recognized as professing the Christian religion is of no avail whatever, unless there be something more added to it—the being "born again," is a matter so *mysterious*, that human words cannot describe it.

> The wind bloweth where it listeth, and thou hearest the sound thereof, but canst not tell whence it cometh, and whither it goeth: so is every one that is born of the Spirit.

Nevertheless, it is a change which is *known and felt*: known by works of holiness, and felt by a gracious experience. This great work is *supernatural*. It is not an operation which a man performs for himself: a new principle is infused, which works in the heart, renews the soul, and affects the entire man. It is not a change of my name, but a renewal of my nature, so that I am not the man I used to be, but a new man in Christ Jesus. To wash and dress a corpse is a far different thing from making it alive: man can do the one, God alone can do the other. If you have then, been "born again," your acknowledgment will be,

> O Lord Jesus, the everlasting Father, thou art my spiritual Parent; unless thy Spirit had breathed into me the breath of a new, holy, and spiritual life, I had been to this day "dead in trespasses and sins." My heavenly life is wholly derived from thee, to thee I ascribe it. "My life is hid with Christ in God." It is no longer I who live, but Christ who liveth in me.

May the Lord enable us to be well assured on this vital point, for to be unregenerate is to be unsaved, unpardoned, without God, and without hope.

MARCH 7

Have faith in God.
—Mark 11:22

FAITH is the foot of the soul by which it can march along the road of the commandments. Love can make the feet move more swiftly; but faith is the foot which carries the soul. Faith is the oil enabling the wheels of holy devotion and of earnest piety to move well; and without faith the wheels are taken from the chariot, and we drag heavily. With faith I can do all things; without faith I shall neither have the inclination nor the power to do anything in the service of God. If you would find the men who serve God the best, you must look for the men of the most faith. Little faith will save a man, but little faith cannot do great things for God. Poor Little-faith could not have fought "Apollyon;" it needed "Christian" to do that. Poor Little-faith could not have slain "Giant Despair;" it required "Great-heart's" arm to knock that monster down. Little-faith will go to heaven most certainly, but it often has to hide itself in a nut-shell, and it frequently loses all but its jewels. Little-faith says, "It is a rough road, beset with sharp thorns, and full of dangers; I am afraid to go;" but Great-faith remembers the promise, "Thy shoes shall be iron and brass; as thy days, so shall thy strength be:" and so she boldly ventures. Little-faith stands desponding, mingling her tears with the flood; but Great-faith sings, "When thou passest through the waters, I will be with thee; and through the rivers, they shall not overflow thee:" and she fords the stream at once. Would you be comfortable and happy? Would you enjoy religion? Would you have the religion of cheerfulness and not that of gloom? Then "have faith in God." If you love darkness, and are satisfied to dwell in gloom and misery, then be content with little faith; but if you love the sunshine, and would sing songs of rejoicing, covet earnestly this best gift, "great faith."

March 8

We must through much tribulation
enter into the kingdom of God.
—Acts 14:22

OD'S people have their trials. It was never designed by God, when he chose his people, that they should be an untried people. They were chosen in the furnace of affliction; they were never chosen to worldly peace and earthly joy. Freedom from sickness and the pains of mortality was never promised them; but when their Lord drew up the charter of privileges, he included chastisements amongst the things to which they should inevitably be heirs. Trials are a part of our lot; they were predestinated for us in Christ's last legacy. So surely as the stars are fashioned by his hands, and their orbits fixed by him, so surely are our trials allotted to us: he has ordained their season and their place, their intensity and the effect they shall have upon us. Good men must never expect to escape troubles; if they do, they will be disappointed, for none of their predecessors have been without them. Mark the patience of Job; remember Abraham, for he had his trials, and by his faith under them, he became the "Father of the faithful." Note well the biographies of all the patriarchs, prophets, apostles, and martyrs, and you shall discover none of those whom God made vessels of mercy, who were not made to pass through the fire of affliction. It is ordained of old that the cross of trouble should be engraved on every vessel of mercy, as the royal mark whereby the King's vessels of honor are distinguished. But although tribulation is thus the path of God's children, they have the comfort of knowing that their Master has traversed it before them; they have his presence and sympathy to cheer them, his grace to support them, and his example to teach them how to endure; and when they reach "the kingdom," it will more than make amends for the "much tribulation" through which they passed to enter it.

MARCH 9

Yea, he is altogether lovely.
—Song of Solomon 5:16

THE superlative beauty of Jesus is all-attracting; it is not so much to be admired as to be loved. He is more than pleasant and fair, he is lovely. Surely the people of God can fully justify the use of this golden word, for he is the object of their warmest love, a love founded on the intrinsic excellence of his person, the complete perfection of his charms. Look, O disciples of Jesus, to your Master's lips, and say, "Are they not most sweet?" Do not his words cause your hearts to burn within you as he talks with you by the way? Ye worshippers of Immanuel, look up to his head of much fine gold, and tell me, are not his thoughts precious unto you? Is not your adoration sweetened with affection as ye humbly bow before that countenance which is as Lebanon, excellent as the cedars? Is there not a charm in his every feature, and is not his whole person fragrant with such a savor of his good ointments, that therefore the virgins love him? Is there one member of his glorious body which is not attractive?—one portion of his person which is not a fresh loadstone to our souls?—one office which is not a strong cord to bind your heart? Our love is not as a seal set upon his heart of love alone; it is fastened upon his arm of power also; nor is there a single part of him upon which it does not fix itself. We anoint his whole person with the sweet spikenard of our fervent love. His whole life we would imitate; his whole character we would transcribe. In all other beings we see some lack, in him there is all perfection. The best even of his favored saints have had blots upon their garments and wrinkles upon their brows; he is nothing but loveliness. All earthly suns have their spots: the fair world itself hath its wilderness; we cannot love the whole of the most lovely thing; but Christ Jesus is gold without alloy—light without darkness—glory without cloud—"Yea, he is *altogether* lovely."

MARCH 10

In my prosperity I said I shall never be moved.
—Psalm 30:6

OAB is settled on his lees, he hath not been emptied from vessel to vessel." Give a man wealth; let his ships bring home continually rich freights; let the winds and waves appear to be his servants to bear his vessels across the bosom of the mighty deep; let his lands yield abundantly: let the weather be propitious to his crops; let uninterrupted success attend him; let him stand among men as a successful merchant; let him enjoy continued health; allow him with braced nerve and brilliant eye to march through the world, and live happily; give him the buoyant spirit; let him have the song perpetually on his lips; let his eye be ever sparkling with joy—and the natural consequence of such an easy state to any man, let him be the best Christian who ever breathed, will be presumption; even David said, "I shall never be moved;" and we are not better than David, nor half so good. Brother, beware of the smooth places of the way; if you are treading them, or if the way be rough, thank God for it. If God should always rock us in the cradle of prosperity; if we were always dandled on the knees of fortune; if we had not some stain on the alabaster pillar; if there were not a few clouds in the sky; if we had not some bitter drops in the wine of this life, we should become intoxicated with pleasure, we should dream "we stand;" and stand we should, but it would be upon a pinnacle; like the man asleep upon the mast, each moment we should be in jeopardy.

We bless God, then, for our afflictions; we thank him for our changes; we extol his name for losses of property; for we feel that had he not chastened us thus, we might have become too secure. Continued worldly prosperity is a fiery trial.

> Afflictions, though they seem severe,
> In mercy oft are sent.

MARCH 11

Sin . . . exceeding sinful.
—Romans 7:13

BEWARE of light thoughts of sin. At the time of conversion, the conscience is so tender, that we are afraid of the slightest sin. Young converts have a holy timidity, a godly fear lest they should offend against God. But alas! very soon the fine bloom upon these first ripe fruits is removed by the rough handling of the surrounding world: the sensitive plant of young piety turns into a willow in after life, too pliant, too easily yielding. It is sadly true, that even a Christian may grow by degrees so callous, that the sin which once startled him does not alarm him in the least. By degrees men get familiar with sin. The ear in which the cannon has been booming will not notice slight sounds. At first a little sin startles us; but soon we say, "Is it not a little one?" Then there comes another, larger, and then another, until by degrees we begin to regard sin as but a little ill; and then follows an unholy presumption:

> We have not fallen into open sin. True, we tripped a little, but we stood upright in the main. We may have uttered one unholy word, but as for the most of our conversation, it has been consistent.

So we palliate sin; we throw a cloak over it; we call it by dainty names. Christian, beware how thou thinkest lightly of sin. Take heed lest thou fall by little and little. Sin, a little thing? Is it not a poison? Who knows its deadliness? Sin, a little thing? Do not the little foxes spoil the grapes? Doth not the tiny coral insect build a rock which wrecks a navy? Do not little strokes fell lofty oaks? Will not continual droppings wear away stones? Sin, a little thing? It girded the Redeemer's head with thorns, and pierced his heart! It made him suffer anguish, bitterness, and woe. Could you weigh the least sin in the scales of eternity, you would fly from it as from a serpent, and abhor the least appearance of evil. Look upon all sin as that which crucified the Savior, and you will see it to be "exceeding sinful."

MARCH 12

Thou shalt love thy neighbor.
—*Matthew 5:43*

OVE thy neighbor." Perhaps he rolls in riches, and thou art poor, and living in thy little cot side-by-side with his lordly mansion; thou seest every day his estates, his fine linen, and his sumptuous banquets; God has given him these gifts, covet not his wealth, and think no hard thoughts concerning him. Be content with thine own lot, if thou canst not better it, but do not look upon thy neighbor, and wish that he were as thyself. Love him, and then thou wilt not envy him.

Mayhap, on the other hand, thou art rich, and near thee reside the poor. Do not scorn to call them neighbor. Own that thou art bound to love them. The world calls them thy inferiors. In what are they inferior? They are far more thine equals than thine inferiors, for "God hath made of one blood all people that dwell upon the face of the earth." It is thy coat which is better than theirs, but thou art by no means better than they. They are men, and what art thou more than that? Take heed that thou love thy neighbor even though he be in rags, or sunken in the depths of poverty.

But, perhaps, you say, "I cannot love my neighbors, because for all I do they return ingratitude and contempt." So much the more room for the heroism of love. Wouldst thou be a feather-bed warrior, instead of bearing the rough fight of love? He who dares the most, shall win the most; and if rough be thy path of love, tread it boldly, still loving thy neighbors through thick and thin. Heap coals of fire on their heads, and if they be hard to please, seek not to please *them,* but to please *thy Master;* and remember if *they* spurn thy love, thy Master hath not spurned it, and thy deed is as acceptable to him as if it had been acceptable to them. Love thy neighbor, for in so doing thou art following the footsteps of Christ.

March 13

Why sit we here until we die?
—2 Kings 7:3

EAR reader, this little book was mainly intended for the edification of believers, but if you are yet unsaved, our heart yearns over you: and we would fain say a word which may be blessed to you. Open your Bible, and read the story of the lepers, and mark their position, which was much the same as yours. If you remain where you are you must perish; if you go to Jesus you can but die. "Nothing venture, nothing win," is the old proverb, and in your case the venture is no great one. If you sit still in sullen despair, no one can pity you when your ruin comes; but if you die with mercy sought, if such a thing were possible, you would be the object of universal sympathy. None escape who refuse to look to Jesus; but you know that, at any rate, some are saved who believe in him, for certain of your own acquaintances have received mercy: then why not you? The Ninevites said, "Who can tell?" Act upon the same hope, and try the Lord's mercy. To perish is so awful, that if there were but a straw to catch at, the instinct of self-preservation should lead you to stretch out your hand. We have thus been talking to you on your own unbelieving ground, we would now assure you, as from the Lord, that if you seek him he will be found of you. Jesus casts out none who come unto him. You shall not perish if you trust him; on the contrary, you shall find treasure far richer than the poor lepers gathered in Syria's deserted camp. May the Holy Spirit embolden you to go at once, and you shall not believe in vain. When you are saved yourself, publish the good news to others. Hold not your peace; tell the King's household first, and unite with them in fellowship; let the porter of the city, the minister, be informed of your discovery, and then proclaim the good news in every place. The Lord save thee ere the sun goes down this day.

🌿

MARCH 14

*Let him that thinketh he standeth
take heed, lest he fall.*
—*1 Corinthians 10:12*

IT is a curious fact, that there is such a thing as being proud of grace. A man says, "I have great faith, I shall not fall; poor little faith may, but I never shall." "I have fervent love," says another, "I can stand, there is no danger of my going astray." He who boasts of grace has little grace to boast of. Some who do this imagine that their graces can keep them, knowing not that the stream must flow constantly from the fountain head, or else the brook will soon be dry. If a continuous stream of oil comes not to the lamp, though it burn brightly today, it will smoke tomorrow, and noxious will be its scent. Take heed that thou gloriest not in thy graces, but let all thy glorying and confidence be in Christ and his strength, for only so canst thou be kept from falling. Be much more in prayer. Spend longer time in holy adoration. Read the Scriptures more earnestly and constantly. Watch your lives more carefully. Live nearer to God. Take the best examples for your pattern. Let your conversation be redolent of heaven. Let your hearts be perfumed with affection for men's souls. So live that men may take knowledge of you that you have been with Jesus, and have learned of him; and when that happy day shall come, when he whom you love shall say, "Come up higher," may it be your happiness to hear him say, "Thou hast fought a good fight, thou hast finished thy course, and henceforth there is laid up for thee a crown of righteousness which fadeth not away." On, Christian, with care and caution! On, with holy fear and trembling! On, with faith and confidence in Jesus alone, and let your constant petition be, "Uphold me according to thy word." He is able, and he alone, "To keep you from falling, and to present you faultless before the presence of his glory with exceeding joy."

March 15

Be strong in the grace that is in Christ Jesus.
—2 Timothy 2:1

CHRIST has grace without measure in himself, but he hath not retained it for himself. As the reservoir empties itself into the pipes, so hath Christ emptied out his grace for his people. "Of his fullness have all we received, and grace for grace." He seems only to have in order to dispense to us. He stands like the fountain, always flowing, but only running in order to supply the empty pitchers and the thirsty lips which draw nigh unto it. Like a tree, he bears sweet fruit, not to hang on boughs, but to be gathered by those who need. Grace, whether its work be to pardon, to cleanse, to preserve, to strengthen, to enlighten, to quicken, or to restore, is ever to be had from him freely and without price; nor is there one form of the work of grace which he has not bestowed upon his people. As the blood of the body, though flowing from the heart, belongs equally to every member, so the influences of grace are the inheritance of every saint united to the Lamb; and herein there is a sweet communion between Christ and his Church, inasmuch as they both receive the same grace. Christ is the head upon which the oil is first poured; but the same oil to the very skirts of the garments, so that the meanest saint has an unction of the same costly moisture as that which fell upon the head. This is true communion when the sap of grace flows from the stem to the branch, and when it is perceived that the stem itself is sustained by the very nourishment which feeds the branch. As we day by day receive grace from Jesus, and more constantly recognize it as coming from him, we shall behold him in communion with us, and enjoy the felicity of communion with him. Let us make daily use of our riches, and ever repair to him as to our own Lord in covenant, taking from him the supply of all we need with as much boldness as men take money from their own purse.

MARCH 16

I am a stranger with thee.—Psalm 39:12

ES, O Lord, *with* thee, but not *to* thee. All my natural alienation from thee, thy grace has effectually removed; and now, in fellowship with thyself, I walk through this sinful world as a pilgrim in a foreign country. *Thou* art a stranger in thine own world. Man forgets thee, dishonors thee, sets up new laws and alien customs, and knows thee not. When thy dear Son came unto his own, his own received him not. He was in the world, and the world was made by him, and the world knew him not. Never was foreigner so speckled a bird among the denizens of any land as thy beloved Son among his mother's brethren. It is no marvel, then, if I who live the life of Jesus, should be unknown and a stranger here below. Lord, I would not be a citizen where Jesus was an alien. His pierced hand has loosened the cords which once bound my soul to earth, and now I find myself a stranger in the land. My speech seems to these Babylonians among whom I dwell an outlandish tongue, my manners are singular, and my actions are strange. A Tartar would be more at home in Cheapside than I could ever be in the haunts of sinners. But here is the sweetness of my lot: I am a stranger *with thee.* Thou art my fellow-sufferer, my fellow pilgrim. Oh, what joy to wander in such blessed society! My heart burns within me by the way when thou dost speak to me, and though I be a sojourner, I am far more blest than those who sit on thrones, and far more at home than those who dwell in their ceiled houses.

> To me remains nor place, nor time:
> My country is in every clime;
> I can be calm and free from care
> On any shore, since God is there.
>
> While place we seek, or place we shun,
> The soul finds happiness in none:
> But with a God to guide our way,
> 'Tis equal joy to go or stay.

MARCH 17

Remember the poor.
—Galatians 2:10

HY does God allow so many of his children to be poor? He could make them all rich if he pleased; he could lay bags of gold at their doors; he could send them a large annual income; or he could scatter round their houses abundance of provisions, as once he made the quails lie in heaps round the camp of Israel, and rained bread out of heaven to feed them. There is no necessity that they should be poor, except that he sees it to be best. "The cattle upon a thousand hills are his"—he could supply them; he could make the richest, the greatest, and the mightiest bring all their power and riches to the feet of his children, for the hearts of all men are in his control. But he does not choose to do so; he allows them to suffer want, he allows them to pine in penury and obscurity. Why is this? There are many reasons: one is, *to give us, who are favored with enough, an opportunity of showing our love to Jesus.* We show our love to Christ when we sing of him and when we pray to him; but if there were no sons of need in the world we should lose the sweet privilege of evidencing our love, by ministering in almsgiving to his poorer brethren; he has ordained that thus we should prove that our love standeth not in word only, but in deed and in truth. If we truly love Christ, we shall care for those who are loved by him. Those who are dear to him will be dear to us. Let us then look upon it not as a duty but as a privilege to relieve the poor of the Lord's flock—remembering the words of the Lord Jesus, "Inasmuch as ye have done it unto one of the least of these my brethren, ye have done it unto me." Surely this assurance is sweet enough, and this motive strong enough to lead us to help others with a willing hand and a loving heart—recollecting that all we do for his people is graciously accepted by Christ as done to himself.

MARCH 18

Ye are all the children of God by faith in Christ Jesus.
—Galatians 3:26

 HE *fatherhood of God is common to all his children.* Ah! Little-faith, you have often said,

> Oh that I had the courage of Great-heart, that I could wield his sword and be as valiant as he! But, alas, I stumble at every straw, and a shadow makes me afraid.

List thee, Littlefaith. Great-heart is God's child, and you are God's child too; and Great-heart is not one whit more God's child than you are. Peter and Paul, the highly-favored apostles, were of the family of the Most High; and so are you also; the weak Christian is as much a child of God as the strong one.

> This cov'nant stands secure,
> Though earth's old pillars bow;
> The strong, the feeble, and the weak,
> Are one in Jesus now.

All the names are in the same family register. One may have more grace than another, but God our heavenly Father has the same tender heart towards all. One may do more mighty works, and may bring more glory to his Father, but he whose name is the least in the kingdom of heaven is as much the child of God as he who stands among the King's mighty men. Let this cheer and comfort us, when we draw near to God and say, "Our Father."

Yet, while we are comforted by knowing this, let us not rest contented with weak faith, but ask, like the Apostles, to have it increased. However feeble our faith may be, if it be real faith in Christ, we shall reach heaven at last, but we shall not honor our Master much on our pilgrimage, neither shall we abound in joy and peace. If then you would live to Christ's glory, and be happy in his service, seek to be filled with the spirit of adoption more and more completely, till perfect love shall cast out fear.

MARCH 19

Strong in faith.
—Romans 4:20

CHRISTIAN, take good care of thy faith; for recollect *faith is the only way whereby thou canst obtain blessings.* If we want blessings from God, nothing can fetch them down but faith. Prayer cannot draw down answers from God's throne except it be the earnest prayer of the man who believes. Faith is the angelic messenger between the soul and the Lord Jesus in glory. Let that angel be withdrawn, we can neither send up prayer, nor receive the answers. Faith is the telegraphic wire which links earth and heaven—on which God's messages of love fly so fast, that before we call he answers, and while we are yet speaking he hears us. But if that telegraphic wire of faith be snapped, how can we receive the promise? Am I in trouble?—I can obtain help for trouble by faith. Am I beaten about by the enemy?—my soul on her dear Refuge leans by faith. But take faith away—in vain I call to God. There is no road betwixt my soul and heaven. In the deepest wintertime faith is a road on which the horses of prayer may travel—ay, and all the better for the biting frost; but blockade the road, and how can we communicate with the Great King? Faith links me with divinity. Faith clothes me with the power of God. Faith engages on my side the omnipotence of Jehovah. Faith ensures every attribute of God in my defense. It helps me to defy the hosts of hell. It makes me march triumphant over the necks of my enemies. But without faith how can I receive anything of the Lord? Let not him that wavereth—who is like a wave of the sea—expect that he will receive anything of God! O, then, Christian, watch well thy faith; for with it thou canst win all things, however poor thou art, but without it thou canst obtain nothing. "If thou canst believe, all things are possible to him that believeth."

MARCH 20

My beloved.
—Song of Solomon 2:8

THIS was a golden name which the ancient Church in her most joyous moments was wont to give to the Anointed of the Lord. When the time of the singing of birds was come, and the voice of the turtle was heard in her land, *her* love-note was sweeter than either, as she sang, "My *beloved* is mine and I am his: he feedeth among the lilies." Ever in her song of songs doth she call him by that delightful name, "My beloved!" Even in the long winter, when idolatry had withered the garden of the Lord, her prophets found space to lay aside the burden of the Lord for a little season, and to say, as Esaias did, "Now will I sing to my well-beloved a song of my beloved touching his vineyard." Though the saints had never seen his face, though as yet he was not made flesh, nor had dwelt among us, nor had man beheld his glory, yet he was the consolation of Israel, the hope and joy of all the chosen, the "beloved" of all those who were upright before the Most High. We, in the summer days of the Church, are also wont to speak of Christ as the best beloved of our soul, and to feel that he is very precious, the "chiefest among ten thousand, and the altogether lovely." So true is it that the Church loves Jesus, and claims him as her beloved, that the apostle dares to defy the whole universe to separate her from the love of Christ, and declares that neither persecutions, distress, affliction, peril, or the sword have been able to do it; nay, he joyously boasts, "In all these things we are more than conquerors through him that loved us."

O that we knew more of thee, thou ever precious one!

> My sole possession is thy love;
> In earth beneath, or heaven above,
> I have no other store;
> And though with fervent suit I pray,
> And importune thee day by day,
> I ask thee nothing more.

MARCH 21

Ye shall be scattered, every man to his own,
and shall leave me alone.
—John 16:32

EW had fellowship with the sorrows of Gethsemane. The majority of the disciples were not sufficiently advanced in grace to be admitted to behold the mysteries of "the agony." Occupied with the Passover feast at their own houses, they represent the many who live upon the letter, but are mere babes as to the spirit of the gospel. To twelve, nay, to eleven only was the privilege given to enter Gethsemane and see "this great sight." Out of the eleven, eight were left at a distance; they had fellowship, but not of that intimate sort to which men greatly beloved are admitted. Only three highly favored ones could approach the veil of our Lord's mysterious sorrow: within that veil even these must not intrude; a stone's-cast distance must be left between. He must tread the wine-press *alone*, and of the people there must be none with him. Peter and the two sons of Zebedee, represent the few eminent, experienced saints, who may be written down as "Fathers;" these having done business on great waters, can in some degree measure the huge Atlantic waves of their Redeemer's passion. To some selected spirits it is given, for the good of others, and to strengthen them for future, special, and tremendous conflict, to enter the inner circle and hear the pleadings of the suffering High Priest; they have fellowship with him in his sufferings, and are made conformable unto his death. Yet even these cannot penetrate the secret places of the Savior's woe. "Thine unknown sufferings" is the remarkable expression of the Greek liturgy: there was an inner chamber in our Master's grief, shut out from human knowledge and fellowship. There Jesus is *"left alone."* Here Jesus was more than ever an "Unspeakable gift!" Is not Watts right when he sings—

> And all the unknown joys he gives,
> Were bought with agonies unknown.

81

MARCH 22

*And he went a little farther,
and fell on his face, and prayed.*
—Matthew 26:39

HERE are several instructive features in our Savior's prayer in his hour of trial. It was *lonely prayer*. He withdrew even from his three favored disciples. Believer, be much in solitary prayer, especially in times of trial. Family prayer, social prayer, prayer in the Church, will not suffice, these are very precious, but the best beaten spice will smoke in your censer in your private devotions, where no ear hears but God's.

It was *humble prayer*. Luke says he knelt, but another evangelist says he "fell on his face." Where, then, must be *thy* place, thou humble servant of the great Master? What dust and ashes should cover *thy* head! Humility gives us good foothold in prayer. There is no hope of prevalence with God unless we abase ourselves that he may exalt us in due time.

It was *filial prayer*. "Abba, Father." You will find it a stronghold in the day of trial to plead your adoption. You have no rights as a subject, you have forfeited them by your treason; but nothing can forfeit a child's right to a father's protection. Be not afraid to say, "My Father, hear my cry."

Observe that it was *persevering prayer*. He prayed three times. Cease not until you prevail. Be as the importunate widow, whose continual coming earned what her first supplication could not win. Continue in prayer, and watch in the same with thanksgiving.

Lastly, *it was the prayer of resignation*. "Nevertheless, not as I will, but as thou wilt." Yield, and God yields. Let it be as God wills, and God will determine for the best. Be thou content to leave thy prayer in his hands, who knows when to give, and how to give, and what to give, and what to withhold. So pleading, earnestly, importunately, yet with humility and resignation, thou shalt surely prevail.

MARCH 23

His sweat was, as it were,
great drops of blood falling down to the ground.
—Luke 22:44

HE mental pressure arising from our Lord's struggle with temptation, so forced his frame to an unnatural excitement, that his pores sent forth great drops of blood which fell down to the ground. This proves *how tremendous must have been the weight of sin* when it was able to crush the Savior so that he distilled great drops of blood! This demonstrates *the mighty power of his love.* It is a very pretty observation of old Isaac Ambrose that the gum which exudes from the tree without cutting is always the best. This precious camphor-tree yielded most sweet spices when it was wounded under the knotty whips, and when it was pierced by the nails on the cross; but see, it giveth forth its best spice when there is no whip, no nail, no wound. This sets forth *the voluntariness of Christ's sufferings,* since without a lance the blood flowed freely. No need to put on the leech, or apply the knife; it flows spontaneously. No need for the rulers to cry, "Spring up, O well;" of itself it flows in crimson torrents. If men suffer great pain of mind apparently the blood rushes *to* the heart. The cheeks are pale; a fainting fit comes on; the blood has gone inward as if to nourish the inner man while passing through its trial. But see our Savior in his agony; he is so utterly oblivious of self, that instead of his agony driving his blood to the heart to nourish himself, it drives it outward to bedew the earth. The agony of Christ, inasmuch as it pours him out upon the ground, pictures the fullness of the offering which he made for men.

Do we not perceive how intense must have been the wrestling through which he passed, and will we not hear its voice *to us?* "Ye have not yet resisted unto blood, striving against sin." Behold the great Apostle and High Priest of our profession, and sweat even to blood rather than yield to the great tempter of your souls.

MARCH 24

He was heard, in that he feared.
—Hebrews 5:7

ID this fear arise from the infernal suggestion that he was utterly forsaken? There may be sterner trials than this, but surely it is *one* of the worst to be utterly forsaken? "See," said Satan,

> . . . thou hast a friend nowhere! Thy Father hath shut up
> the bowels of his compassion against thee. Not an angel in
> his courts will stretch out his hand to help thee. All heaven
is alienated from thee; thou art left alone. See the companions with whom thou hast taken sweet counsel, what are they worth? Son of Mary, see there thy brother James, see there thy loved disciple John, and thy bold apostle Peter, how the cowards sleep when thou art in thy sufferings! Lo! Thou hast no friend left in heaven or earth. All hell is against thee. I have stirred up mine infernal den. I have sent my missives throughout all regions summoning every prince of darkness to set upon thee this night, and we will spare no arrows, we will use all our infernal might to overwhelm thee: and what wilt thou do, thou solitary one?

It may be, this was the temptation; we think it was, because the appearance of an angel unto him, strengthening him, removed that fear. He was heard in that he feared; he was no more alone, but heaven was with him. It may be that this is the reason of his coming three times to his disciples—as Hart puts it—

> Backwards and forwards thrice he ran,
> As if he sought some help from man.

He would see for himself whether it were really true that all men had forsaken him; he found them all asleep; but perhaps he gained some faint comfort from the thought that they were sleeping, not from treachery, but from sorrow, the spirit indeed was willing, but the flesh was weak. At any rate, he was heard in that he feared. Jesus was heard in his deepest woe; my soul, thou shalt be heard also.

MARCH 25

Betrayest thou the Son of Man with a kiss?
—Luke 22:48

HE kisses of an enemy are deceitful." Let me be on my guard when the world puts on a loving face, for it will, if possible, betray me as it did my Master, with a kiss. Whenever a man is about to stab religion, he usually professes very great reverence for it. Let me beware of the sleek-faced hypocrisy which is amour-bearer to heresy and infidelity. Knowing the deceivableness of unrighteousness, let me be wise as a serpent to detect and avoid the designs of the enemy. The young man, void of understanding, was led astray by the kiss of the strange woman: may my soul be so graciously instructed all this day, that "the much fair speech" of the world may have no effect upon me. Holy Spirit, let me not, a poor frail son of man, be betrayed with a kiss!

But what if I should be guilty of the same accursed sin as Judas, that son of perdition? I have been baptized into the name of the Lord Jesus; I am a member of his visible Church; I sit at the communion table: all these are so many kisses of my lips. Am I sincere in them? If not, I am a base traitor. Do I live in the world as carelessly as others do, and yet make a profession of being a follower of Jesus? Then I must expose religion to ridicule, and lead men to speak evil of the holy name by which I am called. Surely if I act thus inconsistently I am a Judas, and it were better for me that I had never been born. Dare I hope that I am clear in this matter? Then, O Lord, keep me so. O Lord, make me sincere and true. Preserve me from every false way. Never let me betray my Savior. I do love thee, Jesus, and though I often grieve thee, yet I would desire to abide faithful even unto death. O God, forbid that I should be a high-soaring professor, and then fall at last into the lake of fire, because I betrayed my Master with a kiss.

MARCH 26

Jesus said unto them, "If ye seek me, let these go their way."
—John 18:8

MARK, my soul, the care which Jesus manifested even in his hour of trial, towards the sheep of his hand! The ruling passion is strong in death. He resigns himself to the enemy, but he interposes a word of power to set his disciples free. As to himself, like a sheep before her shearers he is dumb and opened not his mouth, but for his disciples' sake he speaks with Almighty energy. Herein is love, constant, self-forgetting, faithful love. But is there not far more here than is to be found upon the surface? Have we not the very soul and spirit of the atonement in these words? The Good Shepherd lays down his life for the sheep, and pleads that they must therefore go free. The Surety is bound, and justice demands that those for whom he stands a substitute should go their way. In the midst of Egypt's bondage, that voice rings as a word of power, *"Let these go their way."* Out of the slavery of sin and Satan the redeemed must come. In every cell of the dungeons of Despair, the sound is echoed, *"Let these go their way,"* and forth come Despondency and Muchafraid. Satan hears the well-known voice, and lifts his foot from the neck of the fallen; and Death hears it, and the grave opens her gates to let the dead arise. *Their way* is one of progress, holiness, triumph, glory, and none shall dare to stay them in it. No lion shall be on their way, neither shall any ravenous beast go up thereon. "The hind of the morning" has drawn the cruel hunters upon himself, and now the most timid roes and hinds of the field may graze at perfect peace among the lilies of his loves. The thundercloud has burst over the Cross of Calvary, and the pilgrims of Zion shall never be smitten by the bolts of vengeance. Come, my heart, rejoice in the immunity which thy Redeemer has secured thee, and bless his name all the day, and every day.

MARCH 27

Then all the disciples forsook him and fled.
—Matthew 26:56

HE never deserted them, but they in cowardly fear of their lives, fled from him in the very beginning of his sufferings. This is but one instructive instance of the frailty of all believers if left to themselves; they are but sheep at the best, and they flee when the wolf cometh. They had all been warned of the danger, and had promised to die rather than leave their Master; and yet they were seized with sudden panic, and took to their heels. It may be, that I, at the opening of this day, have braced up my mind to bear a trial for the Lord's sake, and I imagine myself to be certain to exhibit perfect fidelity; but let me be very jealous of myself, lest having the same evil heart of unbelief, I should depart from my Lord as the apostles did. It is one thing to promise, and quite another to perform. It would have been to their eternal honor to have stood at Jesus' side right manfully; they fled from honor; may I be kept from imitating them! Where else could they have been so safe as near their Master, who could presently call for twelve legions of angels? They fled from their true safety. O God, let me not play the fool also. Divine grace can make the coward brave. The smoking flax can flame forth like fire on the altar when the Lord wills it. These very apostles who were timid as hares, grew to be bold as lions after the Spirit had descended upon them, and even so the Holy Spirit can make my recreant spirit brave to confess my Lord and witness for his truth.

What anguish must have filled the Savior as he saw his friends so faithless! This was one bitter ingredient in his cup; but that cup is drained dry; let me not put another drop in it. If I forsake my Lord, I shall crucify him afresh, and put him to an open shame. Keep me, O blessed Spirit, from an end so shameful.

March 28

The love of Christ which passeth knowledge.
—Ephesians 3:19

HE love of Christ in its sweetness, its fullness, its greatness, its faithfulness, passeth all human comprehension. Where shall language be found which shall describe his matchless, his unparalleled love towards the children of men? It is so vast and boundless that, as the swallow but skimmeth the water, and diveth not into its depths, so all descriptive words but touch the surface, while depths immeasurable lie beneath. Well might the poet say,

O love, thou fathomless abyss!

for this love of Christ is indeed measureless and fathomless; none can attain unto it. Before we can have any right idea of the love of Jesus, we must understand his previous glory in its height of majesty, and his incarnation upon the earth in all its depths of shame. But who can tell us the majesty of Christ? When he was enthroned in the highest heavens he was very God of very God; by him were the heavens made, and all the hosts thereof. His own almighty arm upheld the spheres; the praises of cherubim and seraphim perpetually surrounded him; the full chorus of the hallelujahs of the universe unceasingly flowed to the foot of his throne: he reigned supreme above all his creatures, God over all, blessed forever. Who can tell his height of glory then? And who, on the other hand, can tell how low he descended? To be a man was something, to be a man of sorrows was far more; to bleed, and die, and suffer, these were much for him who was the Son of God; but to suffer such unparalleled agony—to endure a death of shame and desertion by his Father, this is a depth of condescending love which the most inspired mind must utterly fail to fathom. Herein is love! and truly it is love that "passeth knowledge." O let this love fill our hearts with adoring gratitude, and lead us to practical manifestations of its power.

March 29

Though he were a Son, yet learned he obedience
by the things which he suffered.
—Hebrews 5:8

E are told that the Captain of our salvation was made perfect through suffering, therefore we who are sinful, and who are far from being perfect, must not wonder if we are called to pass through suffering too. Shall the head be crowned with thorns, and shall the other members of the body be rocked upon the dainty lap of ease? Must Christ pass through seas of his own blood to win the crown, and are we to walk to heaven dryshod in silver slippers? No, our Master's experience teaches us that suffering is necessary, and the true-born child of God must not, would not, escape it if he might. But there is one very comforting thought in the fact of Christ's "being made perfect through suffering"—it is, that he can have complete sympathy with us. "He is not an high priest that cannot be touched with the feeling of our infirmities." In this sympathy of Christ we find a sustaining power. One of the early martyrs said, "I can bear it all, for Jesus suffered, and he suffers in me now; he sympathizes with me, and this makes me strong." Believer, lay hold of this thought in all times of agony. Let the thought of Jesus strengthen you as you follow in his steps. Find a sweet support in his sympathy; and remember that, to suffer is an honorable thing—to suffer for Christ is glory. The apostles rejoiced that they were counted worthy to do this. Just so far as the Lord shall give us grace to suffer *for* Christ, to suffer *with* Christ, just so far does he honor us. The jewels of a Christian are his afflictions. The regalia of the kings whom God hath anointed are their troubles, their sorrows, and their griefs. Let us not, therefore, shun being honored. Let us not turn aside from being exalted. Griefs exalt us, and troubles lift us up. "If we suffer, we shall also reign with him."

MARCH 30

He was numbered with the transgressors.
—Isaiah 53:12

HY did Jesus suffer himself to be enrolled amongst sinners? This wonderful condescension was justified by many powerful reasons. *In such a character he could the better become their advocate.* In some trials there is an identification of the counselor with the client, nor can they be looked upon in the eye of the law as apart from one another. Now, when the sinner is brought to the bar, Jesus appears there himself. He stands to answer the accusation. He points to his side, his hands, his feet, and challenges Justice to bring anything against the sinners whom he represents; he pleads his blood, and pleads so triumphantly, being numbered with them and having a part with them, that the Judge proclaims, "Let them go their way; deliver them from going down into the pit, for he hath found a ransom." Our Lord Jesus was numbered with the transgressors in order that they might *feel their hearts drawn towards him.* Who can be afraid of one who is written in the same list with us? Surely we may come boldly to him, and confess our guilt. He who is numbered with us cannot condemn us. Was he not put down in the transgressor's list *that we might be written in the red roll of the saints?* he was holy, and written among the holy; we were guilty, and numbered among the guilty; he transfers his name from yonder list to this black indictment, and our names are taken from the indictment and written in the roll of acceptance, for there is a complete transfer made between Jesus and his people. All our estate of misery and sin Jesus has taken; and all that Jesus has comes to us. His righteousness, his blood, and everything that he hath he gives us as our dowry. Rejoice, believer, in your union to him who was numbered among the transgressors; and prove that you are truly saved by being manifestly numbered with those who are new creatures in him.

MARCH 31

With his stripes, we are healed.
—Isaiah 53:5

ILATE delivered our Lord to the lictors to be scourged. The Roman scourge was a most dreadful instrument of torture. It was made of the sinews of oxen, and sharp bones were inter-twisted every here and there among the sinews; so that every time the lash came down these pieces of bone inflicted fearful laceration, and tore off the flesh from the bone. The Savior was, no doubt, bound to the column, and thus beaten. He had been beaten before; but this of the Roman lictors was probably the most severe of his flagellations. My soul, stand here and weep over his poor stricken body.

Believer in Jesus, can you gaze upon him without tears, as he stands before you the mirror of agonizing love? He is at once fair as the lily for innocence, and red as the rose with the crimson of his own blood. As we feel the sure and blessed healing which his stripes have wrought in us, does not our heart melt at once with love and grief? If ever we have loved our Lord Jesus, surely we must feel that affection glowing now within our bosoms.

> See how the patient Jesus stands,
> Insulted in his lowest case!
> Sinners have bound the Almighty's hands,
> And spit in their Creator's face.
>
> With thorns his temples gor'd and gash'd
> Send streams of blood from every part;
> His back's with knotted scourges lash'd.
> But sharper scourges tear his heart.

We would fain go to our chambers and weep; but since our business calls us away, we will first pray our Beloved to print the image of his bleeding self upon the tablets of our hearts all the day, and at nightfall we will return to commune with him, and sorrow that our sin should have cost him so dear.

APRIL 1

Let him kiss me with the kisses of his mouth.
—Song of Solomon 1:2

OR several days we have been dwelling upon the Savior's passion, and for some little time to come we shall linger there. In beginning a new month, let us seek the same desires after our Lord as those which glowed in the heart of the elect spouse. See how she leaps at once to *him;* there are no prefatory words; she does not even mention his name; she is in the heart of her theme at once, for she speaks of *him* who was the only him in the world to her. How bold is her love! it was much condescension which permitted the weeping penitent to anoint his feet with spikenard—it was rich love which allowed the gentle Mary to sit at his feet and learn of him—but here, love, strong, fervent love, aspires to higher tokens of regard, and closer signs of fellowship. Esther trembled in the presence of Ahasuerus, but the spouse in joyful liberty of perfect love knows no fear. If we have received the same free spirit, we also may ask the like. By kisses we suppose to be intended those varied manifestations of affection by which the believer is made to enjoy the love of Jesus. The kiss of *reconciliation* we enjoyed at our conversion, and it was sweet as honey dropping from the comb. The kiss of *acceptance* is still warm on our brow, as we know that he hath accepted our persons and our works through rich grace. The kiss of daily, present *communion,* is that which we pant after to be repeated day after day, till it is changed into the kiss of *reception,* which removes the soul from earth, and the kiss of *consummation* which fills it with the joy of heaven. Faith is our walk, but fellowship sensibly felt is our rest. Faith is the road, but communion with Jesus is the well from which the pilgrim drinks. O lover of our souls, be not strange to us; let the lips of thy blessing meet the lips of our asking; let the lips of thy fullness touch the lips of our need, and straightway the kiss will be effected.

APRIL 2

He answered him to never a word.
—Matthew 27:14

HE had never been slow of speech when he could bless the sons of men, but he would not say a single word for himself. "Never man spake like this Man," and never man was silent like him. Was this singular silence *the index of his perfect self-sacrifice?* Did it show that he would not utter a word to stay the slaughter of his sacred person, which he had dedicated as an offering for us? Had he so entirely surrendered himself that he would not interfere in his own behalf, even in the minutest degree, but be bound and slain an unstruggling, uncomplaining victim? Was this silence *a type of the defenselessness of sin?* Nothing can be said in palliation or excuse of human guilt; and, therefore, he who bore its whole weight stood speechless before his judge. Is not patient silence *the best reply to a gainsaying world?* Calm endurance answers some questions infinitely more conclusively than the loftiest eloquence. The best apologists for Christianity in the early days were its martyrs. The anvil breaks a host of hammers by quietly bearing their blows. Did not the silent Lamb of God furnish us with *a grand example of wisdom?* Where every word was occasion for new blasphemy, it was the line of duty to afford no fuel for the flame of sin. The ambiguous and the false, the unworthy and mean, will ere long overthrow and confute themselves, and therefore the true can afford to be quiet, and finds silence to be its wisdom. Evidently our Lord, by his silence, furnished *a remarkable fulfillment of prophecy.* A long defense of himself would have been contrary to Isaiah's prediction. "He is led as a lamb to the slaughter, and as a sheep before her shearers is dumb, so he openeth not his mouth." By his quiet he conclusively proved himself to be the true Lamb of God. As such we salute him this morning. Be with us, Jesus, and in the silence of our heart, let us hear the voice of thy love.

APRIL 3

They took Jesus, and led him away.
—John 19:16

E had been all night in agony, he had spent the early morning at the hall of Caiaphas, he had been hurried from Caiaphas to Pilate, from Pilate to Herod, and from Herod back again to Pilate; he had, therefore, but little strength left, and yet neither refreshment nor rest were permitted him. They were eager for his blood, and therefore led him out to die, loaded with the cross. O dolorous procession! Well may Salem's daughters weep. My soul, do thou weep also.

What learn we here as we see our blessed Lord led forth? Do we not perceive that truth which was set forth in shadow by *the scapegoat?* Did not the high-priest bring the scapegoat, and put both his hands upon its head, confessing the sins of the people, that thus those sins might be laid upon the goat, and cease from the people? Then the goat was led away by a fit man into the wilderness, and it carried away the sins of the people, so that if they were sought for they could not be found. Now we see Jesus brought before the priests and rulers, who pronounce him guilty; God himself imputes our sins *to him,* "the Lord hath laid on him the iniquity of us all;" "he was made sin for us;" and, as the substitute for our guilt, bearing our sin upon his shoulders, represented by the cross; we see the great Scapegoat led away by the appointed officers of justice. Beloved, can you feel assured that he carried *your* sin? As you look at the cross upon his shoulders, does it represent *your* sin? There is one way by which you can tell whether he carried your sin or not. Have you laid your hand upon his head, confessed your sin, and trusted in him? Then your sin lies not on you; it has all been transferred by blessed imputation to Christ, and he bears it on his shoulder as a load heavier than the cross.

Let not the picture vanish till you have rejoiced in your own deliverance, and adored the loving Redeemer upon whom your iniquities were laid.

APRIL 4

For he hath made him to be sin for us, who knew no sin;
that we might be made the righteousness of God in him.
—*2 Corinthians 5:21*

OURNING Christian! why weepest thou? Art thou mourning over thine own corruptions? Look to thy perfect Lord, and remember, thou art complete in him; thou art in God's sight as perfect as if thou hadst never sinned; nay, more than that, the Lord our Righteousness hath put a divine garment upon thee, so that thou hast more than the righteousness of man—thou hast the righteousness of God. O thou who art mourning by reason of inbred sin and depravity, remember, none of thy sins can condemn thee. Thou hast learned to hate sin; but thou hast learned also to know that sin is not thine—it was laid upon Christ's head. thy standing is not in thyself—it is in Christ; thine acceptance is not in thyself, but in thy Lord; thou art as much accepted of God today, with all thy sinfulness, as thou wilt be when thou standest before his throne, free from all corruption. O, I beseech thee, lay hold on this precious thought, *perfection in Christ!* For thou art "complete in him." With thy Savior's garment on, thou art holy as the Holy one.

> Who is he that condemneth? It is Christ that died, yea rather, that is risen again, who is even at the right hand of God, who also maketh intercession for us.

Christian, let thy heart rejoice, for thou art "accepted in the beloved"—what hast thou to fear? Let thy face ever wear a smile; live near thy Master; live in the suburbs of the Celestial City; for soon, when thy time has come, thou shalt rise up where thy Jesus sits, and reign at his right hand; and all this because the divine Lord "was made to be sin for us, who knew no sin; that we might be made the righteousness of God in him."

APRIL 5

On him they laid the cross,
that he might bear it after Jesus.
—Luke 23:26

E see in Simon's carrying the cross a picture of the work of the Church throughout all generations; she is the cross-bearer after Jesus. Mark then, Christian, Jesus does not suffer so as to exclude your suffering. He bears a cross, not that you may escape it, but that you may endure it. Christ exempts you from sin, but not from sorrow. Remember that, and expect to suffer.

But let us comfort ourselves with this thought, that in our case, as in Simon's, *it is not our cross, but Christ's cross which we carry.* When you are molested for your piety; when your religion brings the trial of cruel mockings upon you, then remember it is not *your* cross, it is *Christ's* cross; and how delightful is it to carry the cross of our Lord Jesus!

You carry the cross after him. You have blessed company; your path is marked with the footprints of your Lord. The mark of his blood-red shoulder is upon that heavy burden. 'Tis *his* cross, and he goes before you as a shepherd goes before his sheep. Take up your cross daily, and follow him.

Do not forget, also, *that you bear this cross in partnership.* It is the opinion of some that Simon only carried one end of the cross, and not the whole of it. That is very possible; Christ may have carried the heavier part, against the transverse beam, and Simon may have borne the lighter end. Certainly it is so with you; you do but carry the light end of the cross, Christ bore the heavier end.

And remember, *though Simon had to bear the cross for a very little while, it gave him lasting honor.* Even so the cross we carry is only for a little while at most, and then we shall receive the crown, the glory. Surely we should love the cross, and, instead of shrinking from it, *count it very dear,* when it works out for us "a far more exceeding and eternal weight of glory."

APRIL 6

Let us go forth therefore unto him without the camp.
—Hebrews 13:13

ESUS, bearing his cross, went forth to suffer without the gate. The Christian's reason for leaving the camp of the world's sin and religion is not because he loves to be singular, but because *Jesus did so;* and the disciple must follow his Master. Christ was "not of the world:" his life and his testimony were a constant protest against conformity with the world. Never was such overflowing affection for men as you find in him; but still he was separate from sinners. In like manner Christ's people must "go forth unto him." They must take their position "without the camp," as witness-bearers for the truth. They must be prepared to tread the straight and narrow path. They must have bold, unflinching, lion-like hearts, loving Christ first, and his truth next, and Christ and his truth beyond all the world. Jesus would have his people "go forth without the camp" *for their own sanctification.* You cannot grow in grace to any high degree while you are conformed to the world. The life of separation may be a path of sorrow, but it is the highway of safety; and though the separated life may cost you many pangs, and make every day a battle, yet it is a happy life after all. No joy can excel that of the soldier of Christ: Jesus reveals himself so graciously, and gives such sweet refreshment, that the warrior feels more calm and peace in his daily strife than others in their hours of rest. The highway of holiness is the highway of communion. It is thus we shall hope *to win the crown* if we are enabled by divine grace faithfully to follow Christ "without the camp." The crown of glory will follow the cross of separation. A moment's shame will be well recompensed by eternal honor; a little while of witness-bearing will seem nothing when we are "forever with the Lord."

APRIL 7

O ye sons of men, how long will ye turn my glory into shame?
—Psalm 4:2

N instructive writer has made a mournful list of the honors which the blinded people of Israel awarded to their long-expected King.

1. They gave him *a procession of honor,* in which Roman legionaries, Jewish priests, men and women, took a part, he himself bearing his cross. This is the triumph which the world awards to him who comes to overthrow man's direst foes. Derisive shouts are his only acclamations, and cruel taunts his only paeans of praise.

2. They presented him with *the wine of honor.* Instead of a golden cup of generous wine they offered him the criminal's stupefying death-draught, which he refused because he would preserve an uninjured taste wherewith to taste of death; and afterwards when he cried, "I thirst," they gave him vinegar mixed with gall, thrust to his mouth upon a sponge. Oh! wretched, detestable inhospitality to the King's Son.

3. He was provided with *a guard of honor,* who showed their esteem of him by gambling over his garments, which they had seized as their booty. Such was the body-guard of the adored of heaven; a quaternion of brutal gamblers.

4. A *throne of honor* was found for him upon the bloody tree; no easier place of rest would rebel men yield to their liege Lord. The cross was, in fact, the full expression of the world's feeling towards him; "There," they seemed to say, "Thou Son of God, this is the manner in which God himself should be treated, could we reach him."

(5.) *The title of honor* was nominally "King of the Jews," but that, the blinded nation distinctly repudiated, and really called him "King of thieves," by preferring Barabbas, and by placing Jesus in the place of highest shame between two thieves. His glory was thus in all things turned into shame by the sons of men, but it shall yet gladden the eyes of saints and angels, world without end.

APRIL 8

If they do these things in a green tree, what shall be done in the dry?
—Luke 23:31

MONG other interpretations of this suggestive question, the following is full of teaching:

> If I, the innocent substitute for sinners, suffer thus, what will be done when the sinner himself—the dry tree—shall fall into the hands of an angry God?

When God saw Jesus in the sinner's place, he did not spare him; and when he finds the unregenerate without Christ, he will not spare them. O sinner, Jesus was led away by his enemies: so shall you be dragged away by fiends to the place appointed for you. Jesus was deserted of God; and if he, who was only imputedly a sinner, was deserted, how much more shall you be? *"Eloi, Eloi, lama sabachthani?"* what an awful shriek! But what shall be your cry when you shall say, "O God! O God! why hast thou forsaken me?" and the answer shall come back,

> Because ye have set at naught all my counsel, and would none of my reproof: I also will laugh at your calamity; I will mock when your fear cometh.

If God spared not his own Son, how much less will he spare you! What whips of burning wire will be yours when conscience shall smite you with all its terrors. Ye richest, ye merriest, ye most self-righteous sinners—who would stand in your place when God shall say, "Awake, O sword, against the man that rejected me; smite him, and let him feel the smart forever"? Jesus was spit upon: sinner, what shame will be yours! We cannot sum up in one word all the mass of sorrows which met upon the head of Jesus who died for us, therefore it is impossible for us to tell you what streams, what oceans of grief must roll over *your* spirit if you die as you now are. You may die so, you may die now. By the agonies of Christ, by his wounds and by his blood, do not bring upon yourselves the wrath to come! Trust in the Son of God, and you shall never die.

APRIL 9

And there followed him a great company of people, and of women,
which also bewailed and lamented him.
—Luke 23:27

AMID the rabble rout which hounded the Redeemer to his doom, there were some gracious souls whose bitter anguish sought vent in wailing and lamentations—fit music to accompany that march of woe. When my soul can, in imagination, see the Savior bearing his cross to Calvary, she joins the godly women and weeps with them; for, indeed, there is true cause for grief—cause lying deeper than those mourning women thought. They bewailed innocence maltreated, goodness persecuted, love bleeding, meekness about to die; but my heart has a deeper and more bitter cause to mourn. My sins were the scourges which lacerated those blessed shoulders, and crowned with thorn those bleeding brows: my sins cried "Crucify him! crucify him!" and laid the cross upon his gracious shoulders. His being led forth to die is sorrow enough for one eternity: but my having been his murderer, is more, infinitely more, grief than one poor fountain of tears can express.

Why those women loved and wept it were not hard to guess: but they could not have had greater reasons for love and grief than my heart has. Nain's widow saw her son restored—but I myself have been raised to newness of life. Peter's wife's mother was cured of the fever—but I of the greater plague of sin. Out of Magdalene seven devils were cast—but a whole legion out of me. Mary and Martha were favored with visits—but he dwells with me. His mother bare his body—but he is formed in me the hope of glory. In nothing behind the holy women in debt, let me not be behind them in gratitude or sorrow.

> Love and grief my heart dividing,
> With my tears his feet I'll lave—
> Constant still in heart abiding,
> Weep for him who died to save.

April 10

The place which is called Calvary.
—Luke 23:33

THE hill of comfort is the hill of Calvary; the house of consolation is built with the wood of the cross; the temple of heavenly blessing is founded upon the riven rock—riven by the spear which pierced his side. No scene in sacred history ever gladdens the soul like Calvary's tragedy.

> Is it not strange, the darkest hour
> That ever dawned on sinful earth,
> Should touch the heart with softer power,
> For comfort, than an angel's mirth?
> That to the Cross the mourner's eye should turn,
> Sooner than where the stars of Bethlehem burn?

Light springs from the midday-midnight of Golgotha, and every herb of the field blooms sweetly beneath the shadow of the once accursed tree. In that place of thirst, grace hath dug a fountain which ever gusheth with waters pure as crystal, each drop capable of alleviating the woes of mankind. You who have had your seasons of conflict, will confess that it was not at Olivet that you ever found comfort, not on the hill of Sinai, nor on Tabor; but Gethsemane, Gabbatha, and Golgotha have been a means of comfort to you. The bitter herbs of Gethsemane have often taken away the bitters of your life; the scourge of Gabbatha has often scourged away your cares, and the groans of Calvary yields us comfort rare and rich. We never should have known Christ's love in all its heights and depths if he had not died; nor could we guess the Father's deep affection if he had not given his Son to die. The common mercies we enjoy all sing of love, just as the sea-shell, when we put it to our ears, whispers of the deep sea whence it came; but if we desire to hear the ocean itself, we must not look at every-day blessings, but at the transactions of the crucifixion. He who would know love, let him retire to Calvary and see the Man of sorrows die.

APRIL 11

I am poured out like water, and all my bones are out of joint.
—Psalm 22:14

ID earth or heaven ever behold a sadder spectacle of woe! In soul and body, our Lord felt himself to be weak as water poured upon the ground. The placing of the cross in its socket had shaken him with great violence, had strained all the ligaments, pained every nerve, and more or less dislocated all his bones. Burdened with his own weight, the august sufferer felt the strain increasing every moment of those six long hours. His sense of faintness and general weakness were overpowering; while to his own consciousness he became nothing but a mass of misery and swooning sickness. When Daniel saw the great vision, he thus describes his sensations, "There remained no strength in me, for my vigor was turned into corruption, and I retained no strength:" how much more faint must have been our greater Prophet when he saw the dread vision of the wrath of God, and felt it in his own soul! To us, sensations such as our Lord endured would have been insupportable, and kind unconsciousness would have come to our rescue; but in his case, he was wounded, and *felt* the sword; he drained the cup and *tasted* every drop.

> O King of Grief! (a title strange, yet true
> To thee of all kings only due)
> O King of Wounds! how shall I grieve for thee,
> Who in all grief preventest me!

As we kneel before our now ascended Savior's throne, let us remember well the way by which he prepared it as a throne of grace for us; let us in spirit drink of his cup, that we may be strengthened for our hour of heaviness whenever it may come. In his natural body every member suffered, and so must it be in the spiritual; but as out of all his griefs and woes his body came forth uninjured to glory and power, even so shall his mystical body come through the furnace with not so much as the smell of fire upon it.

APRIL 12

My heart is like wax; it is melted in the midst of my bowels.
—Psalm 22:14

OUR blessed Lord experienced a terrible sinking and melting of soul. "The spirit of a man will sustain his infirmity, but a wounded spirit who can bear?" Deep depression of spirit is the most grievous of all trials; all besides is as nothing. Well might the suffering Savior cry to his God, "Be not far from me," for above all other seasons a man needs his God when his heart is melted within him because of heaviness. Believer, come near the cross this morning, and humbly adore the King of glory as having once been brought far lower, in mental distress and inward anguish, than any one among us; and mark his fitness to become a faithful High Priest, who can be touched with a feeling of our infirmities. Especially let those of us whose sadness springs directly from the withdrawal of a present sense of our Father's love, enter into near and intimate communion with Jesus. Let us not give way to despair, since through this dark room the Master has passed before us. Our souls may sometimes long and faint, and thirst even to anguish, to behold the light of the Lord's countenance: at such times let us stay ourselves with the sweet fact of the sympathy of our great High Priest. Our drops of sorrow may well be forgotten in the ocean of his griefs; but how high ought our love to rise! Come in, O strong and deep love of Jesus, like the sea at the flood in spring tides, cover all my powers, drown all my sins, wash out all my cares, lift up my earth-bound soul, and float it right up to my Lord's feet, and there let me lie, a poor broken shell, washed up by his love, having no virtue or value; and only venturing to whisper to him that if he will put his ear to me, he will hear within my heart faint echoes of the vast waves of his own love which have brought me where it is my delight to lie, even at his feet forever.

APRIL 13

A bundle of myrrh is my well-beloved unto me.
—Song of Solomon 1:13

YRRH may well be chosen as the type of Jesus on account of its *preciousness,* its *perfume,* its *pleasantness, its healing, preserving, disinfecting qualities, and its connection with sacrifice.* But why is he compared to "*a bundle* of myrrh"? First, for *plenty. He* is not a drop of it, he is a casket full. He is not a sprig or flower of it, but a whole bundle. There is enough in Christ for all my necessities; let me not be slow to avail myself of him. Our well-beloved is compared to a "bundle" again, for *variety:* for there is in Christ not only the one thing needful, but in "him dwelleth all the fullness of the Godhead bodily," everything needful is in him. Take Jesus in his different characters, and you will see a marvelous variety—Prophet, Priest, King, Husband, Friend, Shepherd. Consider him in his life, death, resurrection, ascension, second advent; view him in his virtue, gentleness, courage, self-denial, love, faithfulness, truth, righteousness—everywhere he is a bundle of preciousness. He is a "bundle of myrrh" for *preservation*—not loose myrrh tied up, myrrh to be stored in a casket. We must value him as our best treasure; we must prize his words and his ordinances; and we must keep our thoughts of him and knowledge of him as under lock and key, lest the devil should steal anything from us. Moreover, Jesus is a "bundle of myrrh" *for specialty.* The emblem suggests the idea of distinguishing, discriminating grace. From before the foundation of the world, he was set apart for his people; and he gives forth his perfume only to those who understand how to enter into communion with him, to have close dealings with him. Oh! blessed people whom the Lord hath admitted into his secrets, and for whom he sets himself apart. Oh! choice and happy who are thus made to say, "A bundle of myrrh is my well-beloved unto me."

April 14

All they that see me laugh me to scorn: they shoot out the lip,
they shake the head.
—Psalm 22:7

OCKERY was a great ingredient in our Lord's woe. Judas mocked him in the garden; the chief priests and scribes laughed him to scorn; Herod set him at naught; the servants and the soldiers jeered at him, and brutally insulted him; Pilate and his guards ridiculed his royalty; and on the tree all sorts of horrid jests and hideous taunts were hurled at him. Ridicule is always hard to bear, but when we are in intense pain it is so heartless, so cruel, that it cuts us to the quick. Imagine the Savior crucified, racked with anguish far beyond all mortal guess, and then picture that motley multitude, all wagging their heads or thrusting out the lip in bitterest contempt of one poor suffering victim! Surely there must have been something more in the crucified One than they could see, or else such a great and mingled crowd would not unanimously have honored him with such contempt. Was it not evil confessing, in the very moment of its greatest apparent triumph, that after all it could do no more than mock at that victorious goodness which was then reigning on the cross? O Jesus, "despised and rejected of men," how couldst thou die for men who treated thee so ill? Herein is love amazing, love divine, yea, love beyond degree. We, too, have despised thee in the days of our unregeneracy, and even since our new birth we have set the world on high in our hearts, and yet thou bleedest to heal our wounds, and diest to give us life. O that we could set thee on a glorious high throne in all men's hearts! We would ring out thy praises over land and sea till men should as universally adore as once they did unanimously reject.

> Thy creatures wrong thee, O thou sovereign Good!
> *Thou art not loved, because not understood:*
> This grieves me most, that vain pursuits beguile
> Ungrateful men, regardless of thy smile.

APRIL 15

My God, my God, why hast thou forsaken me?
—Psalm 22:1

E here behold the Savior in the depth of his sorrows. No other place so well shows the griefs of Christ as Calvary, and no other moment at Calvary is so full of agony as that in which his cry rends the air—"My God, my God, why hast thou forsaken me?" At this moment physical weakness was united with acute mental torture from the shame and ignominy through which he had to pass; and to make his grief culminate with emphasis, he suffered spiritual agony surpassing all expression, resulting from the departure of his Father's presence. This was the black midnight of his horror; then it was that he descended the abyss of suffering. No man can enter into the full meaning of these words. Some of us think at times that *we* could cry, "My God, my God, why hast thou forsaken me?" There are seasons when the brightness of our Father's smile is eclipsed by clouds and darkness; but let us remember that God never does really forsake us. It is only a seeming forsaking with us, but in Christ's case it was a real forsaking. We grieve at a little withdrawal of our Father's love; but the real turning away of God's face from his Son, who shall calculate how deep the agony which it caused him?

In our case, our cry is often dictated by unbelief: in his case, it was the utterance of a dreadful fact, for God had really turned away from him for a season. O thou poor, distressed soul, who once lived in the sunshine of God's face, but art now in darkness, remember that he has not really forsaken thee. God in the clouds is as much our God as when he shines forth in all the luster of his grace; but since even the *thought* that he has forsaken us gives us agony, what must the woe of the Savior have been when he exclaimed, "My God, my God, why hast thou forsaken me?"

April 16

The precious blood of Christ.
—1 Peter 1:19

STANDING at the foot of the cross, we see hands, and feet, and side, all distilling crimson streams of precious blood. It is "precious" because of its *redeeming* and *atoning efficacy.* By it the sins of Christ's people are atoned for; they are redeemed from under the law; they are reconciled to God, made one with him. Christ's blood is also "precious" in its *cleansing power;* it "cleanseth from all sin." "Though your sins be as scarlet, they shall be as white as snow." Through Jesus' blood, there is not a spot left upon any believer, no wrinkle nor any such thing remains. O precious blood, which makes us clean, removing the stains of abundant iniquity, and permitting us to stand accepted in the Beloved, notwithstanding the many ways in which we have rebelled against our God. The blood of Christ is likewise "precious" in its *preserving power.* We are safe from the destroying angel under the sprinkled blood. Remember it is *God's seeing* the blood which is the true reason for our being spared. Here is comfort for us when the eye of faith is dim, for God's eye is still the same. The blood of Christ is "precious" also in its *sanctifying influence.* The same blood which justifies by taking away sin, does in its after-action, quicken the new nature and lead it onward to subdue sin and to follow out the commands of God. There is no motive for holiness so great as that which streams from the veins of Jesus. And "precious," unspeakably precious, is this blood, because it has *an overcoming power.* It is written, "They overcame through the blood of the Lamb." How could they do otherwise? He who fights with the precious blood of Jesus, fights with a weapon which cannot know defeat. The blood of Jesus! sin dies at its presence, death ceases to be death: heaven's gates are opened. The blood of Jesus! we shall march on, conquering and to conquer, so long as we can trust its power!

APRIL 17

We are come to the blood of sprinkling,
that speaketh better things than that of Abel.
—Hebrews 12:24

READER, have *you* come to the blood of sprinkling? The question is not whether you have come to a knowledge of doctrine, or an observance of ceremonies, or to a certain form of experience, but *have you come to the blood of Jesus?* The blood of Jesus is the life of all vital godliness. If you have truly come to Jesus, we know how you came—the Holy Spirit sweetly brought you there. You came to the blood of sprinkling with no merits of your own. Guilty, lost, and helpless, you came to take that blood, and that blood alone, as your everlasting hope. You came to the cross of Christ, with a trembling and an aching heart; and oh! what a precious sound it was to you to hear the voice of the blood of Jesus! The dropping of his blood is as the music of heaven to the penitent sons of earth. We are full of sin, but the Savior bids us lift our eyes to him, and as we gaze upon his streaming wounds, each drop of blood, as it falls, cries, "It is finished; I have made an end of sin; I have brought in everlasting righteousness." Oh! sweet language of the precious blood of Jesus! If you have come to that blood once, you will come to it constantly. Your life will be "Looking unto Jesus." Your whole conduct will be epitomized in this—"To whom coming." Not to whom I *have* come, but to whom I am *always coming.* If thou hast ever come to the blood of sprinkling, thou wilt feel thy need of coming to it every day. He who does not desire to wash in it *every day*, has never washed in it at all. The believer ever feels it to be his joy and privilege that there is still a fountain opened. Past experiences are doubtful food for Christians; a present coming to Christ alone can give us joy and comfort. This morning let us sprinkle our door-post fresh with blood, and then feast upon the Lamb, assured that the destroying angel must pass us by.

APRIL 18

She bound the scarlet line in the window.
—Joshua 2:21

RAHAB depended for her preservation upon the promise of the spies, whom she looked upon as the representatives of the God of Israel. Her faith was simple and firm, but it was very obedient. To tie the scarlet line in the window was a very trivial act in itself, but she dared not run the risk of omitting it. Come, my soul, is there not here a lesson for thee? Hast thou been attentive to all thy Lord's will, even though some of his commands should seem nonessential? Hast thou observed in his own way the two ordinances of believers' baptism and the Lord's Supper? These neglected, argue much unloving disobedience in thy heart. Be henceforth in all things blameless, even to the tying of a thread, if that be matter of command.

This act of Rahab sets forth a yet more solemn lesson. Have I implicitly trusted in the precious blood of Jesus? Have I tied the scarlet cord, as with a Gordian knot in my window, so that my trust can never be removed? Or can I look out towards the Dead Sea of my sins, or the Jerusalem of my hopes, without seeing the blood, and seeing all things in connection with its blessed power? The passerby can see a cord of so conspicuous a color, if it hangs from the window: it will be well for me if my life makes the efficacy of the atonement conspicuous to all onlookers. What is there to be ashamed of? Let men or devils gaze if they will, the blood is my boast and my song. My soul, there is One who will see that scarlet line, even when from weakness of faith thou canst not see it thyself; Jehovah, the Avenger, will see it and pass over thee. Jericho's walls fell flat: Rahab's house was on the wall, and yet it stood unmoved; my nature is built into the wall of humanity, and yet when destruction smites the race, I shall be secure. My soul, tie the scarlet thread in the window afresh, and rest in peace.

April 19

*Behold, the veil of the temple was rent in twain
from the top to the bottom.*
—Matthew 27:51

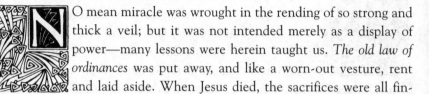NO mean miracle was wrought in the rending of so strong and thick a veil; but it was not intended merely as a display of power—many lessons were herein taught us. *The old law of ordinances* was put away, and like a worn-out vesture, rent and laid aside. When Jesus died, the sacrifices were all finished, because all fulfilled in him, and therefore the place of their presentation was marked with an evident token of decay. That rent also *revealed all the hidden things of the old dispensation:* the mercy-seat could now be seen, and the glory of God gleamed forth above it. By the death of our Lord Jesus we have a clear revelation of God, for he was "not as Moses, who put a veil over his face." Life and immortality are now brought to light, and things which have been hidden since the foundation of the world are manifest in him. *The annual ceremony of atonement was thus abolished. The atoning blood* which was once every year sprinkled within the veil, *was now offered once* for all by the great High Priest, and therefore the place of the symbolical rite was broken up. No blood of bullocks or of lambs is needed now, for Jesus has entered within the veil with his own blood. Hence *access to God is now permitted,* and is the privilege of every believer in Christ Jesus. There is no small space laid open through which we may peer at the mercy-seat, but the rent reaches from the top to the bottom. We may come with boldness to the throne of the heavenly grace. Shall we err if we say that the opening of the Holy of Holies in this marvelous manner by our Lord's expiring cry was *the type of the opening of the gates of paradise* to all the saints by virtue of the Passion? Our bleeding Lord hath the key of heaven; he openeth and no man shutteth; let us enter in with him into the heavenly places, and sit with him there till our common enemies shall be made his footstool.

April 20

That through death he might destroy him that had the power of death.
—*Hebrews 2:14*

child of God, death hath lost its sting, because the devil's power over it is destroyed. Then cease to fear dying. Ask grace from God the Holy Ghost, that by an intimate knowledge and a firm belief of thy Redeemer's death, thou mayst be strengthened for that dread hour. Living near the cross of Calvary thou mayst think of death with pleasure, and welcome it when it comes with intense delight. It is sweet to die in the Lord: it is a covenant-blessing to sleep in Jesus. Death is no longer banishment, it is a return from exile, a going home to the many mansions where the loved ones already dwell. The distance between glorified spirits in heaven and militant saints on earth seems great; but it is not so. We are not far from home—a moment will bring us there. The sail is spread; the soul is launched upon the deep. How long will be its voyage? How many wearying winds must beat upon the sail ere it shall be reefed in the port of peace? How long shall that soul be tossed upon the waves before it comes to that sea which knows no storm? Listen to the answer, "Absent from the body, present with the Lord." Yon ship has just departed, but it is already at its haven. It did but spread its sail and it was there. Like that ship of old, upon the Lake of Galilee, a storm had tossed it, but Jesus said, "Peace, be still," and *immediately* it came to land. Think not that a long period intervenes between the instant of death and the eternity of glory. When the eyes close on earth they open in heaven. The horses of fire are not an instant on the road. Then, O child of God, what is there for thee to fear in death, seeing that through the death of thy Lord its curse and sting are destroyed? and now it is but a Jacob's ladder whose foot is in the dark grave, but its top reaches to glory everlasting.

APRIL 21

I know that my Redeemer liveth.
—Job 19:25

THE marrow of Job's comfort lies in that little word "My"—"My Redeemer," and in the fact that the Redeemer lives. Oh! to get hold of a living Christ. We must get a property in him before we can enjoy him. What is gold in the mine to me? Men are beggars in Peru, and beg their bread in California. It is gold in my purse which will satisfy my necessities, by purchasing the bread I need. So a Redeemer who does not redeem *me*, an avenger who will never stand up for *my* blood, of what avail were such? Rest not content until by faith you can say "Yes, I cast myself upon my living Lord; and he is mine." It may be you hold him with a feeble hand; you half think it presumption to say, "He lives as *my* Redeemer;" yet, remember if you have but faith as a grain of mustard seed, that little faith *entitles* you to say it. But there is also another word here, expressive of Job's strong confidence, *"I know."* To say, "I hope so, I trust so" is comfortable; and there are thousands in the fold of Jesus who hardly ever get much further. But to reach the essence of consolation you *must* say, "I know." Ifs, buts, and perhaps, are sure murderers of peace and comfort. Doubts are dreary things in times of sorrow. Like wasps they sting the soul! If I have any suspicion that Christ is not mine, then there is vinegar mingled with the gall of death; but if I know that Jesus lives for me, then darkness is not dark: even the night is light about me. Surely if Job, in those ages before the coming and advent of Christ, could say, "I know," *we* should not speak less positively. God forbid that our positiveness should be presumption. Let us see that our evidences are right, lest we build upon an ungrounded hope; and then let us not be satisfied with the mere foundation, for it is from the upper rooms that we get the widest prospect. A living Redeemer, truly mine, is joy unspeakable.

APRIL 22

Him hath God exalted.
—Acts 5:31

ESUS, our Lord, once crucified, dead and buried, now sits upon the throne of glory. The highest place that heaven affords is his by undisputed right. It is sweet to remember that the exaltation of Christ in heaven is a *representative exaltation.* He is exalted at the Father's right hand, and though as Jehovah he has eminent glories, in which finite creatures cannot share, yet as the Mediator, the honors which Jesus wears in heaven are the heritage of all the saints. It is delightful to reflect how close is Christ's union with his people. We are actually one with him; we are members of his body; and his exaltation is *our* exaltation. He will give us to sit upon his throne, even as he has overcome, and is set down with his Father on his throne; he has a crown, and he gives us crowns too; he has a throne, but he is not content with having a throne to himself, on his right hand there must be his queen, arrayed in "gold of Ophir." He cannot be glorified without his bride. Look up, believer, to Jesus now; let the eye of your faith behold him with many crowns upon his head; and remember that you will one day be like him, when you shall see him as he is; you shall not be so great as he is, you shall not be so divine, but still you shall, in a measure, share the same honors, and enjoy the same happiness and the same dignity which he possesses. Be content to live unknown for a little while, and to walk your weary way through the fields of poverty, or up the hills of affliction; for by-and-by you shall reign with Christ, for he has "made us kings and priests unto God, and we shall reign forever and ever." Oh! wonderful thought for the children of God! We have Christ for our glorious representative in heaven's courts *now,* and soon he will come and receive us to himself, to be with him there, to behold his glory, and to share his joy.

APRIL 23

Nay, in all these things we are more than conquerors
through him that loved us.
—Romans 8:37

WE go to Christ for forgiveness, and then too often look to the law for power to fight our sins. Paul thus rebukes us,

> O foolish Galatians, who hath bewitched you, that ye should not obey the truth? This only would I learn of you, Received ye the Spirit by the works of the law, or by the hearing of faith? are ye so foolish? having begun in the Spirit, are ye now made perfect by the flesh?

Take your sins to Christ's cross, for the old man can only be crucified there: we are crucified *with him*. The only weapon to fight sin with is the spear which pierced the side of Jesus. To give an illustration—you want to overcome an angry temper, how do you go to work? It is very possible you have never tried the right way of going to Jesus with it. How did I get salvation? I came to Jesus just as I was, and I trusted him to save me. I must kill my angry temper in the same way? It is the only way in which I can ever kill it. I must go to the cross with it, and say to Jesus, "Lord, I trust thee to deliver me from it." This is the only way to give it a death-blow. Are you covetous? Do you feel the world entangle you? You may struggle against this evil so long as you please, but if it be your besetting sin, you will never be delivered from it in any way but by the blood of Jesus. Take it to Christ. Tell him,

> Lord, I have trusted thee, and thy name is Jesus, for thou dost save thy people from their sins; Lord, this is one of my sins; save me from it!

Ordinances are nothing without Christ as a means of mortification. Your prayers, and your repentances, and your tears—the whole of them put together—are worth nothing apart from him. "None but Jesus can do helpless sinners good;" or helpless saints either. You must be conquerors through him who hath loved you, if conquerors at all. Our laurels must grow among his olives in Gethsemane.

April 24

And because of all this we make a sure covenant.
—Nehemiah 9:38

HERE are many occasions in our experience when we may very rightly, and with benefit, renew our covenant with God. After *recovery from sickness* when, like Hezekiah, we have had a new term of years added to our life, we may fitly do it. After any *deliverance from trouble,* when our joys bud forth anew, let us again visit the foot of the cross, and renew our consecration. Especially, let us do this after any *sin which has grieved the Holy Spirit,* or brought dishonor upon the cause of God; let us then look to that blood which can make us whiter than snow, and again offer ourselves unto the Lord. We should not only let our troubles confirm our dedication to God, but *our prosperity* should do the same. If we ever meet with occasions which deserve to be called "crowning mercies" then, surely, if he hath crowned *us,* we ought also to crown our God; let us bring forth anew all the jewels of the divine regalia which have been stored in the jewel-closet of our heart, and let our God sit upon the throne of our love, arrayed in royal apparel. If we would learn to profit by our prosperity, we should not need so much adversity. If we would gather from a kiss all the good it might confer upon us, we should not so often smart under the rod. Have we lately received some blessing which we little expected? Has the Lord put our feet in a large room? Can we sing of mercies multiplied? Then this is the day to put our hand upon the horns of the altar, and say, "Bind me here, my God; bind me here with cords, even forever." Inasmuch as we need the fulfillment of new promises from God, let us offer renewed prayers that our old vows may not be dishonored. Let us this morning make with him a sure covenant, because of the pains of Jesus which for the last month we have been considering with gratitude.

APRIL 25

Rise up my love, my fair one, and come away.
—Song of Solomon 2:10

O, I hear the voice of my Beloved! he speaks to *me!* Fair weather is smiling upon the face of the earth, and he would not have me spiritually asleep while nature is all around me awaking from her winter's rest. He bids me "Rise up," and well he may, for I have long enough been lying among the pots of worldliness. He is risen, I am risen in him, why then should I cleave unto the dust? From lower loves, desires, pursuits, and aspirations, I would rise towards him. He calls me by the sweet title of "My love," and counts me fair; this is a good argument for my rising. If he has thus exalted me, and thinks me thus comely, how can I linger in the tents of Kedar and find congenial associates among the sons of men? He bids me "Come away." Further and further from everything selfish, groveling, worldly, sinful, he calls me; yea, from the outwardly religious world which knows him not, and has no sympathy with the mystery of the higher life, he calls me. "Come away" has no harsh sound in it to my ear, for what is there to hold me in this wilderness of vanity and sin? O my Lord, would that I could come away, but I am taken among the thorns, and cannot escape from them as I would. I would, if it were possible, have neither eyes, nor ears, nor heart for sin. Thou callest me to thyself by saying "Come away," and this is a melodious call indeed. To come to thee is to come home from exile, to come to land out of the raging storm, to come to rest after long labor, to come to the goal of my desires and the summit of my wishes. But Lord, how can a stone rise, how can a lump of clay come away from the horrible pit? O raise me, draw me. Thy grace can do it. Send forth thy Holy Spirit to kindle sacred flames of love in my heart, and I will continue to rise until I leave life and time behind me, and indeed come away.

April 26

This do in remembrance of me.
—1 Corinthians 11:24

IT seems then, that Christians may forget Christ! There could be no need for this loving exhortation, if there were not a fearful supposition that our memories might prove treacherous. Nor is this a bare supposition: it is, alas! too well confirmed in our experience, not as a possibility, but as a lamentable fact. It appears almost impossible that those who have been redeemed by the blood of the dying Lamb, and loved with an everlasting love by the eternal Son of God, should forget that gracious Savior; but, if startling to the ear, it is, alas! too apparent to the eye to allow us to deny the crime. Forget him who never forgot us! Forget him who poured his blood forth for our sins! Forget him who loved us even to the death! Can it be possible? Yes, it is not only possible, but conscience confesses that it is too sadly a fault with all of us, that we suffer him to be as a wayfaring man tarrying but for a night. He whom we should make the abiding tenant of our memories is but a visitor therein. The cross where one would think that memory would linger, and unmindful ness would be an unknown intruder, is desecrated by the feet of forgetfulness. Does not your conscience say that this is true? Do you not find yourselves forgetful of Jesus? Some creature steals away your heart, and you are unmindful of him upon whom your affection ought to be set. Some earthly business engrosses your attention when you should fix your eye steadily upon the cross. It is the incessant turmoil of the world, the constant attraction of earthly things which takes away the soul from Christ. While memory too well preserves a poisonous weed, it suffereth the rose of Sharon to wither. Let us charge ourselves to bind a heavenly forget-me-not about our hearts for Jesus our Beloved, and, whatever else we let slip, let us hold fast to him.

APRIL 27

God, even our own God.
—Psalm 67:6

IT is strange how little use we make of the spiritual blessings which God gives us, but it is stranger still how little use we make of God himself. Though he is "our own God," we apply ourselves but little to him, and ask but little of him. How seldom do we ask counsel at the hands of the Lord! How often do we go about our business, without seeking his guidance! In our troubles how constantly do we strive to bear our burdens ourselves, instead of casting them upon the Lord, that he may sustain us! This is not because we may not, for the Lord seems to say,

> I am thine, soul, come and make use of me as thou wilt; thou mayst freely come to my store, and the oftener the more welcome.

It is our own fault if we make not free with the riches of our God. Then, since thou hast such a friend, and he invites thee, draw from him daily. Never want whilst thou hast a God to go to; never fear or faint whilst thou hast God to help thee; go to thy treasure and take whatever thou needest—there is all that thou canst want. Learn the divine skill of making God all things to thee. He can supply thee with all, or, better still, he can be to thee instead of all. Let me urge thee, then, to make use of thy God. Make use of him *in prayer.* Go to him often, because he is *thy* God. O, wilt thou fail to use so great a privilege? Fly to him, tell him all thy wants. Use him constantly *by faith* at all times. If some dark providence has beclouded thee, use thy God as a "sun;" if some strong enemy has beset thee, find in Jehovah a "shield," for he is a sun and shield to his people. If thou hast lost thy way in the mazes of life, use him as a "guide," for he will direct thee. Whatever thou art, and wherever thou art, remember God is just *what* thou wantest, and just *where* thou wantest, and that he can do *all* thou wantest.

APRIL 28

Remember the word unto thy servant,
upon which thou hast caused me to hope.
—Psalm 119:49

WHATEVER your especial need may be, you may readily find some promise in the Bible suited to it. Are you faint and feeble because your way is rough and you are weary? Here is the promise—"He giveth power to the faint." When you read such a promise, take it back to the great Promiser, and ask him to fulfill his own word. Are you seeking after Christ, and thirsting for closer communion with him? This promise shines like a star upon you—"Blessed are they that hunger and thirst after righteousness, for they shall be filled." Take that promise to the throne continually; do not plead anything else, but go to God over and over again with this—"Lord, thou hast said it, do as thou hast said." Are you distressed because of sin, and burdened with the heavy load of your iniquities? Listen to these words—"I, even I, am he that blotteth out thy transgressions, and will no more remember thy sins." You have no merit of your own to plead why he should pardon you, but plead his written engagements and he will perform them. Are you afraid lest you should not be able to hold on to the end, lest, after having thought yourself a child of God, you should prove a castaway? If that is your state, take this word of grace to the throne and plead it:

> The mountains may depart, and the hills may be removed, but the covenant of my love shall not depart from thee.

If you have lost the sweet sense of the Savior's presence, and are seeking him with a sorrowful heart, remember the promises: "Return unto me, and I will return unto you;" "For a small moment have I forsaken thee, but with great mercies will I gather thee." Banquet your faith upon God's own word, and whatever your fears or wants, repair to the Bank of Faith with your Father's note of hand, saying, "Remember the word unto thy servant, upon which thou hast caused me to hope."

APRIL 29

Thou art my hope in the day of evil.
—*Jeremiah 17:17*

THE path of the Christian is not always bright with sunshine; he has his seasons of darkness and of storm. True, it is written in God's Word, "Her ways are ways of pleasantness, and all her paths are peace;" and it is a great truth, that religion is calculated to give a man happiness below as well as bliss above; but experience tells us that if the course of the just be "As the shining light that shineth more and more unto the perfect day," yet sometimes *that* light is eclipsed. At certain periods clouds cover the believer's sun, and he walks in darkness and sees no light. There are many who have rejoiced in the presence of God for a season; they have basked in the sunshine in the earlier stages of their Christian career; they have walked along the "green pastures" by the side of the "still waters," but suddenly they find the glorious sky is clouded; instead of the Land of Goshen they have to tread the sandy desert; in the place of sweet waters, they find troubled streams, bitter to their taste, and they say, "Surely, if I were a child of God, this would not happen." Oh! say not so, thou who art walking in darkness. The best of God's saints must drink the wormwood; the dearest of his children must bear the cross. No Christian has enjoyed perpetual prosperity; no believer can always keep his harp from the willows. Perhaps the Lord allotted you at first a smooth and unclouded path, because you were weak and timid. He tempered the wind to the shorn lamb, but now that you are stronger in the spiritual life, you must enter upon the riper and rougher experience of God's full-grown children. We need winds and tempests to exercise our faith, to tear off the rotten bough of self-dependence, and to root us more firmly in Christ. The day of evil reveals to us the value of our glorious hope.

APRIL 30

And all the children of Israel murmured.
—Numbers 14:2

THERE are murmurers amongst Christians now, as there were in the camp of Israel of old. There are those who, when the rod falls, cry out against the afflictive dispensation. They ask, "Why am I thus afflicted? What have I done to be chastened in this manner?" A word with thee, O murmurer! Why shouldst thou murmur against the dispensations of thy heavenly Father? Can he treat thee more hardly than thou deservest? Consider what a rebel thou wast once, but he has pardoned thee! Surely, if he in his wisdom sees fit now to chasten thee, thou shouldst not complain. After all, art thou smitten as hardly as thy sins deserve? Consider the corruption which is in thy breast, and then wilt thou wonder that there needs so much of the rod to fetch it out? Weigh thyself, and discern how much dross is mingled with thy gold; and dost thou think the fire too hot to purge away so much dross as thou hast? Does not that proud rebellious spirit of thine prove that thy heart is not thoroughly sanctified? Are not those murmuring words contrary to the holy submissive nature of God's children? Is not the correction needed? But if thou *wilt* murmur against the chastening, take heed, for it will go hard with murmurers. God always chastises his children twice, if they do not bear the first stroke patiently. But know one thing—"He doth not afflict willingly, nor grieve the children of men." All his corrections are sent in love, to purify thee, and to draw thee nearer to himself. Surely it must help thee to bear the chastening with resignation if thou art able to recognize thy *Father's* hand. For "whom the Lord loveth he chasteneth, and scourgeth every son whom he receiveth. If ye endure chastening, God dealeth with you as with sons." "Murmur not as some of them also murmured and were destroyed of the destroyer."

MAY 1

His cheeks are as a bed of spices, as sweet flowers.
—Song of Solomon 5:13

O, the flowery month is come! March winds and April showers have done their work, and the earth is all bedecked with beauty. Come my soul, put on thine holiday attire and go forth to gather garlands of heavenly thoughts. Thou knowest whither to betake thyself, for to thee "the beds of spices" are well known, and thou hast so often smelt the perfume of "the sweet flowers," that thou wilt go at once to thy well-beloved and find all loveliness, all joy in him. That cheek once so rudely smitten with a rod, oft bedewed with tears of sympathy and then defiled with spittle—that cheek as it smiles with mercy is as fragrant aromatic to my heart. Thou didst not hide thy face from shame and spitting, O Lord Jesus, and therefore I will find my dearest delight in praising thee. Those cheeks were furrowed by the plough of grief, and crimsoned with red lines of blood from thy thorn-crowned temples; such marks of love unbounded cannot but charm my soul far more than "pillars of perfume." If I may not see the whole of his face I would behold his cheeks, for the least glimpse of him is exceedingly refreshing to my spiritual sense and yields a variety of delights. In Jesus I find not only fragrance, but a bed of spices; not one flower, but all manner of sweet flowers. He is to me my rose and my lily, my heartsease and my cluster of camphor. When he is with me it is May all the year round, and my soul goes forth to wash her happy face in the morning-dew of his grace, and to solace herself with the singing of the birds of his promises. Precious Lord Jesus, let me in very deed know the blessedness which dwells in abiding, unbroken fellowship with thee. I am a poor worthless one, whose cheek thou hast deigned to kiss! O let me kiss thee in return with the kisses of my lips.

MAY 2

I pray not that thou shouldst take them out of the world.
—John 17:15

T is a sweet and blessed event which will occur to all believers in God's own time—the going home to be with Jesus. In a few more years the Lord's soldiers, who are now fighting "the good fight of faith" will have done with conflict, and have entered into the joy of their Lord. But although Christ prays that his people may eventually be with him where he is, he does not ask that they may be taken at once away from this world to heaven. He wishes them to stay here. Yet how frequently does the wearied pilgrim put up the prayer, "O that I had wings like a dove! for then would I fly away and be at rest;" but Christ does not pray like that, he leaves us in his Father's hands, until, like shocks of corn fully ripe, we shall each be gathered into our Master's garner. Jesus does not plead for our instant removal by death, for to abide in the flesh is needful for others if not profitable for ourselves. He asks that we may be kept from evil, but he never asks for us to be admitted to the inheritance in glory till we are of full age. Christians often want to die when they have any trouble. Ask them why, and they tell you, "Because we would be with the Lord." We fear it is not so much because they are longing to be with the Lord, as because they desire to get rid of their troubles; else they would feel the same wish to die at other times when not under the pressure of trial. They want to go home, not so much for the Savior's company, as to be at rest. Now it is quite right to desire to depart if we can do it in the same spirit that Paul did, because to be with Christ is far better, but the wish to escape from trouble is a selfish one. Rather let your care and wish be to glorify God by your life here as long as he pleases, even though it be in the midst of toil, and conflict, and suffering, and leave him to say when "it is enough."

MAY 3

In the world ye shall have tribulation.
—John 16:33

RT thou asking the reason of this, believer? Look *upward* to thy heavenly Father, and behold him pure and holy. Dost thou know that thou art one day to be like him? Wilt thou easily be conformed to his image? Wilt thou not require much refining in the furnace of affliction to purify thee? Will it be an easy thing to get rid of thy corruptions, and make thee perfect even as thy Father which is in heaven is perfect? Next, Christian, turn thine eye *downward*. Dost thou know what foes thou hast beneath thy feet? Thou wast once a servant of Satan, and no king will willingly lose his subjects. Dost thou think that Satan will let thee alone? No, he will be always at thee, for he "goeth about like a roaring lion, seeking whom he may devour." Expect trouble, therefore, Christian, when thou lookest beneath thee. Then look *around thee.* Where art thou? Thou art in an enemy's country, a stranger and a sojourner. The world is not thy friend. If it be, then thou art not God's friend, for he who is the friend of the world is the enemy of God. Be assured that thou shalt find foemen everywhere. When thou sleepest, think that thou art resting on the battlefield; when thou walkest, suspect an ambush in every hedge. As mosquitoes are said to bite strangers more than natives, so will the trials of earth be sharpest to you. Lastly, look *within thee,* into thine own heart and observe what is there. *Sin* and *self* are still within. Ah! if thou hadst no devil to tempt thee, no enemies to fight thee, and no world to ensnare thee, thou wouldst still find in thyself evil enough to be a sore trouble to thee, for "the heart is deceitful above all things, and desperately wicked." Expect trouble then, but despond not on account of it, for God is with thee to help and to strengthen thee. He hath said, "I will be with thee in trouble; I will deliver thee and honor thee."

MAY 4

Shall a man make gods unto himself, and they are no gods?
—Jeremiah 16:20

ONE great besetting sin of ancient Israel was idolatry, and the spiritual Israel are vexed with a tendency to the same folly. Remphan's star shines no longer, and the women weep no more for Tammuz, but Mammon still intrudes his golden calf, and the shrines of pride are not forsaken. Self in various forms struggles to subdue the chosen ones under its dominion, and the flesh sets up its altars wherever it can find space for them. Favorite children are often the cause of much sin in believers; the Lord is grieved when he sees us doting upon them above measure; they will live to be as great a curse to us as Absalom was to David, or they will be taken from us to leave our homes desolate. If Christians desire to grow thorns to stuff their sleepless pillows, let them dote on their dear ones.

It is truly said that "they are no gods," for the objects of our foolish love are very doubtful blessings, the solace which they yield us now is dangerous, and the help which they can give us in the hour of trouble is little indeed. Why, then, are we so bewitched with vanities? We pity the poor heathen who adore a god of stone, and yet worship a god of gold. Where is the vast superiority between a god of flesh and one of wood? The principle, the sin, the folly is the same in either case, only that in ours the crime is more aggravated because we have more light, and sin in the face of it. The heathen bows to a false deity, but the true God he has never known; we commit two evils, inasmuch as we forsake the living God and turn unto idols. May the Lord purge us all from this grievous iniquity!

> The dearest idol I have known,
> Whate'er that idol be;
> Help me to tear it from thy throne,
> And worship only thee.

MAY 5

I will be their God, and they shall be my people.
—2 Corinthians 6:16

HAT a sweet title: "My people!" What a cheering revelation: "Their God!" How much of meaning is couched in those two words, "My people!" Here is *specialty*. The whole world is God's; the heaven, even the heaven of heavens is the Lord's, and he reigneth among the children of men; but of those whom he hath chosen, whom he hath purchased to himself, he saith what he saith not of others—"My people." In this word there is the idea of *proprietorship*. In a special manner the "Lord's portion is his people; Jacob is the lot of his inheritance." All the nations upon earth are his; the whole world is in his power; yet are his people, his chosen, more especially his possession; for he has done more for them than others; he has bought them with his blood; he has brought them nigh to himself; he has set his great heart upon them; he has loved them with an everlasting love, a love which many waters cannot quench, and which the revolutions of time shall never suffice in the least degree to diminish. Dear friends, can you, by faith, see yourselves in that number? Can you look up to heaven and say,

> My Lord and my God: mine by that sweet *relationship* which entitles me to call thee Father; mine by that hallowed *fellowship* which I delight to hold with thee when thou art pleased to manifest thyself unto me as thou dost not unto the world?

Canst thou read the Book of Inspiration, and find there the indentures of thy salvation? Canst thou read thy title writ in precious blood? Canst thou, by humble faith, lay hold of Jesus' garments, and say, "My Christ"? If thou canst, then God saith of thee, and of others like thee, "My people;" for, if God be your God, and Christ your Christ, the Lord has a special, peculiar favor to you; you are the object of his choice, accepted in his beloved Son.

MAY 6

We dwell in him.
—1 John 4:13

O you want a house for your soul? Do you ask, "What is the purchase?" It is something less than proud human nature will like to give. It is without money and without price. Ah! you would like to pay a respectable rent! You would love to do something to win Christ? Then you cannot have the house, for it is "without price." Will you take my Master's house on a lease for all eternity, with nothing to pay for it, nothing but the ground-rent of loving and serving him forever? Will you take Jesus and "dwell in him?" See, this house is furnished with all you want, it is filled with riches more than you will spend as long as you live. Here you can have intimate communion with Christ and feast on his love; here are tables well stored with food for you to live on forever; in it, when weary, you can find rest with Jesus; and from it you can look out and see heaven itself. Will you have the house? Ah! if you are houseless, you will say, "I should like to have the house; but may I have it?" Yes; there is the key—the key is, "Come to Jesus." "But," you say, "I am too shabby for such a house." Never mind; there are garments inside. If you feel guilty and condemned, come; and though the house is too good for you, Christ will make you good enough for the house by-and-by. He will wash you and cleanse you, and you will yet be able to sing, "We dwell in him." Believer: thrice happy art thou to have such a dwelling-place! Greatly privileged thou art, for thou hast a "strong habitation" in which thou art ever safe. And "dwelling in him," thou hast not only a perfect and secure house, but an *everlasting* one. When this world shall have melted like a dream, our house shall live, and stand more imperishable than marble, more solid than granite, self existent as God, for it is God himself—"We dwell in him."

MAY 7

Great multitudes followed him, and he healed them all.
—*Matthew 12:15*

HAT a mass of hideous sickness must have thrust itself under the eye of Jesus! Yet we read not that he was disgusted, but patiently waited on every case. What a singular variety of evils must have met at his feet! What sickening ulcers and putrefying sores! Yet he was ready for every new shape of the monster evil, and was victor over it in every form. Let the arrow fly from what quarter it might, he quenched its fiery power. The heat of fever, or the cold of dropsy; the lethargy of palsy, or the rage of madness; the filth of leprosy, or the darkness of ophthalmia—all knew the power of his word, and fled at his command. In every corner of the field he was triumphant over evil, and received the homage of delivered captives. He came, he saw, he conquered everywhere. It is even so this morning. Whatever my own case may be, the beloved Physician can heal me; and whatever may be the state of others whom I may remember at this moment in prayer, I may have hope in Jesus that he will be able to heal them of their sins. My child, my friend, my dearest one, I can have hope for each, for all, when I remember the healing power of my Lord; and on my own account, however severe my struggle with sins and infirmities, I may yet be of good cheer. He who on earth walked the hospitals, still dispenses his grace, and works wonders among the sons of men: let me go to him at once in right earnest.

Let me praise him, this morning, as I remember *how* he wrought his spiritual cures, which bring him most renown. It was by taking upon himself our sicknesses. "By his stripes we are healed." The Church on earth is full of souls healed by our beloved Physician; and the inhabitants of heaven itself confess that "he healed them all." Come, then, my soul, publish abroad the virtue of his grace, and let it be "to the Lord for a name, for an everlasting sign which shall not be cut off."

May 8

He that was healed wist not who it was.
—John 5:13

YEARS are short to the happy and healthy; but thirty-eight years of disease must have dragged a very weary length along the life of the poor impotent man. When Jesus, therefore, healed him by a word, while he lay at the pool of Bethesda, he was delightfully *sensible of a change.* Even so the sinner who has for weeks and months been paralyzed with despair, and has wearily sighed for salvation, is very conscious of the change when the Lord Jesus speaks the word of power, and gives joy and peace in believing. The evil removed is too great to be removed without our discerning it; the life imparted is too remarkable to be possessed and remain inoperative; and the change wrought is too marvelous not to be perceived. Yet the poor man was *ignorant of the author* of his cure; he knew not the sacredness of his person, the offices which he sustained, or the errand which brought him among men. Much ignorance of Jesus may remain in hearts which yet feel the power of his blood. We must not hastily condemn men for lack of knowledge; but where we can see the faith which saves the soul, we must believe that salvation has been bestowed. The Holy Spirit makes men penitents long before he makes them divines; and he who believes what he knows, shall soon know more clearly what he believes. Ignorance is, however, an evil; for this poor man was much *tantalized by the Pharisees,* and was quite unable to cope with them. It is good to be able to answer gainsayers; but we cannot do so if we know not the Lord Jesus clearly and with understanding. The cure of his ignorance, however, soon followed the cure of his infirmity, for he was *visited by the Lord in the temple;* and after that gracious manifestation, he was *found testifying* that "it was Jesus who had made him whole." Lord, if thou hast saved me, show me thyself, that I may declare thee to the sons of men.

MAY 9

Who hath blessed us with all spiritual blessings.
—Ephesians 1:3

ALL the goodness of the past, the present, and the future, Christ bestows upon his people. In the mysterious ages of the past the Lord Jesus was his Father's first elect, and in his *election* he gave us an interest, for we were chosen in him from before the foundation of the world. He had from all eternity the prerogatives of *Sonship,* as his Father's only-begotten and well-beloved Son, and he has, in the riches of his grace, by adoption and regeneration, elevated us to sonship also, so that to us he has given "power to become the sons of God." The *eternal covenant,* based upon suretiship and confirmed by oath, is ours, for our strong consolation and security. In the *everlasting settlements of predestinating wisdom* and omnipotent decree, the eye of the Lord Jesus was ever fixed on us; and we may rest assured that in the whole roll of destiny there is not a line which militates against the interests of his redeemed. The *great betrothal* of the Prince of Glory is ours, for it is to us that he is affianced, as the sacred nuptials shall ere long declare to an assembled universe. The *marvelous incarnation* of the God of heaven, with all the amazing condescension and humiliation which attended it, is ours. The bloody sweat, the scourge, the cross, are ours forever. Whatever blissful consequences flow from *perfect obedience, finished atonement, resurrection, ascension, or intercession,* all are ours by his own gift. Upon his breastplate he is now bearing our names; and in his authoritative pleadings at the throne he remembers our persons and pleads our cause. His *dominion* over principalities and powers, and his absolute majesty in heaven, he employs for the benefit of them who trust in him. His high estate is as much at our service as was his condition of abasement. He who gave himself for us in the depths of woe and death, doth not withdraw the grant now that he is enthroned in the highest heavens.

MAY 10

But now is Christ risen from the dead.
—1 Corinthians 15:20

HE whole system of Christianity rests upon the fact that "Christ is risen from the dead;" for, "If Christ be not risen, then is our preaching vain, and your faith is also vain: ye are yet in your sins." The *divinity* of Christ finds its surest proof in his resurrection, since he was "Declared to be the Son of God with power, according to the spirit of holiness, by the resurrection from the dead." It would not be unreasonable to doubt his Deity if he had not risen. Moreover, Christ's *sovereignty* depends upon his resurrection, "For to this end Christ both died, and rose, and revived, that he might be Lord both of the dead and living." Again, our *justification,* that choice blessing of the covenant, is linked with Christ's triumphant victory over death and the grave; for "he was delivered for our offences, and was raised again for our justification." Nay, more, our very *regeneration* is connected with his resurrection, for we are "Begotten again unto a lively hope by the resurrection of Jesus Christ from the dead." And most certainly our *ultimate resurrection* rests here, for,

> If the Spirit of him that raised up Jesus from the dead dwell in you, he that raised up Christ from the dead shall also quicken your mortal bodies by his Spirit that dwelleth in you.

If Christ be not risen, then shall we not rise; but if he be risen then they who are asleep in Christ have not perished, but in their flesh shall surely behold their God. Thus, the silver thread of resurrection runs through all the believer's blessings, from his regeneration onwards to his eternal glory, and binds them together. How important then will this glorious fact be in his estimation, and how will he rejoice that beyond a doubt it is established, that "now is Christ risen from the dead."

> The promise is fulfill'd,
> Redemption's work is done,
> Justice with mercy's reconciled,
> For God has raised his Son.

MAY 11

I am with you alway.
—Matthew 28:20

T is well there is One who is ever the same, and who is ever with us. It is well there is one stable rock amidst the billows of the sea of life. O my soul, set not thine affections upon rusting, moth-eaten, decaying treasures, but set thine heart upon him who abides forever faithful to thee. Build not thine house upon the moving quicksands of a deceitful world, but found thy hopes upon this rock, which, amid descending rain and roaring floods, shall stand immovably secure. My soul, I charge thee, lay up thy treasure in the only secure cabinet; store thy jewels where thou canst never lose them. Put thine all in Christ; set all thine affections on his person, all thy hope in his merit, all thy trust in his efficacious blood, all thy joy in his presence, and so thou mayest laugh at loss, and defy destruction. Remember that all the flowers in the world's garden fade by turns, and the day cometh when nothing will be left but the black, cold earth. Death's black extinguisher must soon put out thy candle. Oh! how sweet to have sunlight when the candle is gone! The dark flood must soon roll between thee and all thou hast; then wed thine heart to him who will never leave thee; trust thyself with him who will go with thee through the black and surging current of death's stream, and who will land thee safely on the celestial shore, and make thee sit with him in heavenly places forever. Go, sorrowing son of affliction, tell thy secrets to the Friend who sticketh closer than a brother. Trust all thy concerns with him who never can be taken from thee, who will never leave thee, and who will never let thee leave him, even "Jesus Christ, the same yesterday, and today, and forever." "Lo, I am with you alway," is enough for my soul to live upon, let who will forsake me.

May 12

And will manifest myself to him.
—John 14:21

HE Lord Jesus gives special revelations of himself to his people. Even if Scripture did not declare this, there are many of the children of God who could testify the truth of it from their own experience. They have had manifestations of their Lord and Savior Jesus Christ in a peculiar manner, such as no mere reading or hearing could afford. In the biographies of eminent saints, you will find many instances recorded in which Jesus has been pleased, in a very special manner to speak to their souls, and to unfold the wonders of his person; yea, so have their souls been steeped in happiness that they have thought themselves to be in heaven, whereas they were not there, though they were well nigh on the threshold of it—for when Jesus manifests himself to his people, it is heaven on earth; it is paradise in embryo; it is bliss begun. Especial manifestations of Christ exercise a holy influence on the believer's heart. One effect will be *humility*. If a man says, "I have had such-and-such spiritual communications, I am a great man," he has never had any communion with Jesus at all; for "God hath respect unto the lowly: but the proud he knoweth afar off." He does not need to come near them to know them, and will never give them any visits of love. Another effect will be *happiness*; for in God's presence there are pleasures for evermore. *Holiness* will be sure to follow. A man who has no holiness has never had this manifestation. Some men profess a great deal; but we must not believe any one unless we see that his deeds answer to what he says. "Be not deceived; God is not mocked." He will not bestow his favors upon the wicked: for while he will not cast away a perfect man, neither will he respect an evil doer. Thus there will be three effects of nearness to Jesus—humility, happiness, and holiness. May God give them to thee, Christian!

MAY 13

Weeping may endure for a night,
but joy cometh in the morning.—Psalm 30:5

HRISTIAN! If thou art in a night of trial, think of the morrow; cheer up thy heart with the thought of the coming of thy Lord. Be patient, for

> Lo! He comes with clouds descending.

Be patient! The Husbandman waits until he reaps his harvest. Be patient; for you know who has said, "Behold, I come quickly; and my reward is with me, to give to every man according as his work shall be." If you are never so wretched now, remember

> A few more rolling suns, at most,
> Will land thee on fair Canaan's coast.

Thy head may be crowned with thorny troubles now, but it shall wear a starry crown ere long; thy hand may be filled with cares—it shall sweep the strings of the harp of heaven soon. Thy garments may be soiled with dust now; they shall be white by-and-by. Wait a little longer. Ah! how despicable our troubles and trials will seem when we look back upon them! Looking at them here in the prospect, they seem immense; but when we get to heaven we shall then

> With transporting joys recount,
> The labors of our feet.

Our trials will then seem light and momentary afflictions. Let us go on boldly; if the night be never so dark, the morning cometh, which is more than they can say who are shut up in the darkness of hell. Do you know what it is thus to live on the future—to live on expectation—to antedate heaven? Happy believer, to have so sure, so comforting a hope. It may be all dark now, but it will soon be light; it may be all trial now, but it will soon be all happiness. What matters it though "weeping may endure for a night," when "joy cometh in the morning"?

May 14

Joint heirs with Christ.
—Romans 8:17

THE boundless realms of his Father's universe are Christ's by prescriptive right. As "heir of all things," he is the sole proprietor of the vast creation of God, and he has admitted us to claim the whole as ours, by virtue of that deed of joint-heirship which the Lord hath ratified with his chosen people. The golden streets of paradise, the pearly gates, the river of life, the transcendent bliss, and the unutterable glory, are, by our blessed Lord, made over to us for our everlasting possession. All that he has he shares with his people. The crown royal he has placed upon the head of his Church, appointing her a kingdom, and calling her sons a royal priesthood, a generation of priests and kings. He uncrowned himself that we might have a coronation of glory; he would not sit upon his own throne until he had procured a place upon it for all who overcome by his blood. Crown the head and the whole body shares the honor. Behold here the reward of every Christian conqueror! Christ's throne, crown, scepter, palace, treasure, robes, heritage, are yours. Far superior to the jealousy, selfishness, and greed, which admit of no participation of their advantages, Christ deems his happiness completed by his people sharing it. "The glory which thou gavest me have I given them." "These things have I spoken unto you, that my joy might remain in you, and that your joy might be full." The smiles of his Father are all the sweeter to him, because his people share them. The honors of his kingdom are more pleasing, because his people appear with him in glory. More valuable to him are his conquests, since they have taught his people to overcome. He delights in his throne, because on it there is a place for them. He rejoices in his royal robes, since over them his skirts are spread. He delights the more in his joy, because he calls them to enter into it.

MAY 15

All that believe are justified.
—Acts 13:39

HE believer in Christ receives a *present* justification. Faith does not produce this fruit by-and-by, but *now.* So far as justification is the result of faith, it is given to the soul in the moment when it closes with Christ, and accepts him as its all in all. Are they who stand before the throne of God justified now?—so are we, as truly and as clearly justified as they who walk in white and sing melodious praises to celestial harps. The thief upon the cross was justified the moment that he turned the eye of faith to Jesus; and Paul, the aged, after years of service, was not more justified than was the thief with no service at all. We are *today* accepted in the Beloved, *today* absolved from sin, *today* acquitted at the bar of God. Oh! soul-transporting thought! There are some clusters of Eshcol's vine which we shall not be able to gather till we enter heaven; but this is a bough which runneth over the wall. This is not as the corn of the land, which we can never eat till we cross the Jordan; but this is part of the manna in the wilderness, a portion of our daily nutriment with which God supplies us in our journeying to and fro. We are *now*—even *now* pardoned; even *now* are our sins put away; even *now* we stand in the sight of God accepted, as though we had never been guilty. "There is therefore *now* no condemnation to them which are in Christ Jesus." There is not a sin in the Book of God, even *now*, against one of his people. Who dareth to lay anything to their charge? There is neither speck, nor spot, nor wrinkle, nor any such thing remaining upon any one believer in the matter of justification in the sight of the Judge of all the earth. Let present privilege awaken us to present duty, and now, while life lasts, let us spend and be spent for our sweet Lord Jesus.

May 16

Who giveth us richly all things to enjoy.
—1 Timothy 6:17

OUR Lord Jesus is ever giving, and does not for a solitary instant withdraw his hand. As long as there is a vessel of grace not yet full to the brim, the oil shall not be stayed. He is a sun ever-shining; he is manna always falling round the camp; he is a rock in the desert, ever sending out streams of life from his smitten side; the rain of his grace is always dropping; the river of his bounty is ever-flowing, and the well-spring of his love is constantly overflowing. As the King can never die, so his grace can never fail. Daily we pluck his fruit, and daily his branches bend down to our hand with a fresh store of mercy. There are seven feast-days in his weeks, and as many as are the days, so many are the banquets in his years. Who has ever returned from his door unblessed? Who has ever risen from his table unsatisfied, or from his bosom un-emparadised? His mercies are new every morning and fresh every evening. Who can know the number of his benefits, or recount the list of his bounties? Every sand which drops from the glass of time is but the tardy follower of a myriad of mercies. The wings of our hours are covered with the silver of his kindness, and with the yellow gold of his affection. The river of time bears from the mountains of eternity the golden sands of his favor. The countless stars are but as the standard bearers of a more innumerable host of blessings. Who can count the dust of the benefits which he bestows on Jacob, or tell the number of the fourth part of his mercies towards Israel? How shall my soul extol him who daily loadeth us with benefits, and who crowneth us with loving-kindness? O that my praise could be as ceaseless as his bounty! O miserable tongue, how canst thou be silent? Wake up, I pray thee, lest I call thee no more my glory, but my shame. "Awake, psaltery and harp: I myself will awake right early."

MAY 17

So to walk even as he walked.
—1 John 2:6

HY should Christians imitate Christ? They should do it for *their own sakes.* If they desire to be in a healthy state of soul—if they would escape the sickness of sin, and enjoy the vigor of growing grace, let Jesus be their model. For their own happiness' sake, if they would drink wine on the lees, well refined; if they would enjoy holy and happy communion with Jesus; if they would be lifted up above the cares and troubles of this world, let them walk even as he walked. There is nothing which can so assist you to walk towards heaven with good speed, as wearing the image of Jesus on your heart to rule all its motions. It is when, by the power of the Holy Spirit, you are enabled to walk with Jesus in his very footsteps, that you are most happy, and most known to be the sons of God. Peter afar off is both unsafe and uneasy. Next, for *religion's sake,* strive to be like Jesus. Ah! poor religion, thou hast been sorely shot at by cruel foes, but thou hast not been wounded one-half so dangerously by thy foes as by thy friends. Who made those wounds in the fair hand of Godliness? The professor who used the dagger of hypocrisy. The man who with pretences, enters the fold, being naught but a wolf in sheep's clothing, worries the flock more than the lion outside. There is no weapon half so deadly as a Judas-kiss. Inconsistent professors injure the gospel more than the sneering critic or the infidel. But, especially for *Christ's own sake,* imitate his example. Christian, lovest thou thy Savior? Is his name precious to thee? Is his cause dear to thee? Wouldst thou see the kingdoms of the world become his? Is it thy desire that he should be glorified? Art thou longing that souls should be won to him? If so, *imitate* Jesus; be an "epistle of Christ, known and read of all men."

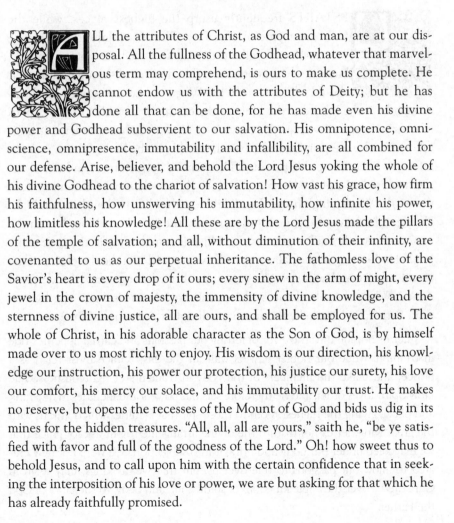

MAY 18

In him dwelleth all the fullness of the Godhead bodily.
And ye are complete in him.
—Colossians 2:9–10

ALL the attributes of Christ, as God and man, are at our disposal. All the fullness of the Godhead, whatever that marvelous term may comprehend, is ours to make us complete. He cannot endow us with the attributes of Deity; but he has done all that can be done, for he has made even his divine power and Godhead subservient to our salvation. His omnipotence, omniscience, omnipresence, immutability and infallibility, are all combined for our defense. Arise, believer, and behold the Lord Jesus yoking the whole of his divine Godhead to the chariot of salvation! How vast his grace, how firm his faithfulness, how unswerving his immutability, how infinite his power, how limitless his knowledge! All these are by the Lord Jesus made the pillars of the temple of salvation; and all, without diminution of their infinity, are covenanted to us as our perpetual inheritance. The fathomless love of the Savior's heart is every drop of it ours; every sinew in the arm of might, every jewel in the crown of majesty, the immensity of divine knowledge, and the sternness of divine justice, all are ours, and shall be employed for us. The whole of Christ, in his adorable character as the Son of God, is by himself made over to us most richly to enjoy. His wisdom is our direction, his knowledge our instruction, his power our protection, his justice our surety, his love our comfort, his mercy our solace, and his immutability our trust. He makes no reserve, but opens the recesses of the Mount of God and bids us dig in its mines for the hidden treasures. "All, all, all are yours," saith he, "be ye satisfied with favor and full of the goodness of the Lord." Oh! how sweet thus to behold Jesus, and to call upon him with the certain confidence that in seeking the interposition of his love or power, we are but asking for that which he has already faithfully promised.

MAY 19

I have seen servants upon horses,
and princes walking as servants upon the earth.—Ecclesiastes 10:7

PSTARTS frequently usurp the highest places, while the truly great pine in obscurity. This is a riddle in providence whose solution will one day gladden the hearts of the upright; but it is so common a fact, that none of us should murmur if it should fall to our own lot. When our Lord was upon earth, although he is the Prince of the kings of the earth, yet he walked the footpath of weariness and service as the Servant of servants: what wonder is it if his followers, who are princes of the blood, should also be looked down upon as inferior and contemptible persons? The world is upside down, and therefore, the first are last and the last first. See how the servile sons of Satan lord it in the earth! What a high horse they ride! How they lift up their horn on high! Haman is in the court, while Mordecai sits in the gate; David wanders on the mountains, while Saul reigns in state; Elijah is complaining in the cave while Jezebel is boasting in the palace; yet who would wish to take the places of the proud rebels? and who, on the other hand, might not envy the despised saints? When the wheel turns, those who are lowest rise, and the highest sink. Patience, then, believer, eternity will right the wrongs of time.

Let us not fall into the error of letting our passions and carnal appetites ride in triumph, while our nobler powers walk in the dust. Grace must reign as a prince, and make the members of the body instruments of righteousness. The Holy Spirit loves order, and he therefore sets our powers and faculties in due rank and place, giving the highest room to those spiritual faculties which link us with the great King; let us not disturb the divine arrangement, but ask for grace that we may keep under our body and bring it into subjection. We were not new created to allow our passions to rule over us, but that we, as kings, may reign in Christ Jesus over the triple kingdom of spirit, soul, and body, to the glory of God the Father.

MAY 20

Marvelous lovingkindness.
—Psalm 17:7

WHEN we give our hearts with our alms, we give well, but we must often plead to a failure in this respect. Not so our Master and our Lord. His favors are always performed with the love of his heart. He does not send to us the cold meat and the broken pieces from the table of his luxury, but he dips our morsel in his own dish, and seasons our provisions with the spices of his fragrant affections. When he puts the golden tokens of his grace into our palms, he accompanies the gift with such a warm pressure of our hand, that the manner of his giving is as precious as the boon itself. He will come into our houses upon his errands of kindness, and he will not act as some austere visitors do in the poor man's cottage, but he sits by our side, not despising our poverty, nor blaming our weakness. Beloved, with what smiles does he speak! What golden sentences drop from his gracious lips! What embraces of affection does he bestow upon us! If he had but given us farthings, the way of his giving would have gilded them; but as it is, the costly alms are set in a golden basket by his pleasant carriage. It is impossible to doubt the sincerity of his charity, for there is a bleeding heart stamped upon the face of all his benefactions. He giveth liberally and upbraideth not. Not one hint that we are burdensome to him; not one cold look for his poor pensioners; but he rejoices in his mercy, and presses us to his bosom while he is pouring out his life for us. There is a fragrance in his spikenard which nothing but his heart could produce; there is a sweetness in his honey-comb which could not be in it unless the very essence of his soul's affection had been mingled with it. Oh! the rare communion which such singular heartiness effecteth! May we continually taste and know the blessedness of it!

MAY 21

If so be, ye have tasted that the Lord is gracious.
—1 Peter 2:3

"F:"—then, this is not a matter to be taken for granted concerning every one of the human race. "If:"—then there is a possibility and a probability that some may not have tasted that the Lord is gracious. "If:"—then this is not a general but a special mercy; and it is needful to enquire whether we know the grace of God by inward experience. There is no spiritual favor which may not be a matter for heart-searching.

But while this should be a matter of earnest and prayerful inquiry, no one ought to be content whilst there is any such thing as an "if" about his having tasted that the Lord is gracious. A jealous and holy distrust of self may give rise to the question even in the believer's heart, but the *continuance* of such a doubt would be an evil indeed. We must not rest without a desperate struggle to clasp the Savior in the arms of faith, and say, "I know whom I have believed, and I am persuaded that he is able to keep that which I have committed unto him." Do not rest, O believer, till thou hast a full assurance of thine interest in Jesus. Let nothing satisfy thee till, by the infallible witness of the Holy Spirit bearing witness with thy spirit, thou art certified that thou art a child of God. Oh, trifle not here; let no "perhaps" and "peradventure" and "if" and "maybe" satisfy thy soul. Build on eternal verities, and verily build upon them. Get the sure mercies of David, and surely get them. Let thine anchor be cast into that which is within the veil, and see to it that thy soul be linked to the anchor by a cable that will not break. Advance beyond these dreary "ifs;" abide no more in the wilderness of doubts and fears; cross the Jordan of distrust, and enter the Canaan of peace, where the Canaanite still lingers, but where the land ceaseth not to flow with milk and honey.

MAY 22

He led them forth by the right way.
—Psalm 107:7

HANGEFUL experience often leads the anxious believer to enquire "Why is it thus with me?" I looked for light, but lo, darkness came; for peace, but behold trouble. I said in my heart, my mountain standeth firm, I shall never be moved. Lord, thou dost hide thy face, and I am troubled. It was but yesterday that I could read my title clear; today my evidences are bedimmed, and my hopes are clouded. Yesterday I could climb to Pisgah's top, and view the landscape o'er, and rejoice with confidence in my future inheritance; today, my spirit has no hopes, but many fears; no joys, but much distress. Is this part of God's plan with me? Can this be the way in which God would bring me to heaven? Yes, it is even so. The eclipse of your faith, the darkness of your mind, the fainting of your hope, all these things are but parts of God's method of making you ripe for the great inheritance upon which you shall soon enter. These trials are for the testing and strengthening of your faith—they are waves that wash you further upon the rock—they are winds which waft your ship the more swiftly towards the desired haven. According to David's words, so it might be said of you, "so he bringeth them to their desired haven." By honor and dishonor, by evil report and by good report, by plenty and by poverty, by joy and by distress, by persecution and by peace, by all these things is the life of your souls maintained, and by each of these are you helped on your way. Oh, think not, believer, that your sorrows are out of God's plan; they are necessary parts of it. "We must, through much tribulation, enter the kingdom." Learn, then, even to "count it all joy when ye fall into divers temptations.

> O let my trembling soul be still,
> And wait thy wise, thy holy will!
> I cannot, Lord, thy purpose see,
> Yet all is well since ruled by thee.

MAY 23

The Lord will perfect that which concerneth me.
—Psalm 138:8

OST manifestly the confidence which the Psalmist here expressed was a *divine confidence.* He did not say,

> I have grace enough to perfect that which concerneth me—my faith is so steady that it will not stagger—my love is so warm that it will never grow cold—my resolution is so firm that nothing can move it;

no, his dependence was on the Lord alone. If we indulge in any confidence which is not grounded on the Rock of ages, our confidence is worse than a dream, it will fall upon us, and cover us with its ruins, to our sorrow and confusion. All that Nature spins time will unravel, to the eternal confusion of all who are clothed therein. The Psalmist was wise, he rested upon nothing short of the *Lord's* work. It is the Lord who has begun the good work within us; it is he who has carried it on; and if he does not finish it, it never will be complete. If there be one stitch in the celestial garment of our righteousness which we are to insert ourselves, then we are lost; but this is our confidence, the Lord who began will perfect. He *has* done it all, *must* do it all, and *will* do it all. Our confidence must not be in what we have done, nor in what we have resolved to do, but entirely in what *the Lord* will do. Unbelief insinuates—

> You will never be able to stand. Look at the evil of your heart, you can never conquer sin; remember the sinful pleasures and temptations of the world that beset you, you will be certainly allured by them and led astray.

Ah! yes, we should indeed perish if left to our own strength. If we had alone to navigate our frail vessels over so rough a sea, we might well give up the voyage in despair; but, thanks be to God, he will perfect that which concerneth us, and bring us to the desired haven. We can never be too confident when we confide in him alone, and never too much concerned to *have such* a trust.

May 24

Blessed be God, which hath not turned away my prayer.
—Psalm 66:20

N looking back upon the character of our prayers, if we do it honestly, we shall be filled with wonder that God has ever answered them. There may be some who think their prayers worthy of acceptance—as the Pharisee did; but the true Christian, in a more enlightened retrospect, weeps over his prayers, and if he could retrace his steps he would desire to pray more earnestly. Remember, Christian, how *cold* thy prayers have been. When in thy closet thou shouldst have wrestled as Jacob did; but instead thereof, thy petitions have been faint and few—far removed from that humble, believing, persevering faith, which cries, "I will not let thee go except thou bless me." Yet, wonderful to say, God has heard these cold prayers of thine, and not only heard, but answered them. Reflect also, how *infrequent* have been thy prayers, unless thou hast been in trouble, and *then* thou hast gone often to the mercy-seat: but when deliverance has come, where has been thy constant supplication? Yet, notwithstanding thou hast ceased to pray as once thou didst, God has not ceased to bless. When thou hast neglected the mercy-seat, God has not deserted it, but the bright light of the Shekinah has always been visible between the wings of the cherubim. Oh! it is marvelous that the Lord should regard those intermittent spasms of importunity which come and go with our necessities. What a God is he thus to hear the prayers of those who come to him when they have pressing wants, but neglect him when they have received a mercy; who approach him when they are forced to come, but who almost forget to address him when mercies are plentiful and sorrows are few. Let his gracious kindness in hearing such prayers touch our hearts, so that we may henceforth be found "Praying always with all prayer and supplication in the Spirit."

MAY 25

Forsake me not, O Lord.
—Psalm 38:21

REQUENTLY we pray that God would not forsake us in the hour of trial and temptation, but we too much forget that we have need to use this prayer *at all times*. There is no moment of our life, however holy, in which we can do without his constant upholding. Whether in light or in darkness, in communion or in temptation, we alike need the prayer, "Forsake me not, O Lord." "Hold thou me up, and I shall be safe." A little child, while learning to walk, always needs the nurse's aid. The ship left by the pilot drifts at once from her course. We cannot do without continued aid from above; let it then be your prayer today,

Forsake me not. Father, forsake not thy child, lest he fall by the hand of the enemy. Shepherd, forsake not thy lamb, lest he wander from the safety of the fold. Great Husbandman, forsake not thy plant, lest it wither and die. "Forsake me not, O Lord," now; and forsake me not at any moment of my life. Forsake me not in my joys, lest they absorb my heart. Forsake me not in my sorrows, lest I murmur against thee. Forsake me not in the day of my repentance, lest I lose the hope of pardon, and fall into despair; and forsake me not in the day of my strongest faith, lest faith degenerate into presumption. Forsake me not, for without thee I am weak, but with thee I am strong. Forsake me not, for my path is dangerous, and full of snares, and I cannot do without thy guidance. The hen forsakes not her brood, do thou then evermore cover me with thy feathers, and permit me under thy wings to find my refuge. "Be not far from me, O Lord, for trouble is near, for there is none to help." "Leave me not, neither forsake me, O God of my salvation!"

> O ever in our cleansed breast,
> Bid thine Eternal Spirit rest;
> And make our secret soul to be
> A temple pure and worthy thee.

MAY 26

Cast thy burden upon the Lord, and he shall sustain thee.
—Psalm 55:22

ARE, even though exercised upon legitimate objects, if carried to excess, has in it the nature of sin. The precept to avoid anxious care is earnestly inculcated by our Savior, again and again; it is reiterated by the apostles; and it is one which cannot be neglected without involving transgression: for the very essence of anxious care is the imagining that we are wiser than God, and the thrusting ourselves into his place to do for him that which he has undertaken to do for us. We attempt to think of that which we fancy he will forget; we labor to take upon ourselves our weary burden, as if he were unable or unwilling to take it for us. Now this disobedience to his plain precept, this unbelief in his Word, this presumption in intruding upon his province, is all sinful. Yet more than this, anxious care often leads to acts of sin. He who cannot calmly leave his affairs in God's hand, but will carry his own burden, is very likely to be tempted to use wrong means to help himself. This sin leads to a forsaking of God as our counselor, and resorting instead to human wisdom. This is going to the "broken cistern" instead of to the "fountain;" a sin which was laid against Israel of old. Anxiety makes us doubt God's lovingkindness, and thus our love to him grows cold; we feel mistrust, and thus grieve the Spirit of God, so that our prayers become hindered, our consistent example marred, and our life one of self-seeking. Thus want of confidence in God leads us to wander far from him; but if through simple faith in his promise, we cast each burden as it comes upon him, and are "careful for nothing" because he undertakes to care for us, it will keep us close to him, and strengthen us against much temptation. "Thou wilt keep him in perfect peace whose mind is stayed on thee, because he trusteth in thee."

MAY 27

So Mephibosheth dwelt in Jerusalem:
for he did eat continually at the king's table;
and was lame on both his feet.
—2 Samuel 9:13

MEPHIBOSHETH was no great ornament to a royal table, yet he had a continual place at David's board, because the king could see in his face the features of the beloved Jonathan. Like Mephibosheth, we may cry unto the King of Glory, "What is thy servant, that thou shouldst look upon such a dead dog as I am?" but still the Lord indulges us with most familiar intercourse with himself, because he sees in our countenances the remembrance of his dearly-beloved Jesus. The Lord's people are *dear for another's sake.* Such is the love which the Father bears to his only begotten, that for his sake he raises his lowly brethren from poverty and banishment, to courtly companionship, noble rank, and royal provision. Their *deformity shall not rob them of their privileges.* Lameness is no bar to sonship; the cripple is as much the heir as if he could run like Asahel. Our right does not limp, though our might may. A king's table is a noble hiding-place for lame legs, and at the gospel feast we learn to glory in infirmities, because the power of Christ resteth upon us. Yet grievous *disability may mar the persons of the best-loved saints.* Here is one feasted by David, and yet so lame in both his feet that he could not go up with the king when he fled from the city, and was therefore maligned and injured by his servant Ziba. Saints whose faith is weak, and whose knowledge is slender, are great losers; they are exposed to many enemies, and cannot follow the king whithersoever he goeth. This *disease frequently arises from falls.* Bad nursing in their spiritual infancy often causes converts to fall into a despondency from which they never recover, and sin in other cases brings broken bones. Lord, help the lame to leap like an hart, and satisfy all thy people with the bread of thy table!

MAY 28

Whom he justified, them he also glorified.
—Romans 8:30

ERE is a precious truth for thee, believer. Thou mayest be poor, or in suffering, or unknown, but for thine encouragement take a review of thy "calling" and the consequences that flow from it, and especially that blessed result here spoken of. As surely as thou art God's child today, so surely shall all thy trials soon be at an end, and thou shalt be rich to all the intents of bliss. Wait awhile, and that weary head shall wear the crown of glory, and that hand of labor shall grasp the palm-branch of victory. Lament not thy troubles, but rather rejoice that ere long thou wilt be where "there shall be neither sorrow, nor crying, neither shall there be any more pain." The chariots of fire are at thy door, and a moment will suffice to bear thee to the glorified. The everlasting song is almost on thy lip. The portals of heaven stand open for thee. Think not that thou canst fail of entering into rest. If he hath called thee, nothing can divide thee from his love. Distress cannot sever the bond; the fire of persecution cannot burn the link; the hammer of hell cannot break the chain. Thou art secure; that voice which called thee at first, shall call thee yet again from earth to heaven, from death's dark gloom to immortality's unuttered splendors. Rest assured, the heart of him who has justified thee beats with infinite love towards thee. Thou shalt soon be with the glorified, where thy portion is; thou art only waiting here to be made meet for the inheritance, and that done, the wings of angels shall waft thee far away, to the mount of peace, and joy, and blessedness, where,

> Far from a world of grief and sin,
> With God eternally shut in,

thou shalt rest forever and ever.

MAY 29

Thou hatest wickedness.
—Psalm 45:7

"BE ye angry, and sin not." There can hardly be goodness in a man if he be not angry at sin; he who loves truth must hate every false way. How our Lord Jesus hated it when the temptation came! Thrice it assailed him in different forms, but ever he met it with, "Get thee behind me, Satan." He hated it in others; none the less fervently because he showed his hate oftener in tears of pity than in words of rebuke; yet what language could be more stern, more Elijah-like, than the words, "Woe unto you, scribes and Pharisees, hypocrites! for ye devour widows' houses, and for a pretence make long prayer." He hated wickedness, so much that he bled to wound it to the heart; he died that it might die; he was buried that he might bury it in his tomb; and he rose that he might forever trample it beneath his feet. Christ is in the Gospel, and that Gospel is opposed to wickedness in every shape. Wickedness arrays itself in fair garments, and imitates the language of holiness; but the precepts of Jesus, like his famous scourge of small cords, chase it out of the temple, and will not tolerate it in the Church. So, too, in the heart where Jesus reigns, what war there is between Christ and Belial! And when our Redeemer shall come to be our Judge, those thundering words, "Depart, ye cursed" which are, indeed, but a prolongation of his life-teaching concerning sin, shall manifest his abhorrence of iniquity. As warm as is his love to sinners, so hot is his hatred of sin; as perfect as is his righteousness, so complete shall be the destruction of every form of wickedness. O thou glorious champion of right, and destroyer of wrong, for this cause hath God, even thy God, anointed thee with the oil of gladness above thy fellows.

MAY 30

Take us the foxes, the little foxes that spoil the vines.
—*Song of Solomon 2:15*

little thorn may cause much suffering. A little cloud may hide the sun. Little foxes spoil the vines; and little sins do mischief to the tender heart. These little sins burrow in the soul, and make it so full of that which is hateful to Christ, that he will hold no comfortable fellowship and communion with us. A great sin cannot destroy a Christian, but a little sin can make him miserable. Jesus will not walk with his people unless they drive out every known sin. He says, "If ye keep my commandments, ye shall abide in my love, even as I have kept my Father's commandments and abide in his love." Some Christians very seldom enjoy their Savior's presence. How is this? Surely it must be an affliction for a tender child to be separated from his father. Art thou a child of God, and yet satisfied to go on without seeing thy Father's face? What! thou the spouse of Christ, and yet content without his company! Surely, thou hast fallen into a sad state, for the chaste spouse of Christ mourns like a dove without her mate, when he has left her. Ask, then, the question, what has driven Christ from thee? He hides his face behind the wall of thy sins. That wall may be built up of *little* pebbles, as easily as of great stones. The sea is made of drops; the rocks are made of grains: and the sea which divides thee from Christ may be filled with the drops of thy little sins; and the rock which has well nigh wrecked thy barque, may have been made by the daily working of the coral insects of thy little sins. If thou wouldst live with Christ, and walk with Christ, and see Christ, and have fellowship with Christ, take heed of "the little foxes that spoil the vines, for our vines have tender grapes." Jesus invites you to go *with him* and take them. He will surely, like Samson, take the foxes at once and easily. Go with him to the hunting.

MAY 31

The king also himself passed over the brook Kidron.
—2 Samuel 15:23

AVID passed that gloomy brook when flying with his mourning company from his traitor son. The man after God's own heart was not exempt from trouble, nay, his life was full of it. He was both the Lord's Anointed, and the Lord's Afflicted. Why then should we expect to escape? At sorrow's gates the noblest of our race have waited with ashes on their heads, wherefore then should we complain as though some strange thing had happened unto us?

The *King* of kings himself was not favored with a more cheerful or royal road. He passed over the filthy ditch of Kidron, through which the filth of Jerusalem flowed. God had one Son without sin, but not a single child without the rod. It is a great joy to believe that Jesus has been tempted in all points like as we are. What is our Kidron this morning? Is it a faithless friend, a sad bereavement, a slanderous reproach, a dark foreboding? The King has passed over all these. Is it bodily pain, poverty, persecution, or contempt? Over each of these Kidrons the King has gone before us. "In all our afflictions he was afflicted." The idea of strangeness in our trials must be banished at once and forever, for he who is the Head of all saints, knows by experience the grief which we think so peculiar. All the citizens of Zion must be free of the Honorable Company of Mourners, of which the Prince Immanuel is Head and Captain.

Notwithstanding the abasement of David, he yet returned in triumph to his city, and David's Lord arose victorious from the grave; let us then be of good courage, for we also shall win the day. We shall yet with joy draw water out of the wells of salvation, though now for a season we have to pass by the noxious streams of sin and sorrow. Courage, soldiers of the Cross, the King himself triumphed after going over Kidron, and so shall you.

JUNE 1

The evening and the morning were the first day.
—Genesis 1:5

WAS it so even in the beginning? Did light and darkness divide the realm of time in the first day? Then little wonder is it if I have also changes in my circumstances from the sunshine of prosperity to the midnight of adversity. It will not always be the blaze of noon even in my soul concerns, I must expect at seasons to mourn the absence of my former joys, and seek my Beloved in the night. Nor am I alone in this, for all the Lord's beloved ones have had to sing the mingled song of judgment and of mercy, of trial and deliverance, of mourning and of delight. It is one of the arrangements of Divine providence that day and night shall not cease either in the spiritual or natural creation till we reach the land of which it is written, "there is no night there." What our heavenly Father ordains is wise and good.

What, then, my soul, is it best for thee to do? Learn first *to be content* with this divine order, and be willing, with Job, to receive evil from the hand of the Lord as well as good. Study next, to *make the outgoings of the morning and the evening to rejoice.* Praise the Lord for the sun of joy when it rises, and for the gloom of evening as it falls. There is beauty both in sunrise and sunset, sing of it, and glorify the Lord. Like the nightingale, pour forth thy notes at all hours. *Believe that the night is as useful as the day.* The dews of grace fall heavily in the night of sorrow. The stars of promise shine forth gloriously amid the darkness of grief. *Continue thy service* under all changes. If in the day thy watchword be *labor*, at night exchange it for *watch.* Every hour has its duty, do thou continue in thy calling as the Lord's servant until he shall suddenly appear in his glory. My soul, thine evening of old age and death is drawing near, dread it not, for it is part of the day; and the Lord has said, "I will cover him all the day long."

JUNE 2

For the flesh lusteth against the Spirit, and the Spirit against the flesh.
—Galatians 5:17

IN every believer's heart there is a constant struggle between the old nature and the new. The old nature is very active, and loses no opportunity of plying all the weapons of its deadly armory against newborn grace; while on the other hand, the new nature is ever on the watch to resist and destroy its enemy. Grace within us will employ prayer, and faith, and hope, and love, to cast out the evil; it takes unto it the "whole armor of God," and wrestles earnestly. These two opposing natures will never cease to struggle so long as we are in this world. The battle of "Christian" with "Apollyon" lasted three hours, but the battle of Christian with himself lasted all the way from the Wicket Gate in the river Jordan. The enemy is so securely entrenched within us that he can never be driven out while we are in this body: but although we are closely beset, and often in sore conflict, we have an Almighty helper, even Jesus, the Captain of our salvation, who is ever with us, and who assures us that we shall eventually come off more than conquerors through him. With such assistance the new-born nature is more than a match for its foes. Are you fighting with the adversary today? Are Satan, the world, and the flesh, all against you? Be not discouraged nor dismayed. Fight on! For God himself is with you; *Jehovah Nissi* is your banner, and *Jehovah Rophi* is the healer of your wounds. Fear not, you shall overcome, for who can defeat Omnipotence? Fight on, "looking unto Jesus;" and though long and stern be the conflict, sweet will be the victory, and glorious the promised reward.

> From strength to strength go on;
> Wrestle, and fight, and pray,
> Tread all the powers of darkness down,
> And win the well-fought day.

JUNE 3

These were potters, and those that dwelt among plants and hedges:
there they dwelt with the king for his work.
—1 Chronicles 4:23

POTTERS were the very highest grade of workers, but "the king" needed potters, and therefore they were in royal service, although the material upon which they worked was nothing but clay. We, too, may be engaged in the most menial part of the Lord's work, but it is a great privilege to do anything for "the king;" and therefore we will abide in our calling, hoping that, "although we have lien among the pots, yet shall we be as the wings of a dove covered with silver, and her feathers with yellow gold." The text tells us of those who *dwelt among plants and hedges,* having rough, rustic, hedging and ditching work to do. They may have desired to live in the city, amid its life, society, and refinement, but they kept their appointed places, for they also were doing the king's work. The place of our habitation is fixed, and we are not to remove from it out of whim and caprice, but seek to serve the Lord in it, by being a blessing to those among whom we reside. These potters and gardeners had *royal company,* for they dwelt "with the king" and although among hedges and plants, they dwelt with the king *there.* No lawful place, or gracious occupation , however mean, can debar us from communion with our divine Lord. In visiting hovels, swarming lodging-houses, workhouses, or gaols, we may go *with the king.* In all works of faith we may count upon Jesus' fellowship. It is when we are in his work that we may reckon upon his smile. Ye unknown workers who are occupied for your Lord amid the dirt and wretchedness of the lowest of the low, be of good cheer, for jewels have been found upon dunghills ere now, earthen pots have been filled with heavenly treasure, and ill weeds have been transformed into precious flowers. Dwell ye with the King for his work, and when he writes his chronicles your name shall be recorded.

JUNE 4

The kindness and love of God our Savior.
—Titus 3:4

HOW sweet it is to behold the Savior communing with his own beloved people! There can be nothing more delightful than, by the Divine Spirit, to be led into this fertile field of delight. Let the mind for an instant consider the history of the Redeemer's love, and a thousand enchanting acts of affection will suggest themselves, all of which have had for their design the weaving of the heart into Christ, and the intertwisting of the thoughts and emotions of the renewed soul with the mind of Jesus. When we meditate upon this amazing love, and behold the all-glorious Kinsman of the Church endowing her with all his ancient wealth, our souls may well faint for joy. Who is he that can endure such a weight of love? That partial sense of it which the Holy Spirit is sometimes pleased to afford, is more than the soul can contain; how transporting must be a complete view of it! When the soul shall have understanding to discern all the Savior's gifts, wisdom wherewith to estimate them, and time in which to meditate upon them, such as the world to come will afford us, we shall then commune with Jesus in a nearer manner than at present. But who can imagine the sweetness of such fellowship? It must be one of the things which have not entered into the heart of man, but which God hath prepared for them that love him. Oh, to burst open the door of our Joseph's granaries, and see the plenty which he hath stored up for us! This will overwhelm us with love. By faith we see, as in a glass darkly, the reflected image of his unbounded treasures, but when we shall actually see the heavenly things themselves, with our own eyes, how deep will be the stream of fellowship in which our soul shall bathe itself! Till then our loudest sonnets shall be reserved for our loving benefactor, Jesus Christ our Lord, whose love to us is wonderful, passing the love of women.

JUNE 5

The Lord shut him in.
—Genesis 7:16

OAH was shut in *away from all the world* by the hand of divine love. The door of electing purpose interposes between us and the world which lieth in the wicked one. We are not of the world even as our Lord Jesus was not of the world. Into the sin, the gaiety, the pursuits of the multitude we cannot enter; we cannot play in the streets of Vanity Fair with the children of darkness, for our heavenly Father has shut us in. Noah was shut in *with his God.* "Come thou into the ark," was the Lord's invitation, by which he clearly showed that he himself intended to dwell in the ark with his servant and his family. Thus all the chosen dwell in God and God in them. Happy people to be enclosed in the same circle which contains God in the Trinity of his persons, Father, Son, and Spirit. Let us never be inattentive to that gracious call,

> Come, my people, enter thou into thy chambers, and shut thy doors about thee, and hide thyself as it were for a little moment until the indignation be overpast.

Noah was so shut in that *no evil could reach him.* Floods did but lift him heavenward, and winds did but waft him on his way. Outside of the ark all was ruin, but inside all was rest and peace. Without Christ we perish, but in Christ Jesus there is perfect safety. Noah was so shut in that *he could not even desire to come out,* and those who are in Christ Jesus are in him forever. They shall go no more out forever, for eternal faithfulness has shut them in, and infernal malice cannot drag them out. The Prince of the house of David shutteth and no man openeth; and when once in the last days as Master of the house he shall rise up and shut the door, it will be in vain for mere professors to knock, and cry Lord, Lord open unto us, for that same door which shuts in the wise virgins will shut out the foolish forever. Lord, shut me in by thy grace.

JUNE 6

Behold, I am vile.—Job 40:4

NE cheering word, poor lost sinner, for thee! You think you must not come to God because you are vile. Now, there is not a saint living on earth but has been made to feel that he is vile. If Job, and Isaiah, and Paul were all obliged to say "I am vile," oh, poor sinner, wilt thou be ashamed to join in the same confession? If divine grace does not eradicate all sin from the believer, how dost thou hope to do it thyself? and if God loves his people while they are yet vile, dost thou think thy vileness will prevent his loving thee? Believe on Jesus, thou outcast of the world's society! Jesus calls *thee*, and such as thou art.

> Not the righteous, not the righteous;
> Sinners, Jesus came to call.

Even now say, "Thou hast died for sinners; I am a sinner, Lord Jesus, sprinkle thy blood on me;" if thou wilt confess thy sin thou shalt find pardon. If, now, with all thy heart, thou wilt say, "I am vile, wash me," thou shalt be washed *now*. If the Holy Spirit shall enable thee from thy heart to cry . . .

> Just as I am, without one plea
> But that thy blood was shed for me,
> And that thou bidd'st me come to thee,
> O Lamb of God, I come!

. . . thou shalt rise from reading this morning's portion with all thy sins pardoned; and though thou didst wake this morning with every sin that man hath ever committed on thy head, thou shalt rest tonight accepted in the Beloved; though once degraded with the rags of sin, thou shalt be adorned with a robe of righteousness, and appear white as the angels are. For "now," mark it, *"Now* is the accepted time." If thou "believest on him who justifieth the ungodly thou art saved." Oh! may the Holy Spirit give thee saving faith in him who receives the vilest.

JUNE 7

Ye that love the Lord hate evil.
—Psalm 97:10

THOU hast good reason to "hate evil," for only consider what harm it has already wrought thee. Oh, what a world of mischief sin has brought into thy heart! Sin blinded thee so that thou couldst not see the beauty of the Savior; it made thee deaf so that thou couldst not hear the Redeemer's tender invitations. Sin turned thy feet into the way of death, and poured poison into the very fountain of thy being; it tainted thy heart, and made it "deceitful above all things, and desperately wicked." Oh, what a creature thou wast when evil had done its utmost with thee, before divine grace interposed! Thou wast an heir of wrath even as others; thou didst "run with the multitude to do evil." Such were all of us; but Paul reminds us, "but ye are washed, but ye are sanctified, but ye are justified in the name of the Lord Jesus, and by the Spirit of our God." We have good reason, indeed, for hating evil when we look back and trace its deadly workings. Such mischief did evil do us, that our souls would have been lost had not omnipotent love interfered to redeem us. Even now it is an active enemy, ever watching to do us hurt, and to drag us to perdition. Therefore "hate evil," O Christians, unless you desire trouble. If you would strew your path with thorns, and plant nettles in your death-pillow, then neglect to "hate evil;" but if you would live a happy life, and die a peaceful death, then walk in all the ways of holiness, hating evil, even unto the end. If you truly love your Savior, and would honor him, then "hate evil." We know of no cure for the love of evil in a Christian like abundant intercourse with the Lord Jesus. Dwell much with him, and it is impossible for you to be at peace with sin.

> Order my footsteps by thy Word,
> And make my heart sincere;
> Let sin have no dominion, Lord,
> But keep my conscience clear.

JUNE 8

There fell down many slain, because the war was of God.
—*1 Chronicles 5:22*

WARRIOR, fighting under the banner of the Lord Jesus, observe this verse with holy joy, for as it was in the days of old so is it now, if the war be of God the victory is sure. The sons of Reuben, and the Gadites, and the half tribe of Manasseh could barely muster five and forty thousand fighting men, and yet in their war with the Hagarites, they slew "men, an hundred thousand," "for they cried to God in the battle, and he was entreated of them, because they put their trust in him." The Lord saveth not by many nor by few; it is ours to go forth in Jehovah's name if we be but a handful of men, for the Lord of Hosts is with us for our Captain. They did not neglect buckler, and sword, and bow, neither did they place their trust in these weapons; we must use all fitting means, but our confidence must rest in the Lord alone, for he is the sword and the shield of his people. The great reason of their extraordinary success lay in the fact that "the war was of God." Beloved, in fighting with sin without and within, with error doctrinal or practical, with spiritual wickedness in high places or low places, with devils and the devil's allies, you are waging Jehovah's war, and unless he himself can be worsted, you need not fear defeat. Quail not before superior numbers, shrink not from difficulties or impossibilities, flinch not at wounds or death, smite with the two-edged sword of the Spirit, and the slain shall lie in heaps. The battle is the Lord's and he will deliver his enemies into our hands. With steadfast foot, strong hand, dauntless heart, and flaming zeal, rush to the conflict, and the hosts of evil shall fly like chaff before the gale.

Stand up! stand up for Jesus!	To him that overcometh,
The strife will not be long;	A crown of life shall be;
This day the noise of battle,	He with the King of glory
The next the victor's song:	Shall reign eternally.

June 9

The Lord hath done great things for us, whereof we are glad.
—Psalm 126:3

OME Christians are sadly prone to *look* on the *dark* side of everything, and to dwell more upon what they have gone through than upon what God has done for them. Ask for their impression of the Christian life, and they will describe their continual conflicts, their deep afflictions, their sad adversities, and the sinfulness of their hearts, yet with scarcely any allusion to the mercy and help which God has vouchsafed them. But a Christian whose soul is in a *healthy* state, will come forward joyously, and say,

> I will speak, not about myself, but to the honor of my God. He hath brought me up out of an horrible pit, and out of the miry clay, and set my feet upon a rock, and established my goings: and he hath put a new song in my mouth, even praise unto our God. The Lord hath done great things for me, whereof I am glad.

Such an abstract of experience as this is the very best that any child of God can present. It is true that we endure trials, but it is just as true that we are delivered out of them. It is true that we have our corruptions, and mournfully do we know this, but it is quite as true that we have an all-sufficient Savior, who overcomes these corruptions, and delivers us from their dominion. In looking back, it would be wrong to deny that we have been in the Slough of Despond, and have crept along the Valley of Humiliation, but it would be equally wicked to forget that we have been *through* them safely and profitably; we have not remained in them, thanks to our Almighty Helper and Leader, who has brought us "out into a wealthy place." The deeper our troubles, the louder our thanks to God, who has led us through all, and preserved us until now. Our griefs cannot mar the melody of our praise, we reckon them to be the bass part of our life's song, "He hath done great things for us, whereof we are glad."

JUNE 10

We live unto the Lord.
—Romans 14:8

F God had willed it, each of us might have entered heaven at the moment of conversion. It was not absolutely necessary for our preparation for immortality that we should tarry here. It is possible for a man to be taken to heaven, and to be found meet to be a partaker of the inheritance of the saints in light, though he has but just believed in Jesus. It is true that our sanctification is a long and continued process, and we shall not be perfected till we lay aside our bodies and enter within the veil; but nevertheless, had the Lord so willed it, he might have changed us from imperfection to perfection, and have taken us to heaven at once. Why then are we here? Would God keep his children out of paradise a single moment longer than was necessary? Why is the army of the living God still on the battle-field when one charge might give them the victory? Why are his children still wandering hither and thither through a maze, when a solitary word from his lips would bring them into the center of their hopes in heaven? The answer is—they are here that they may *"live unto the Lord,"* and may bring others to know his love. We remain on earth as sowers to scatter good seed; as ploughmen to break up the fallow ground; as heralds publishing salvation. We are here as the "salt of the earth," to be a blessing to the world. We are here to glorify Christ in our daily life. We are here as workers for him, and as "workers together with him." Let us see that our life answereth its end. Let us live earnest, useful, holy lives, to "the praise of the glory of his grace." Meanwhile we long to be with him, and daily sing—

> My heart is with him on his throne,
> And ill can brook delay;
> Each moment listening for the voice,
> "Rise up, and come away."

June 11

We love him because he first loved us.
—1 John 4:19

HERE is no light in the planet but that which proceedeth from the sun; and there is no true love to Jesus in the heart but that which cometh from the Lord Jesus himself. From this overflowing fountain of the infinite love of God, all our love to God must spring. This must ever be a great and certain truth, that we love him for no other reason than because he first loved us. Our love to him is *the fair offspring* of his love to us. Cold admiration, when studying the works of God, anyone may have, but the warmth of love can only be kindled in the heart by God's Spirit. How great the wonder that such as we should ever have been brought to love Jesus at all! How marvelous that when we had rebelled against him, he should, by a display of such amazing love, seek to draw us back. No! never should we have had a grain of love towards God unless it had been sown in us by the sweet seed of his love to us. Love, then, has for its parent the love of God shed abroad in the heart: but after it is thus divinely born, it must be *divinely nourished*. Love is an exotic; it is not a plant which will flourish naturally in human soil, it must be watered from above. Love to Jesus is a flower of a delicate nature, and if it received no nourishment but that which could be drawn from the rock of our hearts it would soon wither. As love comes from heaven, so it must feed on heavenly bread. It cannot exist in the wilderness unless it be fed by manna from on high. Love must feed on love. The very soul and life of our love to God is his love to us.

> I love thee, Lord, but with no love of mine,
> For I have none to give;
> I love thee, Lord; but all the love is thine,
> For by thy love I live.
> I am as nothing, and rejoice to be
> Emptied, and lost, and swallowed up in thee.

JUNE 12

Thou art weighed in the balances and art found wanting.
—Daniel 5:27

IT is well frequently to weigh ourselves in the scale of God's Word. You will find it a holy exercise to read some psalm of David, and, as you meditate upon each verse, to ask yourself,

> Can I say this? Have I felt as David felt? Has my heart ever
> been broken on account of sin, as his was when he penned
> his penitential psalms? Has my soul been full of true confi-
> dence in the hour of difficulty as his was when he sang of God's mercies
> in the cave of Adullam, or in the holds of Engedi? Do I take the cup of
> salvation and call upon the name of the Lord?

Then turn to the life of Christ, and as you read, ask yourselves how far you are conformed to his likeness. Endeavor to discover whether you have the meekness, the humility, the lovely spirit which he constantly inculcated and displayed. Take, then, the epistles, and see whether you can go with the apostle in what he said of his experience. Have you ever cried out as he did—"O wretched man that I am! who shall deliver me from the body of this death"? Have you ever felt his self-abasement? Have you seemed to yourself the chief of sinners, and less than the least of all saints? Have you known anything of his devotion? Could you join with him and say, "For me to live is Christ, and to die is gain"? If we thus read God's Word as a test of our spiritual condition, we shall have good reason to stop many a time and say,

> Lord, I feel I have never yet been here, O bring me here! give me true
> penitence, such as this I read of. Give me real faith; give me warmer
> zeal; inflame me with more fervent love; grant me the grace of meek-
> ness; make me more like Jesus. Let me no longer be "found wanting,"
> when weighed in the balances of the sanctuary, lest I be found wanting
> in the scales of judgment.

"Judge yourselves that ye be not judged."

🌱

June 13

Whosoever will, let him take the water of life freely.
—Revelation 22:17

ESUS says, "take freely." He wants no payment or preparation. He seeks no recommendation from our virtuous emotions. If you have no good feelings, if you be but willing, you are invited; therefore come! You have no belief and no repentance,—come to him, and he will give them to you. Come just as you are, and take "Freely," without money and without price. He gives himself to needy ones. The drinking fountains at the corners of our streets are valuable institutions; and we can hardly imagine any one so foolish as to feel for his purse, when he stands before one of them, and to cry, "I cannot drink because I have not five pounds in my pocket." However poor the man is, there is the fountain, and just as he is he may drink of it. Thirsty passengers, as they go by, whether they are dressed in fustian or in broadcloth, do not look for any warrant for drinking; its being there is their warrant for taking its water freely. The liberality of some good friends has put the refreshing crystal there and we take it, and ask no questions. Perhaps the only persons who need go thirsty through the street where there is a drinking fountain, are the fine ladies and gentlemen who are in their carriages. They are very thirsty, but cannot think of being so vulgar as to get out to drink. It would demean them, they think, to drink at a common drinking fountain: so they ride by with parched lips. Oh, how many there are who are rich in their own good works and cannot therefore come to Christ! "I will not be saved," they say, "in the same way as the harlot or the swearer." What! go to heaven in the same way as a chimney sweep. Is there no pathway to glory but the path which led the thief there? I will not be saved that way. Such proud boasters must remain without the living water; but, *"Whosoever will, let him take the water of life freely."*

JUNE 14

Delight thyself also in the Lord.
—Psalm 37:4

THE teaching of these words must seem very surprising to those who are strangers to vital godliness, but to the sincere believer it is only the inculcation of a recognized truth. The life of the believer is here described as a *delight* in God, and we are thus certified of the great fact that true religion overflows with happiness and joy. Ungodly persons and mere professors never look upon religion as a joyful thing; to them it is service, duty, or necessity, but never pleasure or delight. If they attend to religion at all, it is either that they may gain thereby, or else because they dare not do otherwise. The thought of *delight* in religion is so strange to most men, that no two words in their language stand further apart than "holiness" and "delight." But believers who know Christ, understand that delight and faith are so blessedly united, that the gates of hell cannot prevail to separate them. They who love God with all their hearts, find that his ways are ways of pleasantness, and all his paths are peace. Such joys, such brimful delights, such overflowing blessednesses, do the saints discover in their Lord, that so far from serving him from custom, they would follow him though all the world cast out his name as evil. We fear not God because of any compulsion; our faith is no fetter, our profession is no bondage, we are not dragged to holiness, nor driven to duty. No, our piety is our pleasure, our hope is our happiness, our duty is our delight.

Delight and true religion are as allied as root and flower; as indivisible as truth and certainty; they are, in fact, two precious jewels glittering side by side in a setting of gold.

> 'Tis when we taste thy love,
> Our joys divinely grow,
> Unspeakable like those above,
> And heaven begins below.

JUNE 15

And Sarah said, "God hath made me to laugh,
so that all that hear will laugh with me."
—Genesis 21:6

T was far above the power of nature, and even contrary to its laws, that the aged Sarah should be honored with a son; and even so it is beyond all ordinary rules that I, a poor, helpless, undone sinner, should find grace to bear about in my soul the indwelling Spirit of the Lord Jesus. I, who once despaired, as well I might, for my nature was as dry, and withered, and barren, and accursed as a howling wilderness, even I have been made to bring forth fruit unto holiness. Well may my mouth be filled with joyous laughter, because of the singular, surprising grace which I have received of the Lord, for I have found Jesus, the promised seed, and he is mine forever. This day will I lift up psalms of triumph unto the Lord who has remembered my low estate, for "my heart rejoiceth in the Lord; mine horn is exalted in the Lord; my mouth is enlarged over mine enemies, because I rejoice in thy salvation."

I would have all those that hear of my great deliverance from hell, and my most blessed visitation from on high, laugh for joy with me. I would surprise my family with my abundant peace; I would delight my friends with my ever-increasing happiness; I would edify the Church with my grateful confessions; and even impress the world with the cheerfulness of my daily conversation. Bunyan tells us that Mercy laughed in her sleep, and no wonder when she dreamed of Jesus; my joy shall not stop short of hers while my Beloved is the theme of my daily thoughts. The Lord Jesus is a deep sea of joy: my soul shall dive therein, shall be swallowed up in the delights of his society. Sarah looked on her Isaac, and laughed with excess of rapture, and all her friends laughed with her; and thou, my soul, look on thy Jesus, and bid heaven and earth unite in thy joy unspeakable.

JUNE 16

And I give unto them eternal life, and they shall never perish.
—John 10:28

HE Christian should never think or speak lightly of unbelief. For a child of God to mistrust his love, his truth, his faithfulness, must be greatly displeasing to him. How can we ever grieve him by doubting his upholding grace? Christian! it is contrary to every promise of God's precious Word that thou shouldst ever be forgotten or left to perish. If it could be so, how could he be true who has said, "Can a woman forget her sucking child, that she should not have compassion on the son of her womb? Yea, they may forget, yet will I never forget thee." What were the value of that promise—"The mountains shall depart, and the hills be removed; but my kindness shall not depart from thee, neither shall the covenant of my peace be removed, saith the Lord that hath mercy on thee." Where were the truth of Christ's words—

> I give unto my sheep eternal life; and they shall never perish, neither shall any man pluck them out of my hand. My Father, which gave them me, is greater than all; and no man is able to pluck them out of my Father's hand.

Where were the doctrines of grace? They would be all disproved if one child of God should perish. Where were the veracity of God, his honor, his power, his grace, his covenant, his oath, if any of those for whom Christ has died, and who have put their trust in him, should nevertheless be cast away? Banish those unbelieving fears which so dishonor God. Arise, shake thyself from the dust, and put on thy beautiful garments. Remember it is sinful to doubt his Word wherein he has promised thee that thou shalt never perish. Let the eternal life within thee express itself in confident rejoicing.

> The gospel bears my spirit up:
> A faithful and unchanging God
> Lays the foundation for my hope,
> In oaths, and promises, and blood.

June 17

Help, Lord.
—Psalm 12:1

HE prayer itself is remarkable, for it is *short,* but *seasonable, sententious,* and *suggestive.* David mourned the fewness of faithful men, and therefore lifted up his heart in supplication; when the creature failed, he flew to the Creator. He evidently felt his own weakness, or he would not have cried for help; but at the same time he intended honestly to exert himself for the cause of truth, for the word "help" is inapplicable where we ourselves do nothing. There is much of *directness, clearness of perception,* and *distinctness of utterance* in this petition of two words; much more, indeed, than in the long rambling outpourings of certain professors. The Psalmist runs straightforward to his God, with a well-considered prayer; he knows what he is seeking, and where to seek it. Lord, teach us to pray in the same blessed manner.

The occasions for the use of this prayer are frequent. In *providential afflictions* how suitable it is for tried believers who find all helpers failing them. Students, in *doctrinal difficulties,* may often obtain aid by lifting up this cry of "Help, Lord," to the Holy Spirit, the great Teacher. Spiritual warriors in *inward conflicts* may send to the throne for reinforcements, and this will be a model for their request. Workers in *heavenly labor* may thus obtain grace in time of need. Seeking sinners, in *doubts and alarms,* may offer up the same weighty supplication; in fact, in all these cases, times, and places, this will serve the turn of needy souls. "Help, Lord," will suit us living and dying, suffering or laboring, rejoicing or sorrowing. In him our help is found, let us not be slack to cry to him.

The answer to the prayer is certain, if it be sincerely offered through Jesus. The Lord's character assures us that he will not leave his people; his relationship as Father and Husband guarantees us his aid; his gift of Jesus is a pledge of every good thing; and his sure promise stands, "Fear not, *I will help thee.*"

JUNE 18

Thy Redeemer.
—Isaiah 54:5

JESUS, the Redeemer, is altogether ours and ours forever. All the *offices* of Christ are held on our behalf. He is king for us, priest for us, and prophet for us. Whenever we read a new title of the Redeemer, let us appropriate him as ours under that name as much as under any other. The shepherd's staff, the father's rod, the captain's sword, the priest's mitre, the prince's scepter, the prophet's mantle, all are ours. Jesus hath no dignity which he will not employ for our exaltation, and no prerogative which he will not exercise for our defense. His fullness of *Godhead* is our unfailing, inexhaustible treasure-house.

His *manhood* also, which he took upon him for us, is ours in all its perfection. To us our gracious Lord communicates the spotless virtue of a stainless character; to us he gives the meritorious efficacy of a devoted life; on us he bestows the reward procured by obedient submission and incessant service. He makes the unsullied garment of his life our covering beauty; the glittering virtues of his character our ornaments and jewels; and the superhuman meekness of his death our boast and glory. He bequeaths us his manger, from which to learn how God came down to man; and his Cross to teach us how man may go up to God. All his thoughts, emotions, actions, utterances, miracles, and intercessions, were for us. He trod the road of sorrow on our behalf, and hath made over to us as his heavenly legacy the full results of all the labors of his life. He is now as much ours as heretofore; and he blushes not to acknowledge himself *"our* Lord Jesus Christ," though he is the blessed and only Potentate, the King of kings, and Lord of lords. Christ everywhere and every way is our Christ, forever and ever most richly to enjoy. O my soul, by the power of the Holy Spirit! call him this morning, "thy Redeemer."

JUNE 19

And they were all filled with the Holy Ghost.
—Acts 2:4

RICH were the blessings of this day if all of us were filled with the Holy Ghost. The consequences of this sacred filling of the soul it would be impossible to overestimate. Life, comfort, light, purity, power, peace; and many other precious blessings are inseparable from the Spirit's benign presence. As sacred *oil*, he anoints the head of the believer, sets him apart to the priesthood of saints, and gives him grace to execute his office aright. As the only truly purifying *water* he cleanses us from the power of sin and sanctifies us unto holiness, working in us to will and to do of the Lord's good pleasure. As the *light*, he manifested to us at first our lost estate, and now he reveals the Lord Jesus to us and in us, and guides us in the way of righteousness. Enlightened by his pure celestial ray, we are no more darkness but light in the Lord. As *fire*, he both purges us from dross, and sets our consecrated nature on a blaze. He is the sacrificial flame by which we are enabled to offer our whole souls as a living sacrifice unto God. As heavenly *dew*, he removes our barrenness and fertilizes our lives. O that he would drop from above upon us at this early hour! Such morning dew would be a sweet commencement for the day. As the *dove*, with wings of peaceful love he broods over his Church and over the souls of believers, and as a Comforter he dispels the cares and doubts which mar the peace of his beloved. He descends upon the chosen as upon the Lord in Jordan, and bears witness to their sonship by working in them a filial spirit by which they cry "Abba, Father." As the *wind*, he brings the breath of life to men; blowing where he listeth he performs the quickening operations by which the spiritual creation is animated and sustained. Would to God, that we might feel his presence this day and every day.

JUNE 20

For, lo, I will command, and I will sift the house of Israel
among all nations, like as corn is sifted in a sieve,
yet shall not the least grain fall upon the earth.
—Amos 9:9

VERY sifting comes by *divine command and permission.* Satan must ask leave before he can lay a finger upon Job. Nay, more, in some sense our siftings are *directly the work of heaven,* for the text says, "I will sift the house of Israel." Satan, like a drudge, may hold the sieve, hoping to destroy the corn; but the overruling hand of the Master is accomplishing the purity of the grain by the very process which the enemy intended to be destructive. Precious, but much sifted corn of the Lord's floor, be comforted by the blessed fact that the Lord directeth both flail and sieve to his own glory, and to thine eternal profit.

The Lord Jesus will surely use the fan which is in his hand, and will *divide the precious from the vile.* All are not Israel that are of Israel; the heap on the barn floor is not clean provender, and hence the winnowing process must be performed. In the sieve true weight alone has power. Husks and chaff being devoid of substance must fly before the wind, and only solid corn will remain.

Observe the *complete safety of the Lord's wheat;* even the least grain has a promise of preservation. God himself sifts, and therefore it is stern and terrible work; he sifts them in all places, "among all nations;" he sifts them in the most effectual manner, "like as corn is sifted in a sieve;" and yet for all this, not the smallest, lightest, or most shriveled grain, is permitted to fall to the ground. Every individual believer is precious in the sight of the Lord, a shepherd would not lose one sheep, nor a jeweler one diamond, nor a mother one child, nor a man one limb of his body, nor will the Lord lose one of his redeemed people. However little we may be, if we are the Lord's, we may rejoice that we are preserved in Christ Jesus.

JUNE 21

Thou art fairer than the children of men.
—Psalm 45:2

HE entire person of Jesus is but as one gem, and his life is all along but one impression of the seal. He is altogether complete; not only in his several parts, but as a gracious all-glorious whole. His character is not a mass of fair colors mixed confusedly, nor a heap of precious stones laid carelessly one upon another; he is a picture of beauty and a breastplate of glory. In him, all the "things of good repute" are in their proper places, and assist in adorning each other. Not one feature in his glorious person attracts attention at the expense of others; but he is perfectly and altogether lovely.

Oh, Jesus! thy power, thy grace, thy justice, thy tenderness, thy truth, thy majesty, and thine immutability make up such a man, or rather such a God-man, as neither heaven nor earth hath seen elsewhere. Thy infancy, thy eternity, thy sufferings, thy triumphs, thy death, and thine immortality, are all woven in one gorgeous tapestry, without seam or rent. thou art music without discord; thou art many, and yet not divided; thou art all things, and yet not diverse. As all the colors blend into one resplendent rainbow, so all the glories of heaven and earth meet in thee, and unite so wondrously, that there is none like thee in all things; nay, if all the virtues of the most excellent were bound in one bundle, they could not rival thee, thou mirror of all perfection. thou hast been anointed with the holy oil of myrrh and cassia, which thy God hath reserved for thee alone; and as for thy fragrance, it is as the holy perfume, the like of which none other can ever mingle, even with the art of the apothecary; each spice is fragrant, but the compound is divine.

> Oh, sacred symmetry! oh, rare connection
> Of many perfects, to make one perfection!
> Oh, heavenly music, where all parts do meet
> In one sweet strain, to make one perfect sweet!

JUNE 22

He shall build the temple of the Lord; and he shall bear the glory.
—Zechariah 6:13

CHRIST himself is the builder of his spiritual temple, and he has built it on the mountains of his unchangeable affection, his omnipotent grace, and his infallible truthfulness. But as it was in Solomon's temple, so in this; the materials need making ready. There are the "Cedars of Lebanon," but they are not framed for the building; they are not cut down, and shaped, and made into those planks of cedar, whose odoriferous beauty shall make glad the courts of the Lord's house in Paradise. There are also the rough stones still in the quarry, they must be hewn thence, and squared. All this is Christ's own work. Each individual believer is being prepared, and polished, and made ready for his place in the temple; but Christ's own hand performs the preparation-work. Afflictions cannot sanctify, excepting as they are used by him to this end. Our prayers and efforts cannot make us ready for heaven, apart from the hand of Jesus, who fashioneth our hearts aright.

As in the building of Solomon's temple, "there was neither hammer, nor axe, nor any tool of iron, heard in the house," because all was brought perfectly ready for the exact spot it was to occupy—so is it with the temple which Jesus builds; the making ready is all done on earth. When we reach heaven, there will be no sanctifying us there, no squaring us with affliction, no planning us with suffering. No, we must be made meet here—all *that* Christ will do beforehand; and when he has done it, we shall be ferried by a loving hand across the stream of death, and brought to the heavenly Jerusalem, to abide as eternal pillars in the temple of our Lord.

> Beneath his eye and care,
> The edifice shall rise,
> Majestic, strong, and fair,
> And shine above the skies.

JUNE 23

Ephraim is a cake not turned.
—Hosea 7:8

A cake not turned is *uncooked on one side;* and so Ephraim was, in many respects, untouched by divine grace: though there was some partial obedience, there was very much rebellion left. My soul, I charge thee, see whether this be thy case. Art thou thorough in the things of God? Has grace gone through the very center of thy being so as to be felt in its divine operations in all thy powers, thy actions, thy words, and thy thoughts? To be sanctified, spirit, soul, and body, should be thine aim and prayer; and although sanctification may not be perfect in thee anywhere in degree, yet it must be universal in its action; there must not be the appearance of holiness in one place and reigning sin in another, else thou, too, wilt be a cake not turned.

A cake not turned is *soon burnt on the side nearest the fire,* and although no man can have too much religion, there are some who seem burnt black with bigoted zeal for that part of truth which they have received, or are charred to a cinder with a vain-glorious Pharisaic ostentation of those religious performances which suit their humor. The assumed appearance of superior sanctity frequently accompanies a total absence of all vital godliness. The saint in public is a devil in private. He deals in flour by day and in soot by night. The cake which is burned on one side, is dough on the other.

If it be so with me, O Lord, turn me! Turn my unsanctified nature to the fire of thy love and let it feel the sacred glow, and let my burnt side cool a little while I learn my own weakness and want of heat when I am removed from thy heavenly flame. Let me not be found a double minded man, but one entirely under the powerful influence of reigning grace; for well I know if I am left like a cake unturned, and am not on both sides the subject of thy grace, I must be consumed forever amid everlasting burnings.

JUNE 24

A certain woman of the company lifted up her voice,
and said unto him, "Blessed is the womb that bare thee,
and the paps which thou hast sucked."
But he said, "Yea rather, blessed are they
that hear the word of God, and keep it."—Luke 11:27–28

 T is fondly imagined by some that it must have involved very special privileges to have been the mother of our Lord, because they supposed that she had the benefit of looking into his very heart in a way in which we cannot hope to do. There may be an appearance of plausibility in the supposition, but not much. We do not know that Mary knew more than others; what she did know she did well to lay up in her heart; but she does not appear from anything we read in the Evangelists to have been a better-instructed believer than any other of Christ's disciples. All that she knew we also may discover. Do you wonder that we should say so? Here is a text to prove it: "The secret of the Lord is with them that fear him, and he will show them his covenant." Remember the Master's words—

> Henceforth I call you not servants; for the servant knoweth not what his Lord doeth: but I have called you friends; for all things that I have heard of my Father I have made known unto you.

So blessedly does this Divine Revealer of secrets tell us his heart, that he keepeth back nothing which is profitable to us; his own assurance is, "If it were not so, I would have told you." Doth he not this day manifest himself unto us as he doth not unto the world? It is even so; and therefore we will not ignorantly cry out, "Blessed is the womb that bare thee," but we will intelligently bless God that, having heard the Word and kept it, we have first of all as true a communion with the Savior as the Virgin had, and in the second place as true an acquaintance with the secrets of his heart as she can be supposed to have obtained. Happy soul to be thus privileged!

JUNE 25

Get thee up into the high mountain.
—Isaiah 40:9

OUR knowledge of Christ is somewhat like climbing one of our Welsh mountains. When you are at the base you see but little: the mountain itself appears to be but one-half as high as it really is. Confined in a little valley, you discover scarcely anything but the rippling brooks as they descend into the stream at the foot of the mountain. Climb the first rising knoll, and the valley lengthens and widens beneath your feet. Go higher, and you see the country for four or five miles round, and you are delighted with the widening prospect. Mount still, and the scene enlarges; till at last, when you are on the summit, and look east, west, north, and south, you see almost all England lying before you. Yonder is a forest in some distant county, perhaps two hundred miles away, and here the sea, and there a shining river and the smoking chimneys of a manufacturing town, or the masts of the ships in a busy port. All these things please and delight you, and you say, "I could not have imagined that so much could be seen at this elevation." Now, the Christian life is of the same order. When we first believe in Christ we see but little of him. The higher we climb the more we discover of his beauties. But who has ever gained the summit? Who has known all the heights and depths of the love of Christ which passes knowledge? Paul, when grown old, sitting greyhaired, shivering in a dungeon in Rome, could say with greater emphasis than we can, "I know whom I have believed," for each experience had been like the climbing of a hill, each trial had been like ascending another summit, and his death seemed like gaining the top of the mountain, from which he could see the whole of the faithfulness and the love of him to whom he had committed his soul. Get thee up, dear friend, into the high mountain.

JUNE 26

Art thou become like unto us?
—Isaiah 14:10

HAT must be the apostate professor's doom when his naked soul appears before God? How will he bear that voice,

> Depart, ye cursed; thou hast rejected me, and I reject thee; thou hast played the harlot, and departed from me: I also have banished thee forever from my presence, and will not have mercy upon thee.

What will be this wretch's shame at the last great day when, before assembled multitudes, the apostate shall be unmasked? See the profane, and sinners who never professed religion, lifting themselves up from their beds of fire to point at him. "There he is," says one, "will he preach the gospel in hell?" "There he is," says another, "he rebuked me for cursing, and was a hypocrite himself!" "Aha!" says another,

> . . . here comes a psalm-singing Methodist—one who was always at his meeting; he is the man who boasted of his being sure of everlasting life; and here he is!

No greater eagerness will ever be seen among Satanic tormentors, than in that day when devils drag the hypocrite's soul down to perdition. Bunyan pictures this with massive but awful grandeur of poetry when he speaks of the back-way to hell. Seven devils bound the wretch with nine cords, and dragged him from the road to heaven, in which he had professed to walk, and thrust him through the back-door into hell. Mind that back-way to hell, professors! "Examine yourselves, whether ye be in the faith." Look well to your state; see whether you be in Christ or not. It is the easiest thing in the world to give a lenient verdict when oneself is to be tried; but O, be just and true here. Be just to all, but be rigorous to yourself. Remember if it be not a rock on which you build, when the house shall fall, great will be the fall of it. O may the Lord give you sincerity, constancy, and firmness; and in no day, however evil, may you be led to turn aside.

JUNE 27

Only ye shall not go very far away.
—Exodus 8:28

THIS is a crafty word from the lip of the arch tyrant Pharaoh. If the poor bondaged Israelites must needs go out of Egypt, then he bargains with them that it shall not be very far away; not too far for them to escape the terror of his arms, and the observation of his spies. After the same fashion, the world loves not the nonconformity of nonconformity, or the dissidence of dissent, it would have us be more charitable and not carry matters with too severe a hand. Death to the world, and burial with Christ, are experiences which carnal minds treat with ridicule, and hence the ordinance which sets them forth is almost universally neglected, and even contemned. Worldly wisdom recommends the path of compromise, and talks of "moderation." According to this carnal policy, purity is admitted to be very desirable, but we are warned against being too precise; truth is of course to be followed, but error is not to be severely denounced. "Yes," says the world,

> . . . be spiritually minded by all means, but do not deny yourself a little gay society, an occasional ball, and a Christmas visit to a theatre. What's the good of crying down a thing when it is so fashionable, and everybody does it?

Multitudes of professors yield to this cunning advice, to their own eternal ruin. If we would follow the Lord wholly, we must go right away into the wilderness of separation, and leave the Egypt of the carnal world behind us. We must leave its maxims, its pleasures, and its religion too, and go far away to the place where the Lord calls his sanctified ones. When the town is on fire, our house cannot be too far from the flames. When the plague is abroad, a man cannot be too far from its haunts. The further from a viper the better, and the further from worldly conformity the better. To all true believers let the trumpet-call be sounded, "Come ye out from among them, be ye separate."

JUNE 28

Looking unto Jesus.
—Hebrews 12:2

I T is ever the Holy Spirit's work to turn our eyes away from self to Jesus; but Satan's work is just the opposite of this, for he is constantly trying to make us regard ourselves instead of Christ. He insinuates,

Your sins are too great for pardon; you have no faith; you do not repent enough; you will never be able to continue to the end; you have not the joy of his children; you have such a wavering hold of Jesus.

All these are thoughts about self, and we shall never find comfort or assurance by looking within. But the Holy Spirit turns our eyes entirely away from self: he tells us that we are nothing, but that "Christ is all in all." Remember, therefore, it is not *thy hold* of Christ that saves thee—it is Christ; it is not *thy joy* in Christ that saves thee—it is Christ; it is not even faith in Christ, though that be the instrument—it is Christ's blood and merits; therefore, look not so much to thy hand with which thou art grasping Christ, as to Christ; look not to thy hope, but to Jesus, the source of thy hope; look not to thy faith, but to Jesus, the author and finisher of thy faith. We shall never find happiness by looking at our prayers, our doings, or our feelings; it is what *Jesus* is, not what *we* are, that gives rest to the soul. If we would at once overcome Satan and have peace with God, it must be by "looking unto Jesus." Keep thine eye simply on him; let his death, his sufferings, his merits, his glories, his intercession, be fresh upon thy mind; when thou wakest in the morning look to him; when thou liest down at night look to him. Oh! let not thy hopes or fears come between thee and Jesus; follow hard after him, and he will never fail thee.

> My hope is built on nothing less
> Than Jesus' blood and righteousness:
> I dare not trust the sweetest frame,
> But wholly lean on Jesus' name.

JUNE 29

Them also which sleep in Jesus, will God bring with him.
—1 Thessalonians 4:14

ET us not imagine that *the soul* sleeps in insensibility. "Today shalt thou be with me in paradise," is the whisper of Christ to every dying saint. They "sleep in Jesus," but their souls are before the throne of God, praising him day and night in his temple, singing hallelujahs to him who washed them from their sins in his blood. The body sleeps in its lonely bed of earth, beneath the coverlet of grass. But what is this sleep? The idea connected with sleep is *"rest,"* and that is the thought which the Spirit of God would convey to us. Sleep makes each night a Sabbath for the day. Sleep shuts fast the door of the soul, and bids all intruders tarry for a while, that the life within may enter its summer garden of ease. The toil-worn believer quietly sleeps, as does the weary child when it slumbers on its mother's breast. Oh! happy they who die in the Lord; they rest from their labors, and their works do follow them. Their quiet repose shall never be broken until God shall rouse them to give them their full reward. Guarded by angel watchers, curtained by eternal mysteries, they sleep on, the heritors of glory, till the fullness of time shall bring the fullness of redemption. What an awaking shall be theirs! They were laid in their last resting place, weary and worn, but such they shall not rise. They went to their rest with the furrowed brow, and the wasted features, but they wake up in beauty and glory. The shriveled seed, so destitute of form and comeliness, rises from the dust a beauteous flower. The winter of the grave gives way to the spring of redemption and the summer of glory. Blessed is death, since it, through the divine power, disrobes us of this work-day garment, to clothe us with the wedding garment of incorruption. Blessed are those who "sleep in Jesus."

JUNE 30

And the glory which thou gavest me, I have given them.
—John 17:22

BEHOLD the superlative liberality of the Lord Jesus, for he hath given us his all. Although a tithe of his possessions would have made a universe of angels rich beyond all thought, yet was he not content until he had given us all that he had. It would have been surprising grace if he had allowed us to eat the crumbs of his bounty beneath the table of his mercy; but he will do nothing by halves, he makes us sit with him and share the feast. Had he given us some small pension from his royal coffers, we should have had cause to love him eternally; but no, he will have his bride as rich as himself, and he will not have a glory or a grace in which she shall not share. He has not been content with less than making us joint-heirs with himself, so that we might have equal possessions. He has emptied all his estate into the coffers of the Church, and hath all things common with his redeemed. There is not one room in his house the key of which he will withhold from his people. He gives them full liberty to take all that he hath to be their own; he loves them to make free with his treasure, and appropriate as much as they can possibly carry. The boundless fullness of his all-sufficiency is as free to the believer as the air he breathes. Christ hath put the flagon of his love and grace to the believer's lip, and bidden him drink on forever; for could he drain it, he is welcome to do so, and as he cannot exhaust it, he is bidden to drink abundantly, for it is all his own. What truer proof of fellowship can heaven or earth afford?

> When I stand before the throne
> Dressed in beauty not my own;
> When I see thee as thou art,
> Love thee with unsinning heart;
> Then, Lord, shall I fully know—
> Not till then—how much I owe.

JULY 1

In summer and in winter shall it be.
—Zechariah 14:8

THE streams of living water which flow from Jerusalem are not dried up by the parching heats of sultry midsummer any more than they were frozen by the cold winds of blustering winter. Rejoice, O my soul, that thou art spared to testify of the faithfulness of the Lord. The seasons change and thou changest, but thy Lord abides evermore the same, and the streams of his love are as deep, as broad and as full as ever. The heats of business cares and scorching trials make me need the cooling influences of the river of his grace; I may go at once and drink to the full from the inexhaustible fountain, for in summer and in winter it pours forth its flood. The upper springs are never scanty, and blessed be the name of the Lord, the nether springs cannot fail either. Elijah found Cherith dry up, but Jehovah was still the same God of providence. Job said his brethren were like deceitful brooks, but he found his God an overflowing river of consolation. The Nile is the great confidence of Egypt, but its floods are variable; our Lord is evermore the same. By turning the course of the Euphrates, Cyrus took the city of Babylon, but no power, human or infernal, can divert the current of divine grace. The tracks of ancient rivers have been found all dry and desolate, but the streams which take their rise on the mountains of divine sovereignty and infinite love shall ever be full to the brim. Generations melt away, but the course of grace is unaltered. The river of God may sing with greater truth than the brook in the poem—

> Men may come, and men may go,
> But I go on forever.

How happy art thou, my soul, to be led beside such still waters! never wander to other streams, lest thou hear the Lord's rebuke, "What hast thou to do in the way of Egypt to drink of the muddy river?"

JULY 2

Our heart shall rejoice in him.
—Psalm 33:21

BLESSED is the fact that Christians can rejoice even in the deepest distress; although trouble may surround them, they still sing; and, like many birds, they sing best in their cages. The waves may roll over them, but their souls soon rise to the surface and see the light of God's countenance; they have a buoyancy about them which keeps their head always above the water, and helps them to sing amid the tempest, "God is with me still." To whom shall the glory be given? Oh! to *Jesus*—it is all by Jesus. Trouble does not necessarily bring consolation with it to the believer, but the presence of the Son of God in the fiery furnace with him fills his heart with joy. He is sick and suffering, but Jesus visits him and makes his bed for him. He is dying, and the cold chilly waters of Jordan are gathering about him up to the neck, but Jesus puts his arms around him, and cries,

> Fear not, beloved; to die is to be blessed; the waters of death have their fountain-head in heaven; they are not bitter, they are sweet as nectar, for they flow from the throne of God.

As the departing saint wades through the stream, and the billows gather around him, and heart and flesh fail him, the same voice sounds in his ears, "Fear not; I am with thee; be not dismayed; I am thy God." As he nears the borders of the infinite unknown, and is almost affrighted to enter the realm of shades, Jesus says, "Fear not, it is your Father's good pleasure to give you the kingdom." Thus strengthened and consoled, the believer is not afraid to die; nay, he is even willing to depart, for since he has seen Jesus as the morning star, he longs to gaze upon him as the sun in his strength. Truly, the presence of Jesus is all the heaven we desire. He is at once

> The glory of our brightest days;
> The comfort of our nights.

JULY 3

The ill-favored and lean-fleshed kine [cows]
did eat up the seven well-favored and fat kine.
—Genesis 41:4

PHARAOH'S dream has too often been my waking experience. My days of sloth have ruinously destroyed all that I had achieved in times of zealous industry; my seasons of coldness have frozen all the genial glow of my periods of fervency and enthusiasm; and my fits of worldliness have thrown me back from my advances in the divine life. I had need to beware of lean prayers, lean praises, lean duties, and lean experiences, for these will eat up the fat of my comfort and peace. If I neglect prayer for never so short a time, I lose all the spirituality to which I had attained; if I draw no fresh supplies from heaven, the old corn in my granary is soon consumed by the famine which rages in my soul. When the caterpillars of indifference, the cankerworms of worldliness, and the palmerworms of self-indulgence, lay my heart completely desolate, and make my soul to languish, all my former fruitfulness and growth in grace avails me nothing whatever. How anxious should I be to have no lean-fleshed days, no ill-favored hours! If every day I journeyed towards the goal of my desires I should soon reach it, but backsliding leaves me still far off from the prize of my high calling, and robs me of the advances which I had so laboriously made. The only way in which all my days can be as the "fat kine," is to feed them in the right meadow, to spend them with the Lord, in his service, in his company, in his fear, and in his way. Why should not every year be richer than the past, in love, and usefulness, and joy?—I am nearer the celestial hills, I have had more experience of my Lord, and should be more like him. O Lord, keep far from me the curse of leanness of soul; let me not have to cry, "My leanness, my leanness, woe unto me!" but may I be well-fed and nourished in thy house, that I may praise thy name.

JULY 4

Sanctify them through thy truth.
—John 17:17

ANCTIFICATION begins in regeneration. The Spirit of God infuses into man that new living principle by which he becomes "a new creature" in Christ Jesus. This work, which begins in the new birth, is carried on in two ways—mortification, whereby the lusts of the flesh are subdued and kept under; and vivification, by which the life which God has put within us is made to be a well of water springing up unto everlasting life. This is carried on every day in what is called "perseverance," by which the Christian is preserved and continued in a gracious state, and is made to abound in good works unto the praise and glory of God; and it culminates or comes to perfection, in "glory," when the soul, being thoroughly purged, is caught up to dwell with holy beings at the right hand of the Majesty on high. But while the Spirit of God is thus the author of sanctification, yet there is a visible agency employed which must not be forgotten. "Sanctify them," said Jesus, "through thy *truth*: thy word is truth." The passages of Scripture which prove that the instrument of our sanctification is the Word of God are very many. The Spirit of God brings to our minds the precepts and doctrines of truth, and applies them with power. These are heard in the ear, and being received in the heart, they work in us to will and to do of God's good pleasure. The truth is the sanctifier, and if we do not hear or read the truth, we shall not grow in sanctification. We only progress in sound living as we progress in sound understanding. "Thy word is a lamp unto my feet and a light unto my path." Do not say of any error, "It is a mere matter of opinion." No man indulges an error of judgment, without sooner or later tolerating an error in practice. Hold fast the truth, for by so holding the truth shall you be sanctified by the Spirit of God.

JULY 5

Called to be saints.
—*Romans 1:7*

E are very apt to regard the apostolic saints as if they were "saints" in a more especial manner than the other children of God. All are "saints" whom God has called by his grace, and sanctified by his Spirit; but we are apt to look upon the *apostles* as extraordinary beings, scarcely subject to the same weaknesses and temptations as ourselves. Yet in so doing we are forgetful of this truth, that the nearer a man lives to God the more intensely has he to mourn over his own evil heart; and the more his Master honors him in his service, the more also doth the evil of the flesh vex and tease him day by day. The fact is, if we had seen the apostle Paul, we should have thought him remarkably like the rest of the chosen family: and if we had talked with him, we should have said,

> We find that his experience and ours are much the same. He is more faithful, more holy, and more deeply taught than we are, but he has the selfsame trials to endure. Nay, in some respects he is more sorely tried than ourselves.

Do not, then, look upon the ancient saints as being exempt either from infirmities or sins; and do not regard them with that mystic reverence which will almost make us idolaters. Their holiness is attainable even by us. We are "called to be saints" by that same voice which constrained them to their high vocation. It is a Christian's duty to force his way into the inner circle of saintship; and if these saints were superior to us in their attainments, as they certainly were, let us follow them; let us emulate their ardor and holiness. We have the same light that they had, the same grace is accessible to us, and why should we rest satisfied until we have equaled them in heavenly character? They lived *with* Jesus, they lived *for* Jesus, therefore they grew *like* Jesus. Let us live by the same Spirit as they did, "looking unto Jesus," and our saintship will soon be apparent.

JULY 6

Whoso hearkeneth unto me shall dwell safely,
and shall be quiet from fear of evil.
—Proverbs 1:33

IVINE love is rendered conspicuous when it shines in the midst of judgments. Fair is that lone star which smiles through the rifts of the thunder clouds; bright is the oasis which blooms in the wilderness of sand; so fair and so bright is love in the midst of wrath. When the Israelites provoked the Most High by their continued idolatry, he punished them by withholding both dew and rain, so that their land was visited by a sore famine; but while he did this, he took care that his own chosen ones should be secure. If all other brooks are dry, yet shall there be one reserved for Elijah; and when that fails, God shall still preserve for him a place of sustenance; nay, not only so, the Lord had not simply one "Elijah," but he had a remnant according to the election of grace, who were hidden by fifties in a cave, and though the whole land was subject to famine, yet these fifties in the cave were fed, and fed from Ahab's table too by his faithful, God-fearing steward, Obadiah. Let us from this draw the inference, that come what may, God's people are safe. Let convulsions shake the solid earth, let the skies themselves be rent in twain, yet amid the wreck of worlds the believer shall be as secure as in the calmest hour of rest. If God cannot save his people *under* heaven, he will save them *in* heaven. If the world becomes too hot to hold them, then heaven shall be the place of their reception and their safety. Be ye then confident, when ye hear of wars, and rumors of wars. Let no agitation distress you, but be quiet from fear of evil. Whatsoever cometh upon the earth, you, beneath the broad wings of Jehovah, shall be secure. Stay yourself upon his promise; rest in his faithfulness, and bid defiance to the blackest future, for there is nothing in it direful for you. Your sole concern should be to show forth to the world the blessedness of hearkening to the voice of wisdom.

JULY 7

Brethren, pray for us.
—1 Thessalonians 5:25

HIS one morning in the year we reserved to refresh the reader's memory upon the subject of prayer for ministers, and we do most earnestly implore every Christian household to grant the fervent request of the text first uttered by an apostle and now repeated by us. Brethren, our work is Solemnly momentous, involving weal or woe to thousands; we treat with souls for God on eternal business, and our word is either a savor of life unto life, or of death unto death. A very heavy responsibility rests upon us, and it will be no small mercy if at the last we be found clear of the blood of all men. As officers in Christ's army, we are the especial mark of the enmity of men and devils; they watch for our halting, and labor to take us by the heels. Our sacred calling involves us in temptations from which you are exempt, above all it too often draws us away from our personal enjoyment of truth into a ministerial and official consideration of it. We meet with many knotty cases, and our wits are at a non plus; we observe very sad backslidings, and our hearts are wounded; we see millions perishing, and our spirits sink. We wish to profit you by our preaching; we desire to be blest to your children; we long to be useful both to saints and sinners; therefore, dear friends, intercede for us with our God. Miserable men are we if we miss the aid of your prayers, but happy are we if we live in your supplications. You do not look to us but to our Master for spiritual blessings, and yet how many times has he given those blessings through his ministers; ask then, again and again, that we may be the earthen vessels into which the Lord may put the treasure of the gospel. We, the whole company of missionaries, ministers, city missionaries, and students, do in the name of Jesus beseech you

Brethren, pray for us.

189

JULY 8

Tell me I pray thee wherein thy great strength lieth.
—Judges 16:6

HERE lies the secret strength of faith? It lies in the food it feeds on; for faith studies *what* the promise is—an emanation of divine grace, an overflowing of the great heart of God; and faith says,

> My God could not have given this promise, except from love and grace; therefore it is quite certain his Word will be fulfilled.

Then faith thinketh, *"Who gave* this promise?" It considereth not so much its greatness, as, "Who is the author of it?" She remembers that it is God who cannot lie—God omnipotent, God immutable; and therefore concludeth that the promise must be fulfilled; and forward she advances in this firm conviction. She remembereth, *why the promise was given,*—namely, for God's glory, and she feels perfectly sure that God's glory is safe, that he will never stain his own escutcheon, nor mar the luster of his own crown; and therefore the promise must and will stand. Then faith also considereth the amazing *work of Christ* as being a clear proof of the Father's intention to fulfill his word. "He that spared not his own Son, but freely delivered him up for us all, how shall he not with him also freely give us all things?" Moreover faith looks back upon *the past,* for her battles have strengthened her, and her victories have given her courage. She remembers that God never has failed her; nay, that he never did once fail any of his children. She recollecteth times of great peril, when deliverance came; hours of awful need, when as her day her strength was found, and she cries,

> No, I never will be led to think that he can change and leave his servant now. Hitherto the Lord hath helped me, and he will help me still.

Thus faith views each promise in its connection with the promise-giver, and, because she does so, can with assurance say, "Surely goodness and mercy shall follow me all the days of my life!"

July 9

Forget not all his benefits.
—Psalm 103:2

I T is a delightful and profitable occupation to mark the hand of God in the lives of ancient saints, and to observe his goodness in delivering them, his mercy in pardoning them, and his faithfulness in keeping his covenant with them. But would it not be even more interesting and profitable for us to remark the hand of God in our own lives? Ought we not to look upon our own history as being at least as full of God, as full of his goodness and of his truth, as much a proof of his faithfulness and veracity, as the lives of any of the saints who have gone before? We do our Lord an injustice when we suppose that he wrought all his mighty acts, and showed himself strong for those in the early time, but doth not perform wonders or lay bare his arm for the saints who are now upon the earth. Let us review our own lives. Surely in these we may discover some happy incidents, refreshing to ourselves and glorifying to our God. Have you had no *deliverances*? Have you passed through no rivers, supported by the divine presence? Have you walked through no fires unharmed? Have you had no *manifestations*? Have you had no choice *favors*? The God who gave Solomon the desire of his heart, hath he never listened to you and answered your requests? That God of lavish bounty of whom David sang, "Who satisfieth thy mouth with good things," hath he never satiated *you* with fatness? Have you never been made to lie down in green pastures? Have you never been led by the still waters? Surely the goodness of God has been the same to us as to the saints of old. Let us, then, weave his mercies into a song. Let us take the pure gold of thankfulness, and the jewels of praise and make them into another crown for the head of Jesus. Let our souls give forth music as sweet and as exhilarating as came from David's harp, while we praise the Lord whose mercy endureth forever.

JULY 10

Fellow citizens with the saints.
—Ephesians 2:19

WHAT is meant by our being citizens in heaven? It means that *we are under heaven's government.* Christ the king of heaven reigns in our hearts; our daily prayer is, "Thy will be done on earth as it is in heaven." The proclamations issued from the throne of glory are freely received by us: the decrees of the Great King we cheerfully obey. Then as citizens of the New Jerusalem, *we share heaven's honors.* The glory which belongs to beatified saints belongs to us, for we are already sons of God, already princes of the blood imperial; already we wear the spotless robe of Jesus' righteousness; already we have angels for our servitors, saints for our companions, Christ for our Brother, God for our Father, and a crown of immortality for our reward. We share the honors of citizenship, for we have come to the general assembly and Church of the first-born whose names are written in heaven. As citizens, we have *common rights to all the property of heaven.* Ours are its gates of pearl and walls of chrysolite; ours the azure light of the city that needs no candle nor light of the sun; ours the river of the water of life, and the twelve manner of fruits which grow on the trees planted on the banks thereof; there is naught in heaven that belongeth not to us. "Things present, or things to come," all are ours. Also as citizens of heaven we *enjoy its delights.* Do they there rejoice over sinners that repent—prodigals that have returned? So do we. Do they chant the glories of triumphant grace? We do the same. Do they cast their crowns at Jesus' feet? Such honors as we have we cast there too. Are they charmed with his smile? It is not less sweet to us who dwell below. Do they look forward, waiting for his second advent? We also look and long for his appearing. If, then, we are thus *citizens of heaven,* let our walk and actions be consistent with our high dignity.

JULY 11

After that ye have suffered awhile,
make you perfect, stablish, strengthen, settle you.
—1 Peter 5:10

YOU have seen the arch of heaven as it spans the plain: glorious are its colors, and rare its hues. It is beautiful, but, alas, it passes away, and lo, it is not. The fair colors give way to the fleecy clouds, and the sky is no longer brilliant with the tints of heaven. It is not *established*. How can it be? A glorious show made up of transitory sun-beams and passing rain-drops, how can it abide? The graces of the Christian character must not resemble the rainbow in its transitory beauty, but, on the contrary, must be stablished, settled, abiding. Seek, O believer, that every good thing you have may be an abiding thing. May your character not be a writing upon the sand, but an inscription upon the rock! May your faith be no "baseless fabric of a vision," but may it be builded of material able to endure that awful fire which shall consume the wood, hay, and stubble of the hypocrite. May you be rooted and grounded in love. May your convictions be deep, your love real, your desires earnest. May your whole life be so settled and established, that all the blasts of hell, and all the storms of earth shall never be able to remove you. But notice how this blessing of being "stablished in the faith" is gained. The apostle's words point us to *suffering* as the means employed—*"After that ye have suffered awhile."* It is of no use to hope that we shall be well rooted if no rough winds pass over us. Those old gnarlings on the root of the oak tree, and those strange twistings of the branches, all tell of the many storms that have swept over it, and they are also indicators of the depth into which the roots have forced their way. So the Christian is made strong, and firmly rooted by all the trials and storms of life. Shrink not then from the tempestuous winds of trial, but take comfort, believing that by their rough discipline God is fulfilling this benediction to you.

JULY 12

Sanctified by God the Father.—Jude 1
Sanctified in Christ Jesus.—1 Corinthians 1:2
Through sanctification of the Spirit.—1 Peter 1:2

MARK the union of the Three Divine Persons in all their gracious acts. How unwisely do those believers talk who make preferences in the Persons of the Trinity; who think of Jesus as if he were the embodiment of everything lovely and gracious, while the Father they regard as severely just, but destitute of kindness. Equally wrong are those who magnify the decree of the Father, and the atonement of the Son, so as to depreciate the work of the Spirit. In deeds of grace none of the Persons of the Trinity act apart from the rest. They are as united in their deeds as in their essence. In their love towards the chosen they are one, and in the actions which flow from that great central source they are still undivided. Specially notice this in the matter of sanctification. While we may without mistake speak of sanctification as the work of the Spirit, yet we must take heed that we do not view it as if the Father and the Son had no part therein. It is correct to speak of sanctification as the work of the Father, of the Son, and of the Spirit. Still doth Jehovah say, "Let *us* make man in our own image after our likeness," and thus we are "*his* workmanship, created in Christ Jesus unto good works, which God hath before ordained that we should walk in them." See the value which God sets upon real holiness, since the Three Persons in the Trinity are represented as co-working to produce a Church without "spot, or wrinkle, or any such thing." And you, believer, as the follower of Christ, must also set a high value on holiness—upon purity of life and godliness of conversation. Value the blood of Christ as the foundation of your hope, but never speak disparagingly of the work of the Spirit which is your meetness for the inheritance of the saints in light. This day let us so live as to manifest the work of the Triune God in us.

JULY 13

God said to Jonah, "Doest thou well to be angry?"
—Jonah 4:9

ANGER is not always or necessarily sinful, but it has such a tendency to run wild that whenever it displays itself, we should be quick to question its character, with this enquiry, "Doest thou well to be angry?" It may be that we can answer, "YES." Very frequently anger is the madman's firebrand, but sometimes it is Elijah's fire from heaven. We do well when we are angry with sin, because of the wrong which it commits against our good and gracious God; or with ourselves because we remain so foolish after so much divine instruction; or with others when the sole cause of anger is the evil which they do. He who is not angry at transgression becomes a partaker in it. Sin is a loathsome and hateful thing, and no renewed heart can patiently endure it. God himself is angry with the wicked every day, and it is written in his Word, "Ye that love the Lord, hate evil."

Far more frequently it is to be feared that our anger is not commendable or even justifiable, and then we must answer, "NO." Why should we be fretful with children, passionate with servants, and wrathful with companions? Is such anger honorable to our Christian profession, or glorifying to God? Is it not the old evil heart seeking to gain dominion, and should we not resist it with all the might of our newborn nature? Many professors give way to temper as though it were useless to attempt resistance; but let the believer remember that he must be a conqueror in every point, or else he cannot be crowned. If we cannot control our tempers, what has grace done for us? Some one told Mr. Jay that grace was often grafted on a crab[apple]-stump. "Yes," said he, "but the fruit will not be crabs." We must not make natural infirmity an excuse for sin, but we must fly to the cross and pray the Lord to crucify our tempers, and renew us in gentleness and meekness after his own image.

JULY 14

If thou lift up thy tool upon it, thou hast polluted it.
—Exodus 20:25

OD'S altar was to be built of unhewn stones, that no trace of human skill or labor might be seen upon it. Human wisdom delights to trim and arrange the doctrines of the cross into a system more artificial and more congenial with the depraved tastes of fallen nature; instead, however, of improving the gospel carnal wisdom pollutes it, until it becomes another gospel, and not the truth of God at all. All alterations and amendments of the Lord's own Word are defilements and pollutions. The proud heart of man is very anxious to have a hand in the justification of the soul before God; preparations for Christ are dreamed of, humblings and repentings are trusted in, good works are cried up, natural ability is much vaunted, and by all means the attempt is made to lift up human tools upon the divine altar. It were well if sinners would remember that so far from perfecting the Savior's work, their carnal confidences only pollute and dishonor it. The Lord alone must be exalted in the work of atonement, and not a single mark of man's chisel or hammer will be endured. There is an inherent blasphemy in seeking to add to what Christ Jesus in his dying moments declared to be finished, or to improve that in which the Lord Jehovah finds perfect satisfaction. Trembling sinner, away with thy tools, and fall upon thy knees in humble supplication; and accept the Lord Jesus to be the altar of thine atonement, and rest in him alone.

Many professors may take warning from this morning's text as to the doctrines which they believe. There is among Christians far too much inclination to square and reconcile the truths of revelation; this is a form of irreverence and unbelief, let us strive against it, and receive truth as we find it; rejoicing that the doctrines of the Word are unhewn stones, and so are all the more fit to build an altar for the Lord.

July 15

The fire shall ever be burning upon the altar; it shall never go out.
—Leviticus 6:13

KEEP the altar of *private prayer* burning. This is the very life of all piety. The sanctuary and family altars borrow their fires here, therefore let this burn well. Secret devotion is the very essence, evidence, and barometer, of vital and experimental religion.

Burn here the fat of your sacrifices. Let your closet seasons be, if possible, regular, frequent, and undisturbed. Effectual prayer availeth much. Have you nothing to pray for? Let us suggest the Church, the ministry, your own soul, your children, your relations, your neighbors, your country, and the cause of God and truth throughout the world. Let us examine ourselves on this important matter. Do we engage with lukewarmness in private devotion? Is the fire of devotion burning dimly in our hearts? Do the chariot wheels drag heavily? If so, let us be alarmed at this sign of decay. Let us go with weeping, and ask for the Spirit of grace and of supplications. Let us set apart special seasons for extraordinary prayer. For if this fire should be smothered beneath the ashes of a worldly conformity, it will dim the fire on the family altar, and lessen our influence both in the Church and in the world.

The text will also apply to *the altar of the heart.* This is a golden altar indeed. God loves to see the hearts of his people glowing towards himself. Let us give to God our hearts, all blazing with love, and seek his grace, that the fire may never be quenched; for it will not burn if the Lord does not keep it burning. Many foes will attempt to extinguish it; but if the unseen hand behind the wall pour thereon the sacred oil, it will blaze higher and higher. Let us use texts of Scripture as fuel for our heart's fire, they are live coals; let us attend sermons, but above all, let us be much alone with Jesus.

JULY 16

They gathered manna every morning.
—Exodus 16:21

LABOUR to maintain a sense of thine entire dependence upon the Lord's good will and pleasure for the continuance of thy richest enjoyments. Never try to live on the old manna, nor seek to find help in Egypt. All must come from Jesus, or thou art undone forever. Old anointings will not suffice to impart unction to thy spirit; thine head must have fresh oil poured upon it from the golden horn of the sanctuary, or it will cease from its glory. Today thou mayest be upon the summit of the mount of God, but he who has put thee there must keep thee there, or thou wilt sink far more speedily than thou dreamest. Thy mountain only stands firm when he settles it in its place; if he hide his face, thou wilt soon be troubled. If the Savior should see fit, there is not a window through which thou seest the light of heaven which he could not darken in an instant. Joshua bade the sun stand still, but Jesus can shroud it in total darkness. He can withdraw the joy of thine heart, the light of thine eyes, and the strength of thy life; in his hand thy comforts lie, and at his will they can depart from thee. This hourly dependence our Lord is determined that we shall feel and recognize, for he only permits us to pray for "daily bread," and only promises that "as our days our strength shall be." Is it not best for us that it should be so, that we may often repair to his throne, and constantly be reminded of his love? Oh! how rich the grace which supplies us so continually, and doth not refrain itself because of our ingratitude! The golden shower never ceases, the cloud of blessing tarries evermore above our habitation. O Lord Jesus, we would bow at thy feet, conscious of our utter inability to do anything without thee, and in every favor which we are privileged to receive, we would adore thy blessed name and acknowledge thine unexhausted love.

JULY 17

Knowing, brethren beloved, your election of God.
—1 Thessalonians 1:4

MANY persons want to know their election before they look to Christ, but they cannot learn it thus, it is only to be discovered by "looking unto Jesus." If you desire to ascertain your own election;—after the following manner, shall you assure your heart before God. Do you feel yourself to be a lost, guilty sinner? go straightway to the cross of Christ, and tell Jesus so, and tell him that you have read in the Bible, "him that cometh unto me, I will in no wise cast out." Tell him that he has said, "This is a faithful saying, and worthy of all acceptation, that Christ Jesus came into the world to save sinners." Look to Jesus and believe on him, and you shall make proof of your election directly, for so surely as thou believest, thou art elect. If you will give yourself wholly up to Christ and trust him, then you are one of God's chosen ones; but if you stop and say, "I want to know first whether I am elect," you ask you know not what. Go to Jesus, be you never so guilty, just as you are. Leave all curious inquiry about election alone. Go straight to Christ and hide in his wounds, and you shall know your election. The assurance of the Holy Spirit shall be given to you, so that you shall be able to say, "I know whom I have believed, and I am persuaded that he is able to keep that which I have committed to him." Christ was at the everlasting council: he can tell you whether you were chosen or not; but you cannot find it out in any other way. Go and put your trust in him, and his answer will be—"I have loved thee with an everlasting love, therefore with lovingkindness have I drawn thee." There will be no doubt about his having chosen *you*, when you have chosen *him*.

Sons we are through God's election,
Who in Jesus Christ believe.

JULY 18

They shall go hindmost with their standards.
—Numbers 2:31

HE camp of Dan brought up the rear when the armies of Is-rael were on the march. The Danites occupied *the hindmost place*, but what mattered the position, since they were as truly part of the host as were the foremost tribes; they followed the same fiery cloudy pillar, they ate of the same manna, drank of the same spiritual rock, and journeyed to the same inheritance. Come, my heart, cheer up, though last and least; it is thy privilege to be in the army, and to fare as they fare who lead the van. Some one must be hindmost in honor and esteem, some one must do menial work for Jesus, and why should not I? In a poor village, among an ignorant peasantry; or in a back street, among de-graded sinners, I will work on, and "go hindmost with my standard."

The Danites occupied *a very useful place*. Stragglers have to be picked up upon the march, and lost property has to be gathered from the field. Fiery spirits may dash forward over untrodden paths to learn fresh truth, and win more souls to Jesus; but some of a more conservative spirit may be well en-gaged in reminding the church of her ancient faith, and restoring her fainting sons. Every position has its duties, and the slowly moving children of God will find their peculiar state one in which they may be eminently a blessing to the whole host.

The rear guard is *a place of danger*. There are foes behind us as well as be-fore us. Attacks may come from any quarter. We read that Amalek fell upon Israel, and slew some of the hindmost of them. The experienced Christian will find much work for his weapons in aiding those poor doubting, despond-ing, wavering, souls, who are hindmost in faith, knowledge, and joy. These must not be left unaided, and therefore be it the business of well-taught saints to bear their standards among the hindmost. My soul, do thou tenderly watch to help the hindmost this day.

JULY 19

The Lord our God hath shewed us his glory.
—Deuteronomy 5:24

GOD'S great design in all his works is the manifestation of his own glory. Any aim less than this were unworthy of himself. But how shall the glory of God be manifested to such fallen creatures as we are? Man's eye is not single, he has ever a side glance towards his own honor, has too high an estimate of his own powers, and so is not qualified to behold the glory of the Lord. It is clear, then, that self must stand out of the way, that there may be room for God to be exalted; and this is the reason why he bringeth his people ofttimes into straits and difficulties, that, being made conscious of their own folly and weakness, they may be fitted to behold the majesty of God when he comes forth to work their deliverance. He whose life is one even and smooth path, will see but little of the glory of the Lord, for he has few occasions of self-emptying, and hence, but little fitness for being filled with the revelation of God. They who navigate little streams and shallow creeks, know but little of the God of tempests; but they who "do business in great waters," these see his "wonders in the deep." Among the huge Atlantic-waves of bereavement, poverty, temptation, and reproach, we learn the power of Jehovah, because we feel the littleness of man. Thank God, then, if you have been led by a rough road: it is this which has given you your experience of God's greatness and lovingkindness. Your troubles have enriched you with a wealth of knowledge to be gained by no other means: your trials have been the cleft of the rock in which Jehovah has set you, as he did his servant Moses, that you might behold his glory as it passed by. Praise God that you have not been left to the darkness and ignorance which continued prosperity might have involved, but that in the great fight of affliction, you have been capacitated for the outshinings of his glory in his wonderful dealings with you.

CHARLES HADDON SPURGEON

JULY 20

The earnest of our inheritance.
—Ephesians 1:14

H! what enlightenment, what joys, what consolation, what delight of heart is experienced by that man who has learned to feed on Jesus, and on Jesus alone. Yet the realization which we have of Christ's preciousness is, in this life, imperfect at the best. As an old writer says, " 'Tis but a taste!" We have tasted "that the Lord is gracious," but we do not yet know *how* good and gracious he is, although what we know of his sweetness makes us long for more. We have enjoyed the first fruits of the Spirit, and they have set us hungering and thirsting for the fullness of the heavenly vintage. We groan within ourselves, waiting for the adoption. Here we are like Israel in the wilderness, who had but one cluster from Eshcol, *there* we shall be in the vineyard. Here we see the manna falling small, like coriander seed, but there shall we eat the bread of heaven and the old corn of the kingdom. We are but beginners now in spiritual education; for although we have learned the first letters of the alphabet, we cannot read words yet, much less can we put sentences together; but as one says, "He that has been in heaven but five minutes, knows more than the general assembly of divines on earth." We have many ungratified desires at present, but soon every wish shall be satisfied; and all our powers shall find the sweetest employment in that eternal world of joy. O Christian, antedate heaven for a few years. Within a very little time thou shalt be rid of all thy trials and thy troubles. Thine eyes now suffused with tears shall weep no longer. Thou shalt gaze in ineffable rapture upon the splendor of him who sits upon the throne. Nay, more, upon his throne shalt thou sit. The triumph of his glory shall be shared by thee; his crown, his joy, his paradise, these shall be thine, and thou shalt be co-heir with him who is the heir of all things.

202

JULY 21

The daughter of Jerusalem hath shaken her head at thee.
—Isaiah 37:22

EASSURED by the Word of the Lord, the poor trembling citizens of Zion grew bold, and shook their heads at Sennacherib's boastful threats. Strong faith enables the servants of God to look with calm contempt upon their most haughty foes. *We know that our enemies are attempting impossibilities.* They seek to destroy the eternal life, which cannot die while Jesus lives; to overthrow the citadel, against which the gates of hell shall not prevail. They kick against the pricks to their own wounding, and rush upon the bosses of Jehovah's buckler to their own hurt.

We know their weakness. What are they but men? And what is man but a worm? They roar and swell like waves of the sea, foaming out their own shame. When the Lord ariseth, they shall fly as chaff before the wind, and be consumed as crackling thorns. Their utter powerlessness to do damage to the cause of God and his truth, may make the weakest soldiers in Zion's ranks laugh them to scorn.

Above all, *we know that the Most High is with us*, and when he dresses himself in arms, where are his enemies? If he cometh forth from his place, the potsherds of the earth will not long contend with their Maker. His rod of iron shall dash them in pieces like a potter's vessel, and their very remembrance shall perish from the earth. Away, then, all fears, the kingdom is safe in the King's hands. Let us shout for joy, for the Lord reigneth, and his foes shall be as straw for the dunghill.

> As true as God's own word is true;
> Nor earth, nor hell, with all their crew,
> Against us shall prevail.
> A jest, and by-word, are they grown;
> God *is* with us, we *are* his own,
> Our victory cannot fail.

JULY 22

I am married unto you.
—Jeremiah 3:14

HRIST Jesus is joined unto his people in marriage-union. In love he espoused his Church as a chaste virgin, long before she fell under the yoke of bondage. Full of burning affection he toiled, like Jacob for Rachel, until the whole of her purchase-money had been paid, and now, having sought her by his Spirit, and brought her to know and love him, he awaits the glorious hour when their mutual bliss shall be consummated at the marriage-supper of the Lamb. Not yet hath the glorious Bridegroom presented his betrothed, perfected and complete, before the Majesty of heaven; not yet hath she actually entered upon the enjoyment of her dignities as his wife and queen: she is as yet a wanderer in a world of woe, a dweller in the tents of Kedar; but she is even now the bride, the spouse of Jesus, dear to his heart, precious in his sight, written on his hands, and united with his person. On earth he exercises towards her all the affectionate offices of Husband. He makes rich provision for her wants, pays all her debts, allows her to assume his name, and to share in all his wealth. Nor will he ever act otherwise to her. The word divorce he will never mention, for "He hateth putting away." Death must sever the conjugal tie between the most loving mortals, but it cannot divide the links of this immortal marriage. In heaven they marry not, but are as the angels of God; yet there is this one marvelous exception to the rule, for in Heaven Christ and his Church shall celebrate their joyous nuptials. This affinity as it is more lasting, so is it more near than earthly wedlock. Let the love of husband be never so pure and fervent, it is but a faint picture of the flame which burns in the heart of Jesus. Passing all human union is that mystical cleaving unto the Church, for which Christ left his Father, and became one flesh with her.

JULY 23

Even thou wast as one of them.
—Obadiah 1:11

BROTHERLY kindness was due from Edom to Israel in the time of need, but instead thereof, the men of Esau made common cause with Israel's foes. Special stress in the sentence before us is laid upon the word *thou;* as when Caesar cried to Brutus, "and *thou* Brutus;" a bad action may be all the worse, because of the person who has committed it. When *we* sin, who are the chosen favorites of heaven, we sin with an emphasis; ours is a crying offence, because we are so peculiarly indulged. If an angel should lay his hand upon us when we are doing evil, he need not use any other rebuke than the question, "What *thou?* What dost *thou* here?" Much forgiven, much delivered, much instructed, much enriched, much blessed, shall we dare to put forth our hand unto evil? God forbid!

A few minutes of confession may be beneficial to thee, gentle reader, this morning. Hast thou never been as the wicked? At an evening party certain men laughed at uncleanness, and the joke was not altogether offensive to thine ear, *even thou wast as one of them.* When hard things were spoken concerning the ways of God, thou wast bashfully silent; and so, to on-lookers, *thou wast as one of them.* When worldlings were bartering in the market, and driving hard bargains, wast thou not as one of them? When they were pursuing vanity with a hunter's foot, wert thou not as greedy for gain as they were? Could any difference be discerned between thee and them? *Is there any difference? Here* we come to close quarters. Be honest with thine own soul, and make sure that thou art a new creature in Christ Jesus; but when this is sure, walk jealously, lest any should again be able to say, "Even thou wast as one of them." Thou wouldst not desire to share their eternal doom, why then be like them here? Come not thou into their secret, lest thou come into their ruin. Side with the afflicted people of God, and not with the world.

JULY 24

Stand still, and see the salvation of the Lord.
—Exodus 14:13

HESE words contain God's command to the believer when he is reduced to great straits and brought into extraordinary difficulties. He cannot retreat; he cannot go forward; he is shut up on the right hand and on the left; what is he now to do? The Master's word to him is, "Stand still." It will be well for him if at such times he listens only to his Master's word, for other and evil advisers come with their suggestions. *Despair* whispers, "Lie down and die; give it all up." But God would have us put on a cheerful courage, and even in our worst times, rejoice in his love and faithfulness. *Cowardice* says,

> Retreat; go back to the worldling's way of action; you cannot play the Christian's part, it is too difficult. Relinquish your principles.

But, however much Satan may urge this course upon you, you cannot follow it if you are a child of God. His divine fiat has bid thee go from strength to strength, and so thou shalt, and neither death nor hell shall turn thee from thy course. What, if for a while thou art called to stand still, yet this is but to renew thy strength for some greater advance in due time. *Precipitancy* cries, "do something. Stir yourself; to stand still and wait, is sheer idleness." We *must* be doing something at once—*we* must do it so we think—instead of looking to the Lord, who will not only do something but will do everything. *Presumption* boasts, "If the sea be before you, march into it and expect a miracle." But Faith listens neither to Presumption, nor to Despair, nor to Cowardice, nor to Precipitancy, but it hears God say, "Stand still," and immovable as a rock it stands. "*Stand* still;"—keep the posture of an upright man, ready for action, expecting further orders, cheerfully and patiently awaiting the directing voice; and it will not be long ere God shall say to you, as distinctly as Moses said it to the people of Israel, "Go forward."

JULY 25

He left his garment in her hand, and fled, and got him out.
—*Genesis 39:12*

N contending with certain sins there remains no mode of victory but by flight. The ancient naturalists wrote much of basilisks, whose eyes fascinated their victims and rendered them easy victims; so the mere gaze of wickedness puts us in solemn danger. He who would be safe from acts of evil must haste away from occasions of it. A covenant must be made with our eyes not even to look upon the cause of temptation, for such sins only need a spark to begin with and a blaze follows in an instant. Who would wantonly enter the leper's prison and sleep amid its horrible corruption? He only who desires to be leprous himself would thus court contagion. If the mariner knew how to avoid a storm, he would do anything rather than run the risk of weathering it. Cautious pilots have no desire to try how near the quicksand they can sail, or how often they may touch a rock without springing a leak; their aim is to keep as nearly as possible in the midst of a safe channel.

This day I may be exposed to great peril—let me have the serpent's wisdom to keep out of it and avoid it. The wings of a dove may be of more use to me today than the jaws of a lion. It is true I may be an apparent loser by declining evil company, but I had better leave my cloak than lose my character; it is not needful that I should be rich, but it is imperative upon me to be pure. No ties of friendship, no chains of beauty, no flashings of talent, no shafts of ridicule must turn me from the wise resolve to flee from sin. The devil I am to resist and he will flee from me, but the lusts of the flesh, I must flee, or they will surely overcome me. O God of holiness preserve thy Josephs, that Madam Bubble bewitch them not with her vile suggestions. May the horrible trinity of the world, the flesh, and the devil, never overcome us!

JULY 26

Giving all diligence, add to your faith virtue;
and to virtue, knowledge, etc.
—2 Peter 1:5–6

F thou wouldest enjoy the eminent grace of the full assurance of faith, under the blessed Spirit's influence, and assistance, do what the Scripture tells thee, *"Give diligence."* Take care that thy *faith* is of the right kind—that it is not a mere belief of doctrine, but a simple faith, depending on Christ, and on Christ alone. Give diligent heed to thy *courage.* Plead with God that he would give thee the face of a lion, that thou mayest, with a consciousness of right, go on boldly. Study well the Scriptures, and get *knowledge;* for a knowledge of doctrine will tend very much to confirm faith. Try to understand God's Word; let it dwell in thy heart richly.

When thou hast done this, "Add to thy knowledge *temperance.*" Take heed to thy body: be temperate without. Take heed to thy soul: be temperate within. Get temperance of lip, life, heart, and thought. Add to this, by God's Holy Spirit, *patience;* ask him to give thee that patience which endureth affliction, which, when it is tried, shall come forth as gold. Array yourself with patience, that you may not murmur nor be depressed in your afflictions. When that grace is won look to *godliness.* Godliness is something more than religion. Make God's glory your object in life; live in his sight; dwell close to him; seek for fellowship with him; and thou hast "godliness;" and to that add *brotherly love.* Have a love to all the saints: and add to that a *charity,* which openeth its arms to all men, and loves their souls. When you are adorned with these jewels, and just in proportion as you practice these heavenly virtues, will you come to know by clearest evidence "your calling and election." "Give diligence," if you would get assurance, for lukewarmness and doubting very naturally go hand in hand.

July 27

Exceeding great and precious promises.
—2 Peter 1:4

F you would know experimentally the preciousness of the promises, and enjoy them in your own heart, *meditate much upon them.* There are promises which are like grapes in the wine-press; if you will tread them the juice will flow. Thinking over the hallowed words will often be the prelude to their fulfillment. While you are musing upon them, the boon which you are seeking will insensibly come to you. Many a Christian who has thirsted for the promise has found the favor which it ensured gently distilling into his soul even while he has been considering the divine record; and he has rejoiced that ever he was led to lay the promise near his heart.

But besides *meditating* upon the promises, *seek in thy soul to receive them as being the very words of God.* Speak to thy soul thus,

> If I were dealing with a man's promise, I should carefully consider the ability and the character of the man who had covenanted with me. So with the promise of God; my eye must not be so much fixed upon the greatness of the mercy—that may stagger me; as upon the greatness of the promiser—that will cheer me. My soul, it is God, even thy God, God that cannot lie, who speaks to thee. This word of his which thou art now considering is as true as his own existence. He is a God unchangeable. He has not altered the thing which has gone out of his mouth, nor called back one single consolatory sentence. Nor doth he lack any power; it is the God that made the heavens and the earth who has spoken thus. Nor can he fail in wisdom as to the time when he will bestow the favors for he knoweth when it is best to give and when better to withhold. Therefore, seeing that it is the word of a God so true, so immutable, so powerful, so wise, I will and must believe the promise.

If we thus meditate upon the promises, and consider the Promiser, we shall experience their sweetness, and obtain their fulfillment.

July 28

So foolish was I, and ignorant; I was as a beast before thee.
—Psalm 73:22

REMEMBER this is the confession of the man after God's own heart; and in telling us his inner life, he writes, "So foolish was I, and ignorant." The word *"foolish,"* here, means more than it signifies in ordinary language. David, in a former verse of the Psalm, writes, "I was envious at *the foolish* when I saw the prosperity of the wicked," which shows that the folly he intended had *sin* in it. He puts himself down as being thus "foolish," and adds a word which is to give intensity to it; "so foolish was I." *How foolish* he could not tell. It was a sinful folly, a folly which was not to be excused by frailty, but to be condemned because of its perverseness and willful ignorance, for he had been envious of the present prosperity of the ungodly, forgetful of the dreadful end awaiting all such. And are we better than David that *we* should call ourselves wise! Do we profess that we have attained perfection, or to have been so chastened that the rod has taken all our willfulness out of us? Ah, this were pride indeed! If *David* was foolish, how foolish should *we* be in our own esteem if we could but see ourselves! Look back, believer: think of your doubting God when he has been so faithful to you—think of your foolish outcry of "Not so, my Father," when he crossed his hands in affliction to give you the larger blessing; think of the many times when you have read his providences in the dark, misinterpreted his dispensations, and groaned out, "All these things are against me," when they are all working together for your good! Think how often you have chosen sin because of its pleasure, when indeed, that pleasure was a root of bitterness to you! Surely if we know our own heart we must plead guilty to the indictment of a sinful folly; and conscious of this "foolishness," we must make David's consequent resolve our own—*"Thou shalt guide me with thy counsel."*

JULY 29

Nevertheless I am continually with thee.
—*Psalm 73:23*

"NEVERTHELESS,"—As if, notwithstanding all the foolishness and ignorance which David had just been confessing to God, not one atom the less was it true and certain that David was saved and accepted, and that the blessing of being constantly in God's presence was undoubtedly his. Fully conscious of his own lost estate, and of the deceitfulness and vileness of his nature, yet, by a glorious outburst of faith, he sings "nevertheless I am continually with thee." Believer, you are forced to enter into Asaph's confession and acknowledgment, endeavor in like spirit to say "nevertheless, since I belong to Christ I am continually with God!" By this is meant continually upon his mind, he is always thinking of me for my good. Continually before his eye;—the eye of the Lord never sleepeth, but is perpetually watching over my welfare. Continually in his hand, so that none shall be able to pluck me thence. Continually on his heart, worn there as a memorial, even as the high priest bore the names of the twelve tribes upon his heart forever. Thou always thinkest of me, O God. The bowels of thy love continually yearn towards me. Thou art always making providence work for my good. Thou hast set me as a signet upon thine arm; thy love is strong as death, many waters cannot quench it; neither can the floods drown it. Surprising grace! Thou seest me in Christ, and though in myself abhorred, thou beholdest me as wearing Christ's garments, and washed in his blood, and thus I stand accepted in thy presence. I am thus continually in thy favor—"continually with thee." Here is comfort for the tried and afflicted soul; vexed with the tempest within—look at the calm without. "Nevertheless"—O say it in thy heart, and take the peace it gives. "Nevertheless I am continually with thee."

JULY 30

And when he thought thereon, he wept.
—Mark 14:72

T has been thought by some that as long as Peter lived, the fountain of his tears began to flow whenever he remembered his denying his Lord. It is not unlikely that it was so, for his sin was very great, and grace in him had afterwards a perfect work. This same experience is common to all the redeemed family according to the degree in which the Spirit of God has removed the natural heart of stone. We, like Peter, remember *our boastful promise:* "Though all men shall forsake thee, yet will not I." We eat our own words with the bitter herbs of repentance. When we think of what we vowed we would be, and of what we have been, we may weep whole showers of grief. He thought on *his denying his Lord.* The place in which he did it, the little cause which led him into such heinous sin, the oaths and blasphemies with which he sought to confirm his falsehood, and the dreadful hardness of heart which drove him to do so again and yet again. Can we, when we are reminded of our sins, and their exceeding sinfulness, remain stolid and stubborn? Will we not make our house a Bochim, and cry unto the Lord for renewed assurances of pardoning love? May we never take a dry-eyed look at sin, lest ere long we have a tongue parched in the flames of hell. Peter also thought upon *his Master's look of love.* The Lord followed up the cock's warning voice with an admonitory look of sorrow, pity, and love. That glance was never out of Peter's mind so long as he lived. It was far more effectual than ten thousand sermons would have been without the Spirit. The penitent apostle would be sure to weep when he recollected the *Savior's full forgiveness,* which restored him to his former place. To think that we have offended so kind and good a Lord is more than sufficient reason for being constant weepers. Lord, smite our rocky hearts, and make the waters flow.

July 31

I in them.
—John 17:23

IF such be the union which subsists between our souls and the person of our Lord, how deep and broad is the channel of our communion! This is no narrow pipe through which a thread-like stream may wind its way, it is a channel of amazing depth and breadth, along whose glorious length a ponderous volume of living water may roll its floods. Behold he hath set before us an open door, let us not be slow to enter. This city of communion hath many pearly gates, every several gate is of one pearl, and each gate is thrown open to the uttermost that we may enter, assured of welcome. If there were but one small loophole through which to talk with Jesus, it would be a high privilege to thrust a word of fellowship through the narrow door; how much we are blessed in having so large an entrance! Had the Lord Jesus been far away from us, with many a stormy sea between, we should have longed to send a messenger to him to carry him our loves, and bring us tidings from his Father's house; but see his kindness, he has built his house next door to ours, nay, more, he takes lodging with us, and tabernacles in poor humble hearts, that so he may have perpetual intercourse with us. O how foolish must we be, if we do not live in habitual communion with him. When the road is long, and dangerous, and difficult, we need not wonder that friends seldom meet each other, but when they live together, shall Jonathan forget his David? A wife may when her husband is upon a journey, abide many days without holding converse with him, but she could never endure to be separated from him if she knew him to be in one of the chambers of her own house. Why, believer, dost not thou sit at his banquet of wine? Seek thy Lord, for he is near; embrace him, for he is thy Brother. Hold him fast, for he is thine Husband; and press him to thine heart, for he is of thine own flesh.

AUGUST 1

Let me now go to the field, and glean ears of corn.
—Ruth 2:2

OWNCAST and troubled Christian, come and glean today in the broad field of promise. Here are abundance of precious promises, which exactly meet thy wants. Take this one: "He will not break the bruised reed, nor quench the smoking flax." Doth not that suit thy case? A reed, helpless, insignificant, and weak, a bruised reed, out of which no music can come; weaker than weakness itself; a reed, and that reed bruised, yet, he will not break thee; but on the contrary, will restore and strengthen thee. Thou art like the smoking flax: no light, no warmth, can come from thee; but he will not quench thee; he will blow with his sweet breath of mercy till he fans thee to a flame. Wouldst thou glean another ear? "Come unto me all ye that labor and are heavy laden, and I will give you rest." What soft words! Thy heart is tender, and the Master knows it, and therefore he speaketh so gently to thee. Wilt thou not obey him, and come to him even now? Take another ear of corn: "Fear not, thou worm Jacob, I will help thee, saith the Lord and thy Redeemer, the Holy One of Israel." How canst thou fear with such a wonderful assurance as this? Thou mayest gather ten thousand such golden ears as these! "I have blotted out thy sins like a cloud, and like a thick cloud thy transgressions." Or this, "Though your sins be as scarlet, they shall be as white as snow; though they be red like crimson, they shall be as wool." Or this, "The Spirit and the Bride say, Come, and let him that is athirst come, and whosoever will let him take the water of life freely." Our Master's field is very rich; behold the handfuls. See, there they lie before thee, poor timid believer! Gather them up, make them thine own, for Jesus bids thee take them. Be not afraid, only believe! Grasp these sweet promises, thresh them out by meditation and feed on them with joy.

August 2

Who worketh all things after the counsel of his own will.
—Ephesians 1:11

UR belief in God's wisdom supposes and necessitates that he has a settled purpose and plan in the work of salvation. What would *creation* have been without his design? Is there a fish in the sea, or a fowl in the air, which was left to chance for its formation? Nay, in every bone, joint, and muscle, sinew, gland, and blood-vessel, you mark the presence of a God working everything according to the design of infinite wisdom. And shall God be present in creation, ruling over all, and not in *grace?* Shall the new creation have the fickle genius of free will to preside over it when divine counsel rules the old creation? Look at *Providence!* Who knoweth not that not a sparrow falleth to the ground without your Father? Even the hairs of your head are all numbered. God weighs the mountains of our grief in scales, and the hills of our tribulation in balances. And shall there be a God in providence and not in grace? Shall the shell be ordained by wisdom and the kernel be left to blind chance? No; he knows the end from the beginning. He sees in its appointed place, not merely the corner-stone which he has laid in fair colors, in the blood of his dear Son, but he beholds in their ordained position each of the chosen stones taken out of the quarry of nature, and polished by his grace; he sees the whole from corner to cornice, from base to roof, from foundation to pinnacle. He hath in his mind a clear knowledge of every stone which shall be laid in its prepared space, and how vast the edifice shall be, and when the top-stone shall be brought forth with shoutings of "Grace! Grace! unto it." At the last it shall be clearly seen that in every chosen vessel of mercy, Jehovah did as he willed with his own; and that in every part of the work of grace he accomplished his purpose, and glorified his own name.

AUGUST 3

The Lamb is the light thereof.
—Revelation 21:23

QUIETLY contemplate the Lamb as the light of heaven. Light in Scripture is the emblem of *joy*. The joy of the saints in heaven is comprised in this: *Jesus* chose us, loved us, bought us, cleansed us, robed us, kept us, glorified us: we are here entirely through the Lord Jesus. Each one of these thoughts shall be to them like a cluster of the grapes of Eshcol. Light is also the cause of *beauty*. Naught of beauty is left when light is gone. Without light no radiance flashes from the sapphire, no peaceful ray proceedeth from the pearl; and thus all the beauty of the saints above comes from Jesus. As planets, they reflect the light of the Sun of Righteousness; they live as beams proceeding from the central orb. If he withdrew, they must die; if his glory were veiled, their glory must expire. Light is also the emblem of *knowledge*. In heaven our knowledge will be perfect, but the Lord Jesus himself will be the fountain of it. Dark providences, never understood before, will then be clearly seen, and all that puzzles us now will become plain to us in the light of the Lamb. Oh! what unfoldings there will be and what glorifying of the God of love! Light also means *manifestation*. Light manifests. In this world it doth not yet appear what we shall be. God's people are a hidden people, but when Christ receives his people into heaven, he will touch them with the wand of his own love, and change them into the image of his manifested glory. They were poor and wretched, but what a transformation! They were stained with sin, but one touch of his finger, and they are bright as the sun, and clear as crystal. Oh! what a manifestation! All this proceeds from the exalted Lamb. Whatever there may be of effulgent splendor, Jesus shall be the center and soul of it all. Oh! to be present and to see him in his own light, the King of kings, and Lord of lords!

August 4

The people that do know their God shall be strong.
—Daniel 11:32

EVERY believer understands that to know God is the highest and best form of knowledge; and this spiritual knowledge is a source of strength to the Christian. It strengthens his *faith.* Believers are constantly spoken of in the Scriptures as being persons who are enlightened and taught of the Lord; they are said to "have an unction from the Holy One," and it is the Spirit's peculiar office to lead them into all truth, and all this for the increase and the fostering of their faith. Knowledge strengthens *love,* as well as faith. Knowledge opens the door, and then through that door we see our Savior. Or, to use another similitude, knowledge paints the portrait of Jesus, and when we see that portrait then we love him, we cannot love a Christ whom we do not know, at least, in some degree. If we know but little of the excellences of Jesus, what he has done for us, and what he is doing now, we cannot love him much; but the more we know him, the more we shall love him. Knowledge also strengthens *hope.* How can we hope for a thing if we do not know of its existence? Hope may be the telescope, but till we receive instruction, our ignorance stands in the front of the glass, and we can see nothing whatever; knowledge removes the interposing object, and when we look through the bright optic glass we discern the glory to be revealed, and anticipate it with joyous confidence. Knowledge supplies us reasons for *patience.* How shall we have patience unless we know something of the sympathy of Christ, and understand the good which is to come out of the correction which our heavenly Father sends us? Nor is there one single grace of the Christian which, under God, will not be fostered and brought to perfection by holy knowledge. How important, then, is it that we should grow not only in grace, but in the "knowledge" of our Lord and Savior Jesus Christ.

AUGUST 5

We know that all things work together for good to them that love God.
—Romans 8:28

PON some points a believer is absolutely sure. He knows, for instance, that God sits in the stern-sheets of the vessel when it rocks most. He believes that an invisible hand is always on the world's tiller, and that wherever providence may drift, Jehovah steers it. That re-assuring knowledge prepares him for everything. He looks over the raging waters and sees the spirit of Jesus treading the billows, and he hears a voice saying, "It is I, be not afraid." He knows too that God is always wise, and, knowing this, he is confident that there can be no accidents, no mistakes; that nothing can occur which ought not to arise. He can say,

> If I should lose all I have, it is better that I should lose than have, if God so wills: the worst calamity is the wisest and the kindest thing that could befall to me if God ordains it.

"We know that all things work together for good to them that love God." The Christian does not merely hold this as a theory, but *he knows it* as a matter of fact. Everything *has* worked for good as yet; the poisonous drugs mixed in fit proportions have worked the cure; the sharp cuts of the lancet have cleansed out the proud flesh and facilitated the healing. Every event as yet has worked out the most divinely blessed results; and so, believing that God rules all, that he governs wisely, that he brings good out of evil, the believer's heart is assured, and he is enabled calmly to meet each trial as it comes. The believer can in the spirit of true resignation pray, "Send me what thou wilt, my God, so long as it comes from thee; never came there an ill portion from thy table to any of thy children."

> Say not my soul, "From whence can God relieve my care?"
> Remember that Omnipotence has servants everywhere.
> His method is sublime, his heart profoundly kind,
> God never is before his time, and never is behind.

218

AUGUST 6

Watchman, what of the night?—Isaiah 21:11

HAT enemies are abroad? Errors are a numerous horde, and new ones appear every hour: against what heresy am I to be on my guard? Sins creep from their lurking places when the darkness reigns; I must myself mount the watch-tower, and watch unto prayer. Our heavenly Protector foresees all the attacks which are about to be made upon us, and when as yet the evil designed us is but in the desire of Satan, he prays for us that our faith fail not, when we are sifted as wheat. Continue O gracious Watchman, to forewarn us of our foes, and for Zion's sake hold not thy peace.

"Watchman, what of the night?" *What weather is coming* for the Church? Are the clouds lowering, or is it all clear and fair overhead? We must care for the Church of God with anxious love; and now that Popery and infidelity are both threatening, let us observe the signs of the times and prepare for conflict.

"Watchman, what of the night?" *What stars are visible?* What precious promises suit our present case? You sound the alarm, give us the consolation also. Christ, the polestar, is ever fixed in his place, and all the stars are secure in the right hand of their Lord.

But watchman, *when comes the morning?* The Bridegroom tarries. Are there no signs of his coming forth as the Sun of Righteousness? Has not the morning star arisen as the pledge of day? When will the day dawn, and the shadows flee away? O Jesus, if thou come not in person to thy waiting Church this day, yet come in Spirit to my sighing heart, and make it sing for joy.

> Now all the earth is bright and glad
> With the fresh morn;
> But all my heart is cold, and dark and sad:
> Sun of the soul, let me behold thy dawn!
> Come, Jesus, Lord,
> O quickly come, according to thy word.

AUGUST 7

The upright love thee.
—Song of Solomon 1:4

BELIEVERS love Jesus with a deeper affection than they dare to give to any other being. They would sooner lose father and mother than part with Christ. They hold all earthly comforts with a loose hand, but they carry him fast locked in their bosoms. They voluntarily deny themselves for his sake, but they are not to be driven to deny *him*. It is scant love which the fire of persecution can dry up; the true believer's love is a deeper stream than this. Men have labored to divide the faithful from their Master, but their attempts have been fruitless in every age. Neither crowns of honor, now frowns of anger, have untied this more than Gordian knot. This is no every-day attachment which the world's power may at length dissolve. Neither man nor devil have found a key which opens this lock. Never has the craft of Satan been more at fault than when he has exercised it in seeking to rend in sunder this union of two divinely welded hearts. It is written, and nothing can blot out the sentence, *"The upright love thee."* The intensity of the love of the upright, however, is not so much to be judged by what it appears as by what the upright long for. It is our daily lament that we cannot love enough. Would that our hearts were capable of holding more, and reaching further. Like Samuel Rutherford, we sigh and cry,

> Oh, for as much love as would go round about the earth, and over heaven—yea, the heaven of heavens, and ten thousand worlds—that I might let all out upon fair, fair, only fair Christ.

Alas! our longest reach is but a span of love, and our affection is but as a drop of a bucket compared with his deserts. Measure our love by our intentions, and it is high indeed; 'tis thus, we trust, our Lord doth judge of it. Oh, that we could give all the love in all hearts in one great mass, a gathering together of all loves to him who is altogether lovely!

AUGUST 8

They weave the spider's web.
—Isaiah 59:5

EE the spider's web, and behold in it a most suggestive picture of the hypocrite's religion. *It is meant to catch his prey:* the spider fattens himself on flies, and the Pharisee has his reward. Foolish persons are easily entrapped by the loud professions of pretenders, and even the more judicious cannot always escape. Philip baptized Simon Magus, whose guileful declaration of faith was so soon exploded by the stern rebuke of Peter. Custom, reputation, praise, advancement, and other flies, are the small game which hypocrites take in their nets. A spider's web is *a marvel of skill:* look at it and admire the cunning hunter's wiles. Is not a deceiver's religion equally wonderful? How does he make so barefaced a lie appear to be a truth? How can he make his tinsel answer so well the purpose of gold? A spider's web *comes all from the creature's own bowels.* The bee gathers her wax from flowers, the spider sucks no flowers, and yet she spins out her material to any length. Even so hypocrites find their trust and hope within themselves; their anchor was forged on their own anvil, and their cable twisted by their own hands. They lay their own foundation, and hew out the pillars of their own house, disdaining to be debtors to the sovereign grace of God. But a spider's web is *very frail.* It is curiously wrought, but not enduringly manufactured. It is no match for the servant's broom, or the traveler's staff. The hypocrite needs no battery of Armstrongs to blow his hope to pieces, a mere puff of wind will do it. Hypocritical cobwebs will soon come down when the besom of destruction begins its purifying work. Which reminds us of one more thought, viz., that such cobwebs *are not to be endured in the Lord's house:* he will see to it that they and those who spin them shall be destroyed forever. O my soul, be thou resting on something better than a spider's web. Be the Lord Jesus thine eternal hiding-place.

❦

August 9

The city hath no need of the sun, neither of the moon, to shine in it.
—Revelation 21:23

ONDER in the better world, the inhabitants are independent of all creature comforts. They have no need of raiment; their white robes never wear out, neither shall they ever be defiled. They need no medicine to heal diseases, "for the inhabitant shall not say, I am sick." They need no sleep to recruit their frames—they rest not day nor night, but unweariedly praise him in his temple. They need no social relationship to minister comfort, and whatever happiness they may derive from association with their fellows is not essential to their bliss, for their Lord's society is enough for their largest desires. They need no teachers there; they doubtless commune with one another concerning the things of God, but they do not require this by way of instruction; they shall all be taught of the Lord. Ours are the alms at the king's gate, but they feast at the table itself. Here we lean upon the friendly arm, but there they lean upon their Beloved and upon him alone. Here we must have the help of our companions, but there they find all they want in Christ Jesus. Here we look to the meat which perisheth, and to the raiment which decays before the moth, but there they find everything in God. We use the bucket to fetch us water from the well, but there they drink from the fountain head, and put their lips down to the living water. Here the angels bring us blessings, but we shall want no messengers from heaven then. They shall need no Gabriels there to bring their love-notes from God, for there they shall see *him* face to face. Oh! what a blessed time shall that be when we shall have mounted above every second cause and shall rest upon the bare arm of God! What a glorious hour when God, and not his creatures; the Lord, and not his works, shall be our daily joy! Our souls shall then have attained the perfection of bliss.

AUGUST 10

Christ, who is our life.
—Colossians 3:4

PAUL'S marvelously rich expression indicates, that Christ is the *source* of our life. "You hath he quickened who were dead in trespasses and sins." That same voice which brought Lazarus out of the tomb raised us to newness of life. He is now the *substance* of our spiritual life. It is by his life that we live; he is in us, the hope of glory, the spring of our actions, the central thought which moves every other thought. *Christ is the sustenance of our life.* What can the Christian feed upon but Jesus' flesh and blood? "This is the bread which cometh down from heaven, that a man may eat thereof, and not die." O wayworn pilgrims in this wilderness of sin, you never get a morsel to satisfy the hunger of your spirits, except ye find it in him! *Christ is the solace of our life.* All our true joys come from him; and in times of trouble, his presence is our consolation. There is nothing worth living for but him; and his lovingkindness is better than life! *Christ is the object of our life.* As speeds the ship towards the port, so hastens the believer towards the haven of his Savior's bosom. As flies the arrow to its goal, so flies the Christian towards the perfecting of his fellowship with Christ Jesus. As the soldier fights for his captain, and is crowned in his captain's victory, so the believer contends for Christ, and gets his triumph out of the triumphs of his Master. "For him to live is Christ." *Christ is the exemplar of our life.* Where there is the same life within, there will, there must be, to a great extent, the same developments without; and if we live in near fellowship with the Lord Jesus we shall grow like him. We shall set him before us as our Divine copy, and we shall seek to tread in his footsteps, until he shall become *the crown of our life in glory.* Oh! how safe, how honored, how happy is the Christian, since Christ is our life!

AUGUST 11

Oh that I were as in months past.
—Job 29:2

UMBERS of Christians can view the past with pleasure, but regard the present with dissatisfaction; they look back upon the days which they have passed in communing with the Lord as being the sweetest and the best they have ever known, but as to the present, it is clad in a sable garb of gloom and dreariness. Once they lived near to Jesus, but now they feel that they have wandered from him, and they say, "O that I were as in months past!" They complain that they have lost their evidences, or that they have not present peace of mind, or that they have no enjoyment in the means of grace, or that conscience is not so tender, or that they have not so much zeal for God's glory. The causes of this mournful state of things are manifold. It may arise through a comparative *neglect of prayer,* for a neglected closet is the beginning of all spiritual decline. Or it may be the result of *idolatry.* The heart has been occupied with something else, more than with God; the affections have been set on the things of earth, instead of the things of heaven. A jealous God will not be content with a divided heart; he must be loved first and best. He will withdraw the sunshine of his presence from a cold, wandering heart. Or the cause may be found in *self-confidence* and *self-righteousness.* Pride is busy in the heart, and self is exalted instead of lying low at the foot of the cross. Christian, if you are not now as you "were in months past," do not rest satisfied with *wishing* for a return of former happiness, but go at once to seek your Master, and tell him your sad state. Ask his grace and strength to help you to walk more closely with him; humble yourself before him, and he will lift you up, and give you yet again to enjoy the light of his countenance. Do not sit down to sigh and lament; while the beloved Physician lives there is hope, nay there is a certainty of recovery for the worst cases.

AUGUST 12

The Lord reigneth, let the earth rejoice.—Psalm 97:1

AUSES for disquietude there are none so long as this blessed sentence is true. *On earth* the Lord's power as readily controls the rage of the wicked as the rage of the sea; his love as easily refreshes the poor with mercy as the earth with showers. Majesty gleams in flashes of fire amid the tempest's horrors, and the glory of the Lord is seen in its grandeur in the fall of empires, and the crash of thrones. In all our conflicts and tribulations, we may behold the hand of the divine King.

> God is God; he sees and hears
> All our troubles, all our tears.
> Soul, forget not, 'mid thy pains,
> God o'er all forever reigns.

In hell, evil spirits own, with misery, his undoubted supremacy. When permitted to roam abroad, it is with a chain at their heel; the bit is in the mouth of behemoth, and the hook in the jaws of leviathan. Death's darts are under the Lord's lock, and the grave's prisons have divine power as their warder. The terrible vengeance of the Judge of all the earth makes fiends cower down and tremble, even as dogs in the kennel fear the hunter's whip.

> Fear not death, nor Satan's thrusts,
> God defends who in him trusts;
> Soul, remember, in thy pains,
> God o'er all forever reigns.

In heaven none doubt the sovereignty of the King Eternal, but all fall on their faces to do him homage. Angels are his courtiers, the redeemed his favorites, and all delight to serve him day and night. May we soon reach the city of the great King!

> For this life's long night of sadness
> He will give us peace and gladness.
> Soul, remember, in thy pains,
> God o'er all forever reigns.

AUGUST 13

The cedars of Lebanon which he hath planted.
—Psalm 104:16

EBANON'S cedars are emblematic of the Christian, in that *they owe their planting entirely to the Lord.* This is quite true of every child of God. He is not man-planted, nor self planted, but God-planted. The mysterious hand of the divine Spirit dropped the living seed into a heart which he had himself prepared for its reception. Every true heir of heaven owns the great Husbandman as his planter. Moreover, the cedars of Lebanon *are not dependent upon man for their watering;* they stand on the lofty rock, unmoistened by human irrigation; and yet our heavenly Father supplieth them. Thus it is with the Christian who has learned to live by faith. He is independent of man, even in temporal things; for his continued maintenance he looks to the Lord his God, and to him alone. The dew of heaven is his portion, and the God of heaven is his fountain. Again, the cedars of Lebanon *are not protected by any mortal power.* They owe nothing to man for their preservation from stormy wind and tempest. They are God's trees, kept and preserved by him, and by him alone. It is precisely the same with the Christian. He is not a hot-house plant, sheltered from temptation; he stands in the most exposed position; he has no shelter, no protection, except this, that the broad wings of the eternal God always cover the cedars which he himself has planted. Like cedars, believers are *full of sap,* having vitality enough to be ever green, even amid winter's snows. Lastly, the flourishing and majestic condition of the cedar *is to the praise of God only.* The Lord, even the Lord alone hath been everything unto the cedars, and, therefore David very sweetly puts it in one of the psalms, "Praise ye the Lord, fruitful trees and all cedars." In the believer there is nothing that can magnify man; he is planted, nourished, and protected by the Lord's own hand, and to him let all the glory be ascribed.

AUGUST 14

Thou, Lord, hast made me glad through thy work.
—Psalm 92:4

O you believe that your sins are forgiven, and that Christ has made a full atonement for them? Then what a joyful Christian *you ought to be!* How you should live above the common trials and troubles of the world! Since sin is forgiven, can it matter what happens to you now? Luther said, "Smite, Lord, smite, for my sin is forgiven; if thou hast but forgiven me, smite as hard as thou wilt;" and in a similar spirit you may say, "Send sickness, poverty, losses, crosses, persecution, what thou wilt, *thou hast forgiven me,* and my soul is glad." Christian, if thou art thus saved, whilst thou art glad, *be grateful and loving.* Cling to that cross which took thy sin away; serve thou him who served thee.

> I beseech you therefore, by the mercies of God, that ye present your bodies a living sacrifice, holy, acceptable unto God, which is your reasonable service.

Let not your zeal evaporate in some little ebullition of song. Show your love in expressive tokens. Love the brethren of him who loved you. If there be a Mephibosheth anywhere who is lame or halt, help him for Jonathan's sake. If there be a poor tried believer, weep with him, and bear his cross for the sake of him who wept for thee and carried thy sins. Since thou art thus forgiven freely for Christ's sake, go and tell to others the joyful news of pardoning mercy. Be not contented with this unspeakable blessing for thyself alone, but publish abroad the story of the cross. Holy gladness and holy boldness will make you a good preacher, and all the world will be a pulpit for you to preach in. Cheerful holiness is the most forcible of sermons, but the Lord must give it you. Seek it this morning before you go into the world. When it is the Lord's work in which we rejoice, we need not be afraid of being too glad.

AUGUST 15

Isaac went out to meditate in the field at the eventide.
—Genesis 24:63

ERY admirable was his occupation. If those who spend so many hours in idle company, light reading, and useless pastimes, could learn wisdom, they would find more profitable society and more interesting engagements in meditation than in the vanities which now have such charms for them. We should all know more, live nearer to God, and grow in grace, if we were more alone. Meditation chews the cud and extracts the real nutriment from the mental food gathered elsewhere. When Jesus is the theme, meditation is sweet indeed. Isaac found Rebecca while engaged in private musings; many others have found their best beloved there.

Very admirable was the choice of place. In the field we have a study hung round with texts for thought. From the cedar to the hyssop, from the soaring eagle down to the chirping grasshopper, from the blue expanse of heaven to a drop of dew, all things are full of teaching, and when the eye is divinely opened, that teaching flashes upon the mind far more vividly than from written books. Our little rooms are neither so healthy, so suggestive, so agreeable, or so inspiring as the fields. Let us count nothing common or unclean, but feel that all created things point to their Maker, and the field will at once be hallowed.

Very admirable was the season. The season of sunset as it draws a veil over the day, befits that repose of the soul when earthborn cares yield to the joys of heavenly communion. The glory of the setting sun excites our wonder, and the solemnity of approaching night awakens our awe. If the business of this day will permit it, it will be well, dear reader, if you can spare an hour to walk in the field at eventide, but if not, the Lord is in the town too, and will meet with thee in thy chamber or in the crowded street. Let thy heart go forth to meet him.

AUGUST 16

Give unto the Lord the glory due unto his name.
—Psalm 29:2

OD'S glory is the result of his nature and acts. He is glorious in his character, for there is such a store of everything that is holy, and good, and lovely in God, that he must be glorious. The actions which flow from his character are also glorious; but while he intends that they should manifest to his creatures his goodness, and mercy, and justice, he is equally concerned that the glory associated with them should be given only to himself. Nor is there aught in ourselves in which we may glory; for who maketh us to differ from another? And what have we that we did not receive from the God of all grace? Then how careful ought we to be *to walk humbly before the Lord!* The moment we glorify ourselves, since there is room for one glory only in the universe, we set ourselves up as rivals to the Most High. Shall the insect of an hour glorify itself against the sun which warmed it into life? Shall the potsherd exalt itself above the man who fashioned it upon the wheel? Shall the dust of the desert strive with the whirlwind? Or the drops of the ocean struggle with the tempest? Give unto the Lord, all ye righteous, give unto the Lord glory and strength; give unto him the honor that is due unto his name. Yet it is, perhaps, one of the hardest struggles of the Christian life to learn this sentence—"Not unto us, not unto us, but unto thy name be glory." It is a lesson which God is ever teaching us, and teaching us sometimes by most painful discipline. Let a Christian begin to boast, "I can do all things," without adding "through Christ which strengtheneth me," and before long he will have to groan, "I can do nothing," and bemoan himself in the dust. When we do anything for the Lord, and he is pleased to accept of our doings, let us lay our crown at his feet, and exclaim, "Not I, but the grace of God which was with me!"

AUGUST 17

The mercy of God.
—Psalm 52:8

MEDITATE a little on this mercy of the Lord. It is *tender mercy*. With gentle, loving touch, he healeth the broken in heart, and bindeth up their wounds. He is as gracious in the manner of his mercy as in the matter of it. It *is great mercy*. There is nothing little in God; his mercy is like himself—it is infinite. You cannot measure it. His mercy is so great that it forgives great sins to great sinners, after great lengths of time, and then gives great favors and great privileges, and raises us up to great enjoyments in the great heaven of the great God. It is *undeserved mercy*, as indeed all true mercy must be, for deserved mercy is only a misnomer for justice. There was no right on the sinner's part to the kind consideration of the Most High; had the rebel been doomed at once to eternal fire he would have richly merited the doom, and if delivered from wrath, sovereign love alone has found a cause, for there was none in the sinner himself. It *is rich mercy*. Some things are great, but have little efficacy in them, but this mercy is a cordial to your drooping spirits; a golden ointment to your bleeding wounds; a heavenly bandage to your broken bones; a royal chariot for your weary feet; a bosom of love for your trembling heart. It *is manifold mercy*. As Bunyan says, "All the flowers in God's garden are double." There is no single mercy. You may think you have but one mercy, but you shall find it to be a whole cluster of mercies. It *is abounding mercy*. Millions have received it, yet far from its being exhausted, it is as fresh, as full, and as free as ever. It *is unfailing mercy*. It will never leave thee. If mercy be thy friend, mercy will be with thee in temptation to keep thee from yielding; with thee in trouble to prevent thee from sinking; with thee living to be the light and life of thy countenance; and with thee dying to be the joy of thy soul when earthly comfort is ebbing fast.

AUGUST 18

Strangers are come into the sanctuaries of the Lord's house.
—Jeremiah 51:51

ON this account the faces of the Lord's people were covered with shame, for it was a terrible thing that men should intrude into the Holy Place reserved for the priests alone. Everywhere about us we see like cause for sorrow. How many ungodly men are now educating with the view of entering into the ministry! What a crying sin is that solemn lie by which our whole population is nominally comprehended in a National Church! How fearful it is that ordinances should be pressed upon the unconverted, and that among the more enlightened churches of our land there should be such laxity of discipline. If the thousands who will read this portion shall all take this matter before the Lord Jesus this day, he will interfere and avert the evil which else will come upon his Church. To adulterate the Church is to pollute a well, to pour water upon fire, to sow a fertile field with stones. May we all have grace to maintain in our own proper way the purity of the Church, as being an assembly of believers, and not a nation, an unsaved community of unconverted men.

Our zeal must, however, begin at home. Let us examine *ourselves* as to our right to eat at the Lord's table. Let us see to it that we have on our wedding garment, lest we ourselves be intruders in the Lord's sanctuaries. Many are called, but few are chosen; the way is narrow, and the gate is strait. O for grace to come to Jesus aright, with the faith of God's elect. He who smote Uzzah for touching the ark is very jealous of his two ordinances; as a true believer I may approach them freely, as an alien I must not touch them lest I die. Heartsearching is the duty of all who are baptized or come to the Lord's table. "Search me, O God, and know my way, try me and know my heart."

AUGUST 19

He shall stand and feed in the strength of the Lord.
—Micah 5:4

HRIST'S reign in his Church is that of a *shepherd-king. He* has supremacy, but it is the superiority of a wise and tender shepherd over his needy and loving flock; he commands and receives obedience, but it is the willing obedience of the well-cared-for sheep, rendered joyfully to their beloved Shepherd, whose voice they know so well. He rules by the force of love and the energy of goodness.

His reign is *practical in its character.* It is said, "He shall *stand and feed.*" The great Head of the Church is actively engaged in providing for his people. He does not sit down upon the throne in empty state, or hold a scepter without wielding it in government. No, he stands and feeds. The expression "feed," in the original, is like an analogous one in the Greek, which means to shepherdize, to do everything expected of a shepherd: to guide, to watch, to preserve, to restore, to tend, as well as to feed.

His reign is *continual in its duration.* It is said, *"He shall stand and feed;"* not "He shall feed now and then, and leave his position;" not, "He shall one day grant a revival, and then next day leave his Church to barrenness." His eyes never slumber, and his hands never rest; his heart never ceases to beat with love, and his shoulders are never weary of carrying his people's burdens.

His reign is *effectually powerful in its action;* "He shall feed in the strength of Jehovah." Wherever Christ is, there is God; and whatever Christ does is the act of the Most High. Oh! it is a joyful truth to consider that he who stands today representing the interests of his people is very God of very God, to whom every knee shall bow. Happy are we who belong to such a shepherd, whose humanity communes with us, and whose divinity protects us. Let us worship and bow down before him as the people of his pasture.

AUGUST 20

The sweet psalmist of Israel.
—2 Samuel 23:1

AMONG all the saints whose lives are recorded in Holy Writ, David possesses an experience of the most striking, varied, and instructive character. In his history we meet with trials and temptations not to be discovered, as a whole, in other saints of ancient times, and hence he is all the more suggestive a type of our Lord. David knew the trials of all ranks and conditions of men. Kings have their troubles, and David wore a crown: the peasant has his cares, and David handled a shepherd's crook: the wanderer has many hardships, and David abode in the caves of Engedi: the captain has his difficulties, and David found the sons of Zeruiah too hard for him. The psalmist was also tried in his friends, his counselor Ahithophel forsook him, "He that eateth bread with me, hath lifted up his heel against me." His worst foes were they of his own household: his children were his greatest affliction. The temptations of poverty and wealth, of honor and reproach, of health and weakness, all tried their power upon him. He had temptations from without to disturb his peace, and from within to mar his joy. David no sooner escaped from one trial than he fell into another; no sooner emerged from one season of despondency and alarm, than he was again brought into the lowest depths, and all God's waves and billows rolled over him. It is probably from this cause that David's psalms are so universally the delight of experienced Christians. Whatever our frame of mind, whether ecstasy or depression, David has exactly described our emotions. He was an able master of the human heart, because he had been tutored in the best of all schools—the school of heart-felt, personal experience. As we are instructed in the same school, as we grow matured in grace and in years, we increasingly appreciate David's psalms, and find them to be "green pastures." My soul, let David's experience cheer and counsel thee this day.

AUGUST 21

He that watereth shall be watered also himself.
—Proverbs 11:25

E are here taught the great lesson, that to get, we must give; that to accumulate, we must scatter; that to make ourselves happy, we must make others happy; and that in order to become spiritually vigorous, we must seek the spiritual good of others. In watering others, we are ourselves watered. How? Our efforts to be useful, *bring out our powers for usefulness.* We have latent talents and dormant faculties, which are brought to light by exercise. Our strength for labor is hidden even from ourselves, until we venture forth to fight the Lord's battles, or to climb the mountains of difficulty. We do not know what tender sympathies we possess until we try to dry the widow's tears, and soothe the orphan's grief. We often find in attempting to teach others, that we *gain instruction for ourselves.* Oh, what gracious lessons some of us have learned at sick beds! We went to teach the Scriptures, we came away blushing that we knew so little of them. In our converse with poor saints, we are taught the way of God more perfectly for ourselves and get a deeper insight into divine truth. So that watering others *makes us humble.* We discover how much grace there is where we had not looked for it; and how much the poor saint may outstrip us in knowledge. Our own *comfort is also increased* by our working for others. We endeavor to cheer them, and the consolation gladdens our own heart. Like the two men in the snow; one chafed the other's limbs to keep him from dying, and in so doing kept his own blood in circulation, and saved his own life. The poor widow of Sarepta gave from her scanty store a supply for the prophet's wants, and from that day she never again knew what want was. Give then, and it shall be given unto you, good measure, pressed down, and running over.

AUGUST 22

I charge you, O daughters of Jerusalem, if ye find my beloved,
that ye tell him, that I am sick of [from] love.
—Song of Solomon 5:8

UCH is the language of the believer panting after present fellowship with Jesus, *he is sick for his Lord.* Gracious souls are never perfectly at ease except they are in a state of nearness to Christ; for when they are away from him they lose their peace. The nearer to him, the nearer to the perfect calm of heaven; the nearer to him, the fuller the heart is, not only of peace, but of life, and vigor, and joy, for these all depend on constant intercourse with Jesus. What the sun is to the day, what the moon is to the night, what the dew is to the flower, such is Jesus Christ to us. What bread is to the hungry, clothing to the naked, the shadow of a great rock to the traveler in a weary land, such is Jesus Christ to us; and, therefore, if we are not consciously one with him, little marvel if our spirit cries in the words of the Song, "I charge you, O ye daughters of Jerusalem, if ye find my beloved, tell him that I am sick of love." *This earnest longing after Jesus has* a blessing attending it: "Blessed are they that do hunger and thirst after righteousness;" and therefore, supremely blessed are they who thirst after the Righteous One. Blessed is that hunger, since it comes from God: if I may not have the full-blown blessedness of being filled, I would seek the same blessedness in its sweet bud-pining in emptiness and eagerness till I am filled with Christ. If I may not feed on Jesus, it shall be next door to heaven to hunger and thirst after him. There is a hallowedness about that hunger, since it sparkles among the beatitudes of our Lord. But the blessing *involves a promise.* Such hungry ones *"shall be filled"* with what they are desiring. If Christ thus causes us to long after himself, he will certainly satisfy those longings; and when he does come to us, as come he will, *oh, how sweet it will be!*

AUGUST 23

The voice of weeping shall be no more heard.
—Isaiah 65:19

HE glorified weep no more, for *all outward* causes of grief are gone. There are no broken friendships, nor blighted prospects in heaven. Poverty, famine, peril, persecution, and slander, are unknown there. No pain distresses, no thought of death or bereavement saddens. They weep no more, for *they are perfectly sanctified.* No "evil heart of unbelief" prompts them to depart from the living God; they are without fault before his throne, and are fully conformed to his image. Well may they cease to mourn who have ceased to sin. They weep no more, because *all fear of change is past.* They know that they are eternally secure. Sin is shut out, and they are shut in. They dwell within a city which shall never be stormed; they bask in a sun which shall never set; they drink of a river which shall never dry; they pluck fruit from a tree which shall never wither. Countless cycles may revolve, but eternity shall not be exhausted, and while eternity endures, their immortality and blessedness shall co-exist with it. They are for ever with the Lord. They weep no more, because *every desire is fulfilled.* They cannot wish for anything which they have not in possession. Eye and ear, heart and hand, judgment, imagination, hope, desire, will, all the faculties, are completely satisfied; and imperfect as our present ideas are of the things which God hath prepared for them that love him, yet we know enough, by the revelation of the Spirit, that the saints above are supremely blessed. The joy of Christ, which is an infinite fullness of delight, is in them. They bathe themselves in the bottomless, shoeless sea of infinite beatitude. That same joyful rest remains for us. It may not be far distant. Ere long the weeping willow shall be exchanged for the palm-branch of victory, and sorrow's dewdrops will be transformed into the pearls of everlasting bliss. "Wherefore comfort one another with these words."

AUGUST 24

The breaker is come up before them.
—Micah 2:13

INASMUCH as Jesus has gone before us, things remain not as they would have been had he never passed that way. He has *conquered every foe* that obstructed the way. Cheer up now thou faint-hearted warrior. Not only has Christ traveled the road, but he has slain thine enemies. Dost thou dread sin? He has nailed it to his cross. Dost thou fear death? He has been the death of Death. Art thou afraid of hell? He has barred it against the advent of any of his children; they shall never see the gulf of perdition. Whatever foes may be before the Christian, they are all overcome. There are lions, but their teeth are broken; there are serpents, but their fangs are extracted; there are rivers, but they are bridged or fordable; there are flames, but we wear that matchless garment which renders us invulnerable to fire. The sword that has been forged against us is already blunted; the instruments of war which the enemy is preparing have already lost their point. God has taken away in the person of Christ all the power that anything can have to hurt us. Well then, the army may safely march on, and you may go joyously along your journey, for all your enemies are conquered beforehand. What shall you do but march on to take the prey? They are beaten, they are vanquished; all you have to do is to divide the spoil. You shall, it is true, often engage in combat; but your fight shall be with a vanquished foe. His head is broken; he may attempt to injure you, but his strength shall not be sufficient for his malicious design. Your victory shall be easy, and your treasure shall be beyond all count.

> Proclaim aloud the Savior's fame,
> Who bears *the Breaker's* wond'rous name;
> Sweet name; and it becomes him well,
> Who breaks down earth, sin, death, and hell.

AUGUST 25

His fruit was sweet to my taste.
—Song of Solomon 2:3

AITH, in the Scripture, is spoken of under the emblem of all the senses. It is *sight*: "Look unto me and be ye saved." It is *hearing*: "Hear, and your soul shall live." Faith is *smelling*: "All thy garments smell of myrrh, and aloes, and cassia;" "thy name is as ointment poured forth." Faith is spiritual *touch*. By this faith the woman came behind and touched the hem of Christ's garment, and by this we handle the things of the good word of life. Faith is equally the spirit's *taste*. "How sweet are thy words to my taste! yea, sweeter than honey to my lips." "Except a man eat my flesh," saith Christ, "and drink my blood, there is no life in him."

This *"taste"* is faith *in one of its highest operations.* One of the first performances of faith is *hearing.* We hear the voice of God, not with the outward ear alone, but with the inward ear; we hear it as God's Word, and we believe it to be so; that is the "hearing" of faith. Then our mind *looketh* upon the truth as it is presented to us; that is to say, we understand it, we perceive its meaning; that is the "seeing" of faith. Next we discover its preciousness; we begin to admire it, and find how fragrant it is; that is faith in its *"smell."* Then we appropriate the mercies which are prepared for us in Christ; that is faith in its *"touch."* Hence follow the enjoyments, peace, delight, communion; which are faith in its *"taste."* Any one of these acts of faith is saving. To hear Christ's voice as the sure voice of God in the soul will save us; but that which gives true enjoyment is the aspect of faith wherein Christ, by holy taste, is received into us, and made, by inward and spiritual apprehension of his sweetness and preciousness, to be the food of our souls. It is then we sit "under his shadow with great delight," and find his fruit sweet to our taste.

AUGUST 26

He hath commanded his covenant forever.
—Psalms 111:9

HE Lord's people delight in the covenant itself. It is an un-failing source of consolation to them so often as the Holy Spirit leads them into its banqueting house and waves its banner of love. They delight to contemplate *the antiquity* of that covenant, remembering that before the day-star knew its place, or planets ran their round, the interests of the saints were made secure in Christ Jesus. It is peculiarly pleasing to them to remember *the sureness* of the covenant, while meditating upon "the sure mercies of David." They delight to celebrate it as "signed, and sealed, and ratified, in all things ordered well." It often makes their hearts dilate with joy to think of its *immutability*, as a covenant which neither time nor eternity, life nor death, shall ever be able to violate—a covenant as old as eternity and as everlasting as the Rock of ages. They rejoice also to feast upon *the fullness* of this covenant, for they see in it all things provided for them. God is their portion, Christ their companion, the Spirit their Comforter, earth their lodge, and heaven their home. They see in it an inheritance reserved and entailed to every soul possessing an interest in its ancient and eternal deed of gift. Their eyes sparkled when they saw it as a treasure-trove in the Bible; but oh! how their souls were gladdened when they saw in the last will and testament of their divine kinsman, that it was bequeathed to them! More especially it is the pleasure of God's people to contemplate *the graciousness* of this covenant. They see that the law was made void because it was a covenant of works and depended upon merit, but this they perceive to be enduring because grace is the basis, grace the condition, grace the strain, grace the bulwark, grace the foundation, grace the topstone. The covenant is a treasury of wealth, a granary of food, a fountain of life, a store-house of salvation, a charter of peace, and a haven of joy.

AUGUST 27

How long will it be ere they believe me?
—Numbers 14:11

STRIVE with all diligence to keep out that monster unbelief. It so dishonors Christ, that he will withdraw his visible presence if we insult him by indulging it. It is true it is a weed, the seeds of which we can never entirely extract from the soil, but we must aim at its root with zeal and perseverance. Among hateful things it is the most to be abhorred. Its injurious nature is so venomous that he that exerciseth it and he upon whom it is exercised are both hurt thereby. In thy case, O believer! it is most wicked, for the mercies of thy Lord in the past, increase thy guilt in doubting him now. When thou dost distrust the Lord Jesus, he may well cry out, "Behold I am pressed under you, as a cart is pressed that is full of sheaves." This is crowning his head with thorns of the sharpest kind. It is very cruel for a well-beloved wife to mistrust a kind and faithful husband. The sin is needless, foolish, and unwarranted. Jesus has never given the slightest ground for suspicion, and it is hard to be doubted by those to whom our conduct is uniformly affectionate and true. Jesus is the Son of the Highest, and has unbounded wealth; it is shameful to doubt Omnipotence and distrust all-sufficiency. The cattle on a thousand hills will suffice for our most hungry feeding, and the granaries of heaven are not likely to be emptied by our eating. If Christ were only a cistern, we might soon exhaust his fullness, but who can drain a fountain? Myriads of spirits have drawn their supplies from him, and not one of them has murmured at the scantiness of his resources. Away, then, with this lying traitor unbelief, for his only errand is to cut the bonds of communion and make us mourn an absent Savior. Bunyan tells us that unbelief has "as many lives as a cat:" if so, let us kill one life now, and continue the work till the whole nine are gone. Down with thee, thou traitor, my heart abhors thee.

AUGUST 28

Oil for the light.
—*Exodus 25:6*

MY soul, how much thou needest this, for thy lamp will not long continue to burn without it. thy snuff will smoke and become an offence if light be gone, and gone it will be if oil be absent. Thou hast no oil well springing up in thy human nature, and therefore thou must go to them that sell and buy for thyself, or like the foolish virgins, thou wilt have to cry, "My lamp is gone out." Even the consecrated lamps could not give light without oil; though they shone in the tabernacle they needed to be fed, though no rough winds blew upon them they required to be trimmed, and thy need is equally as great. Under the most happy circumstances thou canst not give light for another hour unless fresh oil of grace be given thee.

It was not every oil that might be used in the Lord's service; neither the petroleum which exudes so plentifully from the earth, nor the produce of fishes, nor that extracted from nuts would be accepted; one oil only was selected, and that the best olive oil. Pretended grace from natural goodness, fancied grace from priestly hands, or imaginary grace from outward ceremonies will never serve the true saint of God; he knows that the Lord would not be pleased with rivers of such oil. He goes to the olive-press of Gethsemane, and draws his supplies from him who was crushed therein. The oil of gospel grace is pure and free from lees and dregs, and hence the light which is fed thereon is clear and bright. Our churches are the Savior's golden candelabra, and if they are to be lights in this dark world, they must have much holy oil. Let us pray for ourselves, our ministers, and our churches, that they may never lack oil for the light. Truth, holiness, joy, knowledge, love, these are all beams of the sacred light, but we cannot give them forth unless in private we receive oil from God the Holy Ghost.

August 29

Have mercy upon me, O God.
—Psalm 51:1

HEN Dr. Carey was suffering from a dangerous illness, the enquiry was made, "If this sickness should prove fatal, what passage would you select as the text for your funeral sermon?" He replied,

> ... Oh, I feel that such a poor sinful creature is unworthy to have anything said about him; but if a funeral sermon must be preached, let it be from the words, "Have mercy upon me, O God, according to thy lovingkindness; according unto the multitude of thy tender mercies blot out my transgressions."

In the same spirit of humility he directed in his will that the following inscription and nothing more should be cut on his gravestone:—

WILLIAM CAREY, BORN AUGUST 17th, 1761, DIED——

A wretched, poor, and helpless worm
On thy kind arms I fall.

Only on the footing of free grace can the most experienced and most honored of the saints approach their God. The best of men are conscious above all others that they are men at the best. Empty boats float high, but heavily laden vessels are low in the water; mere professors can boast, but true children of God cry for mercy upon their unprofitableness. We have need that the Lord should have mercy upon our good works, our prayers, our preachings, our alms-givings, and our holiest things. The blood was not only sprinkled upon the doorposts of Israel's dwelling houses, but upon the sanctuary, the mercy-seat, and the altar, because as sin intrudes into our holiest things, the blood of Jesus is needed to purify them from defilement. If mercy be needed to be exercised towards our duties, what shall be said of our sins? How sweet the remembrance that inexhaustible mercy is waiting to be gracious to us, to restore our backslidings, and make our broken bones rejoice!

August 30

Wait on the Lord.
—Psalm 27:14

IT may seem an easy thing to *wait,* but it is one of the postures which a Christian soldier learns not without years of teaching. Marching and quick-marching are much easier to God's warriors than standing still. There are hours of perplexity when the most willing spirit, anxiously desirous to serve the Lord, knows not what part to take. Then what shall it do? Vex itself by despair? Fly back in cowardice, turn to the right hand in fear, or rush forward in presumption? No, but simply wait. *Wait in prayer,* however. Call upon God, and spread the case before him; tell him your difficulty, and plead his promise of aid. In dilemmas between one duty and another, it is sweet to be humble as a child, and *wait with simplicity of soul* upon the Lord. It is sure to be well with us when we feel and know our own folly, and are heartily willing to be guided by the will of God. But *wait in faith.* Express your unstaggering confidence in him; for unfaithful, untrusting waiting, is but an insult to the Lord. Believe that if he keep you tarrying even till midnight, yet he will come at the right time; the vision shall come and shall not tarry. *Wait in quiet patience,* not rebelling because you are under the affliction, but blessing your God for it. Never murmur against the second cause, as the children of Israel did against Moses; never wish you could go back to the world again, but accept the case as it is, and put it as it stands, simply and with your whole heart, without any self-will, into the hand of your covenant God, saying,

> Now, Lord, not my will, but thine be done. I know not what to do; I am brought to extremities, but I will wait until thou shalt cleave the floods, or drive back my foes. I will wait, if thou keep me many a day, for my heart is fixed upon thee alone, O God, and my spirit waiteth for thee in the full conviction that thou wilt yet be my joy and my salvation, my refuge and my strong tower.

AUGUST 31

On mine arm shall they trust.
—Isaiah 51:5

IN seasons of severe trial, the Christian has nothing on earth that he can trust to, and is therefore compelled to cast himself on his God alone. When his vessel is on its beamends, and no human deliverance can avail, he must simply and entirely trust himself to the providence and care of God. Happy storm that wrecks a man on such a rock as this! O blessed hurricane that drives the soul to God and God alone! There is no getting at our God sometimes because of the multitude of our friends; but when a man is so poor, so friendless, so helpless that he has nowhere else to turn, he flies into his Father's arms, and is blessedly clasped therein! When he is burdened with troubles so pressing and so peculiar, that he cannot tell them to any but his God, he may be thankful for them; for he will learn more of his Lord then than at any other time. Oh, tempest-tossed believer, it is a happy trouble that drives thee to thy Father! Now that thou hast only thy God to trust to, see that thou puttest thy full confidence in him. Dishonor not thy Lord and Master by unworthy doubts and fears; but be strong in faith, giving glory to God. Show the world that thy God is worth ten thousand worlds to thee. Show rich men how rich thou art in thy poverty when the Lord God is thy helper. Show the strong man how strong thou art in thy weakness when underneath thee are the everlasting arms. Now is the time for feats of faith and valiant exploits. Be strong and very courageous, and the Lord thy God shall certainly, as surely as he built the heavens and the earth, glorify himself in thy weakness, and magnify his might in the midst of thy distress. The grandeur of the arch of heaven would be spoiled if the sky were supported by a single visible column, and your faith would lose its glory if it rested on anything discernible by the carnal eye. May the Holy Spirit give you to rest in Jesus this closing day of the month.

September 1

Thou shalt guide me with thy counsel,
and afterward receive me to glory.
—Psalm 73:24

HE Psalmist felt his need of divine guidance. He had just been discovering the foolishness of his own heart, and lest he should be constantly led astray by it, he resolved that God's counsel should henceforth guide him. A sense of our own folly is a great step towards being wise, when it leads us to rely on the wisdom of the Lord. The blind man leans on his friend's arm and reaches home in safety, and so would we give ourselves up implicitly to divine guidance, nothing doubting; assured that though we cannot see, it is always safe to trust the All-seeing God. *"Thou shalt,"* is a blessed expression of confidence. He was sure that the Lord would not decline the condescending task. There is a word for thee, O believer; rest thou in it. Be assured that thy God will be thy counselor and friend; he shall guide thee; he will direct all thy ways. In his written Word thou hast this assurance in part fulfilled, for holy Scripture is his counsel to thee. Happy are we to have God's Word always to guide us! What were the mariner without his compass? And what were the Christian without the Bible? This is the unerring chart, the map in which every shoal is described, and all the channels from the quicksands of destruction to the haven of salvation mapped and marked by one who knows all the way. Blessed be thou, O God, that we may trust thee to guide us now, and guide us even to the end! After this guidance through life, the Psalmist anticipates a divine reception at last—*"and afterward receive me to glory."* What a thought for thee, believer! *God* himself will receive *thee* to glory—*thee!* Wandering, erring, straying, yet he will bring thee safe at last *to glory!* This is thy portion; live on it this day, and if perplexities should surround thee, go in the strength of this text straight to the throne.

SEPTEMBER 2

But Simon's wife's mother lay sick of a fever,
and anon they tell Him of her.
—Mark 1:30

ERY interesting is this little peep into the house of the Apostolic Fisherman. We see at once that household joys and cares are no hindrance to the full exercise of ministry, nay, that since they furnish an opportunity for personally witnessing the Lord's gracious work upon one's own flesh and blood, they may even instruct the teacher better than any other earthly discipline. Papists and other sectaries may decry marriage, but true Christianity and household life agree well together. Peter's house was probably a poor fisherman's hut, but the Lord of Glory entered it, lodged in it, and wrought a miracle in it. Should our little book be read this morning in some very humble cottage, let this fact encourage the inmates to seek the company of King Jesus. God is oftener in little huts than in rich palaces. Jesus is looking round your room now, and is waiting to be gracious to you. Into Simon's house sickness had entered, fever in a deadly form had prostrated his mother-in-law, and as soon as Jesus came they told him of the sad affliction, and he hastened to the patient's bed. Have you any sickness in the house this morning? You will find Jesus by far the best physician, go to him at once and tell him all about the matter. Immediately lay the case before him. It concerns one of his people, and therefore will not be trivial to him. Observe, that *at once* the Savior restored the sick woman; none can heal as he does. We may not make sure that the Lord will at once remove all disease from those we love, but we may know that believing prayer for the sick is far more likely to be followed by restoration than anything else in the world; and where this avails not, we must meekly bow to his will by whom life and death are determined. The tender heart of Jesus waits to hear our griefs, let us pour them into his patient ear.

SEPTEMBER 3

Thou whom my soul loveth.
—Song of Solomon 1:7

T is well to be able, without any "if" or "but," to say of the Lord Jesus—*"Thou whom my soul loveth."* Many can only say of Jesus that they *hope* they love him; they *trust* they love him; but only a poor and shallow experience will be content to stay here. No one ought to give any rest to his spirit till he feels quite sure about a matter of such vital importance. We ought not to be satisfied with a superficial *hope* that Jesus loves us, and with a bare *trust* that we love him. The old saints did not generally speak with "buts," and "ifs," and "hopes," and "trusts," but they spoke positively and plainly. "I *know* whom I have believed," saith Paul. "I *know* that my Redeemer liveth," saith Job. Get positive knowledge of your love of Jesus, and be not satisfied till you can speak of your interest in him as a reality, which you have made sure by having received the witness of the Holy Spirit, and his seal upon your soul by faith.

True love to Christ is in every case the Holy Spirit's work, and must be wrought in the heart by him. He is the *efficient cause* of it; but the logical reason why we love Jesus lies in *himself. Why* do we love Jesus? *Because he first loved us. Why* do we love Jesus? Because he *"gave himself for us."* We have life through his death; we have peace through his blood. Though he was rich, yet *for our sakes* he became poor. *Why* do we love Jesus? Because of the *excellency* of his person. We are filled with a sense of his beauty! an admiration of his charms! a consciousness of his infinite perfection! his greatness, goodness, and loveliness, in one resplendent ray, combine to enchant the soul till it is so ravished that it exclaims, "Yea, he is altogether lovely." Blessed love this—a love which binds the heart with chains more soft than silk, and yet more firm than adamant!

SEPTEMBER 4

I will; be thou clean.
—Mark 1:41

RIMEVAL darkness heard the Almighty fiat, "light be," and straightway light was, and the word of the Lord Jesus is equal in majesty to that ancient word of power. Redemption like Creation has its word of might. Jesus speaks and it is done. Leprosy yielded to no human remedies, but it fled at once at the Lord's "I will." The disease exhibited no hopeful signs or tokens of recovery, nature contributed nothing to its own healing, but the unaided word effected the entire work on the spot and forever. The sinner is in a plight more miserable than the leper; let him imitate his example and go to Jesus, "beseeching him and kneeling down to him." Let him exercise what little faith he has, even though it should go no further than "Lord, if thou wilt, thou canst make me clean;" and there need be no doubt as to the result of the application. Jesus heals all who come, and casts out none. In reading the narrative in which our morning's text occurs, it is worthy of devout notice that Jesus touched the leper. This unclean person had broken through the regulations of the ceremonial law and pressed into the house, but Jesus so far from chiding him broke through the law himself in order to meet him. He made an interchange with the leper, for while he cleansed him, he contracted by that touch a Levitical defilement. Even so Jesus Christ was made sin for us, although in himself he knew no sin, that we might be made the righteousness of God in him. O that poor sinners would go to Jesus, believing in the power of his blessed substitutionary work, and they would soon learn the power of his gracious touch. That hand which multiplied the loaves, which saved sinking Peter, which upholds afflicted saints, which crowns believers, that same hand will touch every seeking sinner, and in a moment make him clean. The love of Jesus is the source of salvation. He loves, he looks, he touches us, *we live.*

SEPTEMBER 5

Woe is me, that I sojourn in Mesech,
that I dwell in the tents of Kedar!
—Psalm 120:5

AS a Christian you have to live in the midst of an ungodly world, and it is of little use for you to cry "Woe is me." Jesus did not pray that you should be taken out of the world, and what he did not pray for you need not desire. Better far in the Lord's strength to meet the difficulty, and glorify him in it. The enemy is ever on the watch to detect inconsistency in your conduct; be therefore very *holy*. Remember that the eyes of all are upon you, and that more is expected from you than from other men. Strive to give no occasion for blame. Let your goodness be the only fault they can discover in you. Like Daniel, compel them to say of you, "We shall not find any occasion against this Daniel, except we find it against him concerning the law of his God." Seek to be *useful* as well as consistent. Perhaps you think, "If I were in a more favorable position I might serve the Lord's cause, but I cannot do any good where I am;" but the worse the people are among whom you live, the more need have they of your exertions; if they be crooked, the more necessity that you should set them straight; and if they be perverse, the more need have you to turn their proud hearts to the truth. Where should the physician be but where there are many sick? Where is honor to be won by the soldier but in the hottest fire of the battle? And when weary of the strife and sin that meets you on every hand, consider that all the saints have endured the same trial. They were not carried on beds of down to heaven, and you must not expect to travel more easily than they. They had to hazard their lives unto the death in the high places of the field, and you will not be crowned till you also have endured hardness as a good soldier of Jesus Christ. Therefore, "stand fast in the faith, quit you like men, be strong."

SEPTEMBER 6

*In the midst of a crooked and perverse nation,
among whom ye shine as lights in the world.*
—Philippians 2:15

WE use lights to *make manifest*. A Christian man should so shine in his life, that a person could not live with him a week without knowing the gospel. His conversation should be such that all who are about him should clearly perceive whose he is, and whom he serves; and should see the image of Jesus reflected in his daily actions. Lights are intended for *guidance*. We are to help those around us who are in the dark. We are to hold forth to them the Word of life. We are to point sinners to the Savior, and the weary to a divine resting-place. Men sometimes read their Bibles, and fail to understand them; we should be ready, like Philip, to instruct the inquirer in the meaning of God's Word, the way of salvation, and the life of godliness. Lights are also used for *warning*. On our rocks and shoals a light-house is sure to be erected. Christian men should know that there are many false lights shown everywhere in the world, and therefore the right light is needed. The wreckers of Satan are always abroad, tempting the ungodly to sin under the name of pleasure; they hoist the wrong light, be it ours to put up the true light upon every dangerous rock, to point out every sin, and tell what it leads to, that so we may be clear of the blood of all men, shining as lights in the world. Lights also have a very *cheering* influence, and so have Christians. A Christian ought to be a comforter, with kind words on his lips, and sympathy in his heart; he should carry sunshine wherever he goes, and diffuse happiness around him.

> Gracious Spirit dwell with me;
> I myself would gracious be,
> And with words that help and heal
> Would thy life in mine reveal,
> And with actions bold and meek
> Would for Christ my Savior speak.

SEPTEMBER 7

And when they could not come nigh unto him for the press,
they uncovered the roof where he was: and when they had broken it up,
they let down the bed wherein the [man] sick of the palsy lay.
—Mark 2:4

FAITH is full of inventions. The house was full, a crowd blocked up the door, but faith found a way of getting at the Lord and placing the palsied man before him. If we cannot get sinners where Jesus is by ordinary methods we must use extraordinary ones. It seems, according to Luke 5:19, that a tiling had to be removed, which would make dust and cause a measure of danger to those below, but where the case is very urgent we must not mind running some risks and shocking some proprieties. Jesus was there to heal, and therefore fall what might, faith ventured all so that her poor paralyzed charge might have his sins forgiven. O that we had more daring faith among us! Cannot we, dear reader, seek it this morning for ourselves and for our fellow-workers, and will we not try today to perform some gallant act for the love of souls and the glory of the Lord.

The world is constantly inventing; genius serves all the purposes of human desire: cannot faith invent too, and reach by some new means the outcasts who lie perishing around us? It was the presence of Jesus which excited victorious courage in the four bearers of the palsied man: is not the Lord among us now? Have we seen his face for ourselves this morning? Have we felt his healing power in our own souls? If so, then through door, through window, or through roof, let us, breaking through all impediments, labor to bring poor souls to Jesus. All means are good and decorous when faith and love are truly set on winning souls. If hunger for bread can break through stone walls, surely hunger for souls is not to be hindered in its efforts. O Lord, make us quick to suggest methods of reaching thy poor sin-sick ones, and bold to carry them out at all hazards.

SEPTEMBER 8

From me is thy fruit found.—Hosea 14:8

UR fruit is found from our God as to *union*. The fruit of the branch is directly traceable to the root. Sever the connection, the branch dies, and no fruit is produced. By virtue of our union with Christ we bring forth fruit. Every bunch of grapes have been first in the root, it has passed through the stem, and flowed through the sap vessels, and fashioned itself externally into fruit, but it was first in the stem; so also every good work was first in Christ, and then is brought forth in us. O Christian, prize this precious union to Christ; for it must be the source of all the fruitfulness which thou canst hope to know. If thou wert not joined to Jesus Christ, thou wouldst be a barren bough indeed.

Our fruit comes from God as to *spiritual providence*. When the dew-drops fall from heaven, when the cloud looks down from on high, and is about to distil its liquid treasure, when the bright sun swells the berries of the cluster, each heavenly boon may whisper to the tree and say, "From me is thy fruit found." The fruit owes much to the root—that is essential to fruitfulness—but it owes very much also to external influences. How much we owe to God's grace-providence! in which he provides us constantly with quickening, teaching, consolation, strength, or whatever else we want. To this we owe our all of usefulness or virtue.

Our fruit comes from God as to *wise husbandry*. The gardener's sharp-edged knife promotes the fruitfulness of the tree, by thinning the clusters, and by cutting off superfluous shoots. So is it, Christian, with that pruning which the Lord gives to thee.

> My Father is the husbandman. Every branch in me that beareth not fruit he taketh away; and every branch that beareth fruit he purgeth it, that it may bring forth more fruit.

Since our God is the author of our spiritual graces, let us give to him all the glory of our salvation.

SEPTEMBER 9

I will answer thee, and shew thee
great and mighty things which thou knowest not.
—Jeremiah 33:3

THERE are different translations of these words. One version renders it, "I will shew thee great and *fortified* things." Another, "Great and *reserved* things." Now, there are reserved and special things in Christian experience: all the developments of spiritual life are not alike easy of attainment. There are the common frames and feelings of repentance, and faith, and joy, and hope, which are enjoyed by the entire family; but there is an upper realm of rapture, of communion, and conscious union with Christ, which is far from being the common dwelling-place of believers. We have not all the high privilege of John, to lean upon Jesus' bosom; nor of Paul, to be caught up into the third heaven. There are heights in experimental knowledge of the things of God which the eagle's eye of acumen and philosophic thought hath never seen: God alone can bear us there; but the chariot in which he takes us up, and the fiery steeds with which that chariot is dragged, are prevailing prayers. Prevailing prayer is victorious over the God of mercy,

> By his strength he had power with God: yea, he had power over the angel, and prevailed: he wept, and made supplication unto him: he found him in Beth-el, and there he spake with us.

Prevailing prayer takes the Christian to Carmel, and enables him to cover heaven with clouds of blessing, and earth with floods of mercy. Prevailing prayer bears the Christian aloft to Pisgah, and shows him the inheritance reserved; it elevates us to Tabor and transfigures us, till in the likeness of his Lord, as he is, so are we also in this world. If you would reach to something higher than ordinary groveling experience, look to the Rock that is higher than you, and gaze with the eye of faith through the window of importunate prayer. When you open the window on your side, it will not be bolted on the other.

SEPTEMBER 10

And he goeth up into a mountain,
and calleth unto him whom he would: and they came unto him.
—Mark 3:13

HERE was sovereignty. Impatient spirits may fret and fume, because they are not called to the highest places in the ministry; but reader be it thine to rejoice that Jesus calleth whom he wills. If he shall leave me to be a doorkeeper in his house, I will cheerfully bless him for his grace in permitting me to do anything in his service. The call of Christ's servants comes from above. Jesus stands on the mountain, evermore above the world in holiness, earnestness, love and power. Those whom he calls must go up the mountain to him, they must seek to rise to his level by living in constant communion with him. They may not be able to mount to classic honors, or attain scholastic eminence, but they must like Moses go up into the mount of God and have familiar intercourse with the unseen God, or they will never be fitted to proclaim the gospel of peace. Jesus went apart to hold high fellowship with the Father, and we must enter into the same divine companionship if we would bless our fellowmen. No wonder that the apostles were clothed with power when they came down fresh from the mountain where Jesus was. This morning we must endeavor to ascend the mount of communion, that there we may be ordained to the lifework for which we are set apart. Let us not see the face of man today till we have seen Jesus. Time spent with him is laid out at blessed interest. We too shall cast out devils and work wonders if we go down into the world girded with that divine energy which Christ alone can give. It is of no use going to the Lord's battle till we are armed with heavenly weapons. We *must* see Jesus, this is essential. At the mercy-seat we will linger till he shall manifest himself unto us as he doth not unto the world, and until we can truthfully say, "We were with him in the Holy Mount."

SEPTEMBER 11

Be ye separate.—2 Corinthians 6:17

T HE Christian, while in the world, is not to be of the world. He should be distinguished from it in *the great object of his life.* To him, "to live," should be "Christ." Whether he eats, or drinks, or whatever he does, he should do all to God's glory. You may lay up treasure; but lay it up in heaven, where neither moth nor rust doth corrupt, where thieves break not through nor steal. You may strive to be rich; but be it your ambition to be "rich in faith," and good works. You may have pleasure; but when you are merry, sing psalms and make melody in your hearts to the Lord. In your *spirit,* as well as in your aim, you should differ from the world. Waiting humbly before God, always conscious of his presence, delighting in communion with him, and seeking to know his will, you will prove that you are of heavenly race. And you should be separate from the world in your *actions.* If a thing be right, though you lose by it, it must be done; if it be wrong, though you would gain by it, you must scorn the sin for your Master's sake. You must have no fellowship with the unfruitful works of darkness, but rather reprove them. Walk worthy of your high calling and dignity. Remember, O Christian, that thou art a son of the King of kings. Therefore, keep thyself unspotted from the world. Soil not the fingers which are soon to sweep celestial strings; let not these eyes become the windows of lust which are soon to see the King in his beauty—let not those feet be defiled in miry places, which are soon to walk the golden streets—let not those hearts be filled with pride and bitterness which are ere long to be filled with heaven, and to overflow with ecstatic joy.

> Then rise my soul! and soar away,
> Above the thoughtless crowd;
> Above the pleasures of the gay,
> And splendors of the proud;
> Up where eternal beauties bloom,
> And pleasures all divine;
> Where wealth, that never can consume,
> And endless glories shine.

SEPTEMBER 12

God is jealous.
—Nahum 1:2

YOUR Lord is very jealous of your love, O believer. Did he choose you? He cannot bear that you should choose another. Did he buy you with his own blood? He cannot endure that you should think that you are your own, or that you belong to this world. He loved you with such a love that he would not stop in heaven without you; he would sooner die than you should perish, and he cannot endure that anything should stand between your heart's love and himself. He *is very jealous of your trust. He* will not permit you to trust in an arm of flesh. He cannot bear that you should hew out broken cisterns, when the overflowing fountain is always free to you. When we lean upon him, he is glad, but when we transfer our dependence to another, when we rely upon our own wisdom, or the wisdom of a friend—worst of all, when we trust in any works of our own, he is displeased, and will chasten us that he may bring us to himself. He *is also very jealous of our company.* There should be no one with whom we converse so much as with Jesus. To abide in him only, this is true love; but to commune with the world, to find sufficient solace in our carnal comforts, to prefer even the society of our fellow Christians to secret intercourse with him, this is grievous to our jealous Lord. He would fain have us abide in him, and enjoy constant fellowship with himself; and many of the trials which he sends us are for the purpose of weaning our hearts from the creature, and fixing them more closely upon himself. Let this jealousy which would keep us near to Christ *be also a comfort* to us, for if he loves us so much as to care thus about *our* love we may be sure that he will suffer nothing to harm us, and will protect us from all our enemies. Oh that we may have grace this day to keep our hearts in sacred chastity for our Beloved alone, with sacred jealousy shutting our eyes to all the fascinations of the world!

SEPTEMBER 13

Who, passing through the valley of Baca, make it a well,
the rain also filleth the pools.
—Psalm 84:6

THIS teaches us that the *comfort* obtained by one may often prove serviceable to another; just as wells would be used by the company who came after. We read some book full of consolation, which is like Jonathan's rod, dropping with honey. Ah! we think our brother has been here before us, and digged this well for us as well as for himself. Many a "Night of Weeping," "Midnight Harmonies," an "Eternal Day," "A Crook in the Lot," a "Comfort for Mourners," has been a well digged by a pilgrim for himself, but has proved quite as useful to others. Specially we notice this in the Psalms, such as that beginning, "Why art thou cast down, O my soul?" Travelers have been delighted to see the footprint of man on a barren shore, and we love to see the waymarks of pilgrims while passing through the vale of tears.

The pilgrims dig the well, but, strange enough, it fills from the top instead of the bottom. We use the means, but the blessing does not spring from the means. We dig a well, but heaven fills it with rain. The horse is prepared against the day of battle, but safety is of the Lord. The means are connected with the end, but they do not of themselves produce it. See here the rain fills the pools, so that the wells become useful as reservoirs for the water; labor is not lost, but yet it does not supersede divine help.

Grace may well be compared to rain for its purity, for its refreshing and vivifying influence, for its coming alone from above, and for the sovereignty with which it is given or withheld. May our readers have showers of blessing, and may the wells they have digged be filled with water! Oh, what are means and ordinances without the smile of heaven! They are as clouds without rain, and pools without water. O God of love, open the windows of heaven and pour us out a blessing!

SEPTEMBER 14

There were also with him other little ships.
—Mark 4:36

ESUS was the Lord High Admiral of the sea that night, and his presence preserved the whole convoy. It is well to sail with Jesus, even though it be in a little ship. When we sail in Christ's company, we may not make sure of fair weather, for great storms may toss the vessel which carries the Lord himself, and we must not expect to find the sea less boisterous around our little boat. If we go with Jesus we must be content to fare as he fares; and when the waves are rough to him, they will be rough to us. It is by tempest and tossing that we shall come to land, as he did before us.

When the storm swept over Galilee's dark lake all faces gathered blackness, and all hearts dreaded shipwreck. When all creature help was useless, the slumbering Savior arose, and with a word, transformed the riot of the tempest into the deep quiet of a calm; then were the little vessels at rest as well as that which carried the Lord. Jesus is the star of the sea; and though there be sorrow upon the sea, when Jesus is on it there is joy too. May our hearts make Jesus their anchor, their rudder, their lighthouse, their life-boat, and their harbor. His Church is the Admiral's flagship, let us attend her movements, and cheer her officers with our presence. He himself is the great attraction; let us follow ever in his wake, mark his signals, steer by his chart, and never fear while he is within hail. Not one ship in the convoy shall suffer wreck; the great Commodore will steer every barque in safety to the desired haven. By faith we will slip our cable for another day's cruise, and sail forth with Jesus into a sea of tribulation. Winds and waves will not spare us, but they all obey him; and, therefore, whatever squalls may occur without, faith shall feel a blessed calm within. He is ever in the center of the weather-beaten company: let us rejoice in him. His vessel has reached the haven, and so shall ours.

SEPTEMBER 15

He shall not be afraid of evil tidings.
—Psalm 112:7

HRISTIAN, you ought not to dread the arrival of evil tidings; because if you are distressed by them, *what do you more than other men?* Other men have not your God to fly to; they have never proved his faithfulness as you have done, and it is no wonder if they are bowed down with alarm and cowed with fear: but you profess to be of another spirit; you have been begotten again unto a lively hope, and your heart lives in heaven and not on earthly things; now, if you are seen to be distracted as other men, what is the value of that grace which you profess to have received? Where is the dignity of that new nature which you claim to possess?

Again, if you should be filled with alarm, as others are, *you would, doubtless, be led into the sins so common to others under trying circumstances.* The ungodly, when they are overtaken by evil tidings, rebel against God; they murmur, and think that God deals hardly with them. Will you fall into that same sin? Will you provoke the Lord as they do?

Moreover, unconverted men often run to wrong means in order to escape from difficulties, and you will be sure to do the same if your mind yields to the present pressure. Trust in the Lord, and wait patiently for him. Your wisest course is to do as Moses did at the Red Sea, "Stand still and see the salvation of God." For if you give way to fear when you hear of evil tidings, you will be unable to meet the trouble with that calm composure which nerves for duty, and sustains under adversity. How can you glorify God if you play the coward? Saints have often sung God's high praises in the fires, but will your doubting and desponding, as if you had none to help you, magnify the Most High? Then take courage, and relying in sure confidence upon the faithfulness of your covenant God, "let not your heart be troubled, neither let it be afraid."

SEPTEMBER 16

Partakers of the divine nature.
—2 Peter 1:4

TO be a partaker of the divine nature is not, of course, to become God. That cannot be. The essence of Deity is not to be participated in by the creature. Between the creature and the Creator there must ever be a gulf fixed in respect of essence; but as the first man Adam was made in the image of God, so we, by the renewal of the Holy Spirit, are in a yet diviner sense made in the image of the Most High, and are partakers of the divine nature. We are, by grace, made like God. "God is love;" we become love—"He that loveth is born of God." God is truth; we become true, and we love that which is true: God is good, and he makes us good by his grace, so that we become the pure in heart who shall see God. Moreover, we become partakers of the divine nature in even a higher sense than this—in fact, in as lofty a sense as can be conceived, short of our being absolutely divine. Do we not become members of the body of the divine person of Christ? Yes, the same blood which flows in the head flows in the hand: and the same life which quickens Christ quickens his people, for "Ye are dead, and your life is hid with Christ in God." Nay, as if this were not enough, we are married unto Christ. He hath betrothed us unto himself in righteousness and in faithfulness, and he who is joined unto the Lord is one spirit. Oh! marvelous mystery! we look into it, but who shall understand it? One with Jesus—so one with him that the branch is not more one with the vine than we are a part of the Lord, our Savior, and our Redeemer! While we rejoice in this, let us remember that those who are made partakers of the divine nature will manifest their high and holy relationship in their intercourse with others, and make it evident by their daily walk and conversation that they have escaped the corruption that is in the world through lust. O for more divine holiness of life!

SEPTEMBER 17

Bring him unto me.
—Mark 9:19

ESPAIRINGLY the poor disappointed father turned away from the disciples to their Master. His son was in the worst possible condition, and all means had failed, but the miserable child was soon delivered from the evil one when the parent in faith obeyed the Lord Jesus' word, "Bring him unto me." Children are a precious gift from God, but much anxiety comes with them. They may be a great joy or a great bitterness to their parents; they may be filled with the Spirit of God, or possessed with the spirit of evil. In all cases, the Word of God gives us one receipt for the curing of all their ills, "Bring him unto me." O for more agonizing prayer on their behalf while they are yet babes! Sin is there, let our prayers begin to attack it. Our cries for our offspring should precede those cries which betoken their actual advent into a world of sin. In the days of their youth we shall see sad tokens of that dumb and deaf spirit which will neither pray aright, nor hear the voice of God in the soul, but Jesus still commands, "Bring them unto me." When they are grown up they may wallow in sin and foam with enmity against God; then when our hearts are breaking we should remember the great Physician's words, "Bring them unto me." Never must we cease to pray until they cease to breathe. No case is hopeless while Jesus lives.

The Lord sometimes suffers his people to be driven into a corner that they may experimentally know how necessary he is to them. Ungodly children, when they show us our own powerlessness against the depravity of their hearts, drive us to flee to the strong for strength, and this is a great blessing to us. Whatever our morning's need may be, let it like a strong current bear us to the ocean of divine love. Jesus can soon remove our sorrow, he delights to comfort us. Let us hasten to him while he waits to meet us.

SEPTEMBER 18

If we live in the Spirit, let us also walk in the Spirit.
—Galatians 5:25

T HE two most important things in our holy religion are the *life of faith* and the *walk of faith*. *He* who shall rightly understand these is not far from being a master in experimental theology, for they are vital points to a Christian. You will never find true faith unattended by true godliness; on the other hand, you will never discover a truly holy life which has not for its root a living faith upon the righteousness of Christ. Woe unto those who seek after the one without the other! There are some who cultivate faith and forget holiness; these may be very high in orthodoxy, but they shall be very deep in condemnation, for they hold the truth in unrighteousness; and there are others who have strained after holiness of life, but have denied the faith, like the Pharisees of old, of whom the Master said, they were "whitewashed sepulchers." We must have faith, for this is the foundation; we must have holiness of life, for this is the superstructure. Of what service is the mere foundation of a building to a man in the day of tempest? Can he hide himself therein? He wants a house to cover him, as well as a foundation for that house. Even so we need the superstructure of spiritual life if we would have comfort in the day of doubt. But seek not a holy life without faith, for that would be to erect a house which can afford no permanent shelter, because it has no foundation on a rock. Let faith and life be put together, and, like the two abutments of an arch, they will make our piety enduring. Like light and heat streaming from the same sun, they are alike full of blessing. Like the two pillars of the temple, they are for glory and for beauty. They are two streams from the fountain of grace; two lamps lit with holy fire; two olive trees watered by heavenly care. O Lord, give us this day life within, and it will reveal itself without to thy glory.

SEPTEMBER 19

The liberty wherewith Christ hath made us free.
—Galatians 5:1

THIS "liberty" makes us *free to* heaven's charter—*the Bible.* Here is a choice passage, believer, "When thou passest through the rivers I will be with thee." You are free to that. Here is another: "The mountains shall depart, and the hills be removed, but my kindness shall not depart from thee;" you are free to that. You are a welcome guest at the table of the promises. Scripture is a neverfailing treasury filled with boundless stores of grace. It is the bank of heaven; you may draw from it as much as you please, without let or hindrance. Come in faith and you are welcome to all *covenant blessings.* There is not a promise in the Word which shall be withheld. In the depths of tribulations let this freedom comfort you; amidst waves of distress let it cheer you; when sorrows surround thee let it be thy solace. This is thy Father's love-token; thou art free to it at all times. Thou art also *free to the throne of grace.* It is the believer's privilege to have access at all times to his heavenly Father. Whatever our desires, our difficulties, our wants, we are at liberty to spread all before him. It matters not how much we may have sinned, we may ask and expect pardon. It signifies nothing how poor we are, we may plead his promise that he will provide all things needful. We have permission to approach his throne at all times—in midnight's darkest hour, or in noontide's most burning heat. Exercise thy right, O believer, and live up to thy privilege. Thou art free to all that is treasured up *in Christ*—wisdom, righteousness, sanctification, and redemption. It matters not what thy need is, for there is fullness of supply in Christ, and it is there *for thee.* O what a "freedom" is thine! freedom from condemnation, freedom to the promises, freedom to the throne of grace, and at last freedom to enter heaven!

SEPTEMBER 20

The sword of the Lord, and of Gideon.
—Judges 7:20

IDEON ordered his men to do two things: covering up a torch in an earthen pitcher, he bade them, at an appointed signal, break the pitcher and let the light shine, and then sound with the trumpet, crying, "The sword of the Lord, and of Gideon! the sword of the Lord, and of Gideon!" This is precisely what all Christians must do. First, *you must shine;* break the pitcher which conceals your light; throw aside the bushel which has been hiding your candle, and shine. Let your light shine before men; let your good works be such, that when men look upon you, they shall know that you have been with Jesus. Then *there must be the sound,* the blowing of the trumpet. There must be active exertions for the ingathering of sinners by proclaiming Christ crucified. Take the gospel to them; carry it to their door; put it in their way; do not suffer them to escape it; blow the trumpet right against their ears. Remember that the true war-cry of the Church is Gideon's watchword, *"The sword of the Lord,* and of Gideon!" God must do it, it is his own work. But we are not to be idle; instrumentality is to be used—"The sword of the Lord, *and of Gideon!"* If we only cry, "The sword of the Lord!" we shall be guilty of an idle presumption; and if we shout, "The sword of Gideon!" alone, we shall manifest idolatrous reliance on an arm of flesh: we must blend the two in practical harmony, "The sword of the Lord, and of Gideon!" We can do nothing of ourselves, but we can do everything by the help of our God; let us, therefore, in his name determine to go out personally and serve with our flaming torch of holy example, and with our trumpet tones of earnest declaration and testimony, and God shall be with us, and Midian shall be put to confusion, and the Lord of hosts shall reign for ever and ever.

September 21

I will rejoice over them to do them good.
—Jeremiah 32:41

OW heart-cheering to the believer is the delight which God has in his saints! We cannot see any reason in ourselves why the Lord should take pleasure in us; we cannot take delight in ourselves, for we often have to groan, being burdened; conscious of our sinfulness, and deploring our unfaithfulness; and we fear that God's people cannot take much delight in us, for they must perceive so much of our imperfections and our follies, that they may rather lament our infirmities than admire our graces. But we love to dwell upon this transcendent truth, this glorious mystery: that as the bridegroom rejoiceth over the bride, so does the Lord rejoice over us. We do not read anywhere that God delighteth in the cloudcapped mountains, or the sparkling stars, but we do read that he delighteth in the habitable parts of the earth, and that his delights are with the sons of men. We do not find it written that even angels give his soul delight; nor doth he say, concerning cherubim and seraphim, "Thou shalt be called Hephzibah, for the Lord delighteth in thee;" but he does say all that to poor fallen creatures like ourselves, debased and depraved by sin, but saved, exalted, and glorified by his grace. In what strong language he expresses his delight in his people! Who could have conceived of the eternal One as bursting forth into a song? Yet it is written, "He will rejoice over thee with joy, he will rest in his love, he will joy over thee with singing." As he looked upon the world he had made, he said, "It is very good;" but when he beheld those who are the purchase of Jesus' blood, his own chosen ones, it seemed as if the great heart of the Infinite could restrain itself no longer, but overflowed in divine exclamations of joy. Should not we utter our grateful response to such a marvelous declaration of his love, and sing, "I will rejoice in the Lord, I will joy in the God of my salvation"?

SEPTEMBER 22

Let Israel rejoice in him.
—Psalm 149:2

BE glad of heart, O believer, but take care that thy gladness has its spring *in the Lord.* Thou hast much cause for gladness in thy God, for thou canst sing with David, "God, my exceeding joy." Be glad that the Lord reigneth, that Jehovah is King! Rejoice that he sits upon the throne, and ruleth all things! Every attribute of God should become a fresh ray in the sunlight of our gladness. That he is *wise* should make us glad, knowing as we do our own foolishness. That he is *mighty,* should cause us to rejoice who tremble at our weakness. That he is *everlasting,* should always be a theme of joy when we know that *we* wither as the grass. That he is *unchanging,* should perpetually yield us a song, since *we* change every hour. That he is full of grace, that he is overflowing with it, and that this grace in covenant he has given to us; that it is ours to cleanse us, ours to keep us, ours to sanctify us, ours to perfect us, ours to bring us to glory—all this should tend to make us glad in him. This gladness in God is as a deep river; we have only as yet touched its brink, we know a little of its clear sweet, heavenly streams, but onward the depth is greater, and the current more impetuous in its joy. The Christian feels that he may delight himself not only in what God *is,* but also in all that God *has done* in the past. The Psalms show us that God's people in olden times were wont to think much of God's actions, and to have a song concerning each of them. So let God's people now rehearse the deeds of the Lord! Let them tell of his mighty acts, and "sing unto the Lord, for he hath triumphed gloriously." Nor let them ever cease to sing, for as new mercies flow to them day by day, so should their gladness in the Lord's loving acts in providence and in grace show itself in continued thanksgiving. Be glad ye children of Zion and rejoice in the Lord your God.

September 23

Accepted in the beloved.
—Ephesians 1:6

WHAT a state of privilege! It includes our *justification* before God, but the term "acceptance" in the Greek means more than that. It signifies that we are the objects of *divine complacency*, nay, even of *divine delight*. How marvelous that we, worms, mortals, sinners, should be the objects of divine love! But it is only *"in the beloved."* Some Christians seem to be accepted in their own experience, at least, that is their apprehension. When their spirit is lively, and their hopes bright, they think God accepts them, for they feel so high, so heavenlyminded, so drawn above the earth! But when their souls cleave to the dust, they are the victims of the fear that they are no longer accepted. If they could but see that all their high joys do not exalt them, and all their low despondencies do not really depress them in their Father's sight, but that they stand accepted in One who never alters, in One who is always the beloved of God, always perfect, always without spot or wrinkle, or any such thing, how much happier they would be, and how much more they would honor the Savior! Rejoice then, believer, in this: thou art accepted "in the beloved." Thou lookest within, and thou sayest, "There is nothing acceptable *here!*" But look at Christ, and see if there is not everything acceptable *there.* Thy sins trouble thee; but God has cast thy sins behind his back, and thou art accepted in the Righteous One. Thou hast to fight with corruption, and to wrestle with temptation, but thou art already accepted in him who has overcome the powers of evil. The devil tempts thee; be of good cheer, he cannot destroy thee, for thou art accepted in him who has broken Satan's head. Know by full assurance thy glorious standing. Even glorified souls are not more accepted than thou art. They are only accepted in heaven "in the beloved," and thou art even now accepted in Christ after the same manner.

SEPTEMBER 24

*For I was ashamed to require of the king a band of soldiers
and horsemen to help us against the enemy in the way:
because we had spoken unto the king, saying,
"The hand of our God is upon all them for good that seek him;
but his power and his wrath is against all them that forsake him."
—Ezra 8:22*

A convoy on many accounts would have been desirable for the pilgrim band, but a holy shame-facedness would not allow Ezra to seek one. He feared lest the heathen king should think his professions of faith in God to be mere hypocrisy, or imagine that the God of Israel was not able to preserve his own worshippers. He could not bring his mind to lean on an arm of flesh in a matter so evidently of the Lord, and therefore the caravan set out with no visible protection, guarded by him who is the sword and shield of his people. It is to be feared that few believers feel this holy jealousy for God; even those who in a measure walk by faith, occasionally mar the luster of their life by craving aid from man. It is a most blessed thing to have no props and no buttresses, but to stand upright on the Rock of Ages, upheld by the Lord alone. Would any believers seek state endowments for their Church, if they remembered that the Lord is dishonored by their asking Caesar's aid? as if the Lord could not supply the needs of his own cause! Should we run so hastily to friends and relations for assistance, if we remembered that the Lord is magnified by our implicit reliance upon his solitary arm? My soul, wait thou only upon God. "But," says one, "are not means to be used?" Assuredly they are; but our fault seldom lies in their neglect: far more frequently it springs out of foolishly believing in them instead of believing in God. Few run too far in neglecting the creature's arm; but very many sin greatly in making too much of it. Learn, dear reader, to glorify the Lord by leaving means untried, if by using them thou wouldst dishonor the name of the Lord.

SEPTEMBER 25

Just, and the justifier of him which believeth.
—*Romans 3:26*

BEING justified by faith, we have peace with God. Conscience accuses no longer. Judgment now decides for the sinner instead of against him. Memory looks back upon past sins, with deep sorrow for the sin, but yet with no dread of any penalty to come; for Christ has paid the debt of his people to the last jot and tittle, and received the divine receipt; and unless God can be so unjust as to demand double payment for one debt, no soul for whom Jesus died as a substitute can ever be cast into hell. It seems to be one of the very principles of our enlightened nature to believe that God is just; we feel that it must be so, and this gives us our terror at first; but is it not marvelous that this very same belief that God is just, becomes afterwards the pillar of our confidence and peace! If God be just, I, a sinner, alone and without a substitute, must be punished; but Jesus stands in my stead and is punished for me; and now, if God be just, I, a sinner, standing in Christ, can never be punished. God must change his nature before one soul, for whom Jesus was a substitute, can ever by any possibility suffer the lash of the law. Therefore, Jesus having taken the place of the believer—having rendered a full equivalent to divine wrath for all that his people ought to have suffered as the result of sin, the believer can shout with glorious triumph, "Who shall lay anything to the charge of God's elect?" Not God, for he hath justified; not Christ, for he hath died, "yea rather hath risen again." My hope lives not because I am not a sinner, but because I am a sinner for whom Christ died; my trust is not that I am holy, but that being unholy, *he* is my righteousness. My faith rests not upon what I am, or shall be, or feel, or know, but in what Christ is, in what he has done, and in what he is now doing for me. On the lion of justice, the fair maid of hope rides like a queen.

SEPTEMBER 26

The myrtle trees that were in the bottom.
—Zechariah 1:8

THE vision in this chapter describes the condition of Israel in Zechariah's day; but being interpreted in its aspect towards *us*, it describes the Church of God as we find it now in the world. The Church is compared to a myrtle grove flourishing in a valley. It is *hidden*, unobserved, secreted; courting no honor and attracting no observation from the careless gazer. The Church, like her head, has a glory, but it is concealed from carnal eyes, for the time of her breaking forth in all her splendor is not yet come. The idea of *tranquil security* is also suggested to us: for the myrtle grove in the valley is still and calm, while the storm sweeps over the mountain summits. Tempests spend their force upon the craggy peaks of the Alps, but down yonder where flows the stream which maketh glad the city of our God, the myrtles flourish by the still waters, all unshaken by the impetuous wind. How great is the inward tranquility of God's Church! Even when opposed and persecuted, she has a peace which the world gives not, and which, therefore, it cannot take away: the peace of God which passeth all understanding keeps the hearts and minds of God's people. Does not the metaphor forcibly picture the peaceful, *perpetual growth* of the saints ? The myrtle sheds not her leaves, she is always green; and the Church in her worst time still hath a blessed verdure of grace about her; nay, she has sometimes exhibited *most* verdure when her winter has been sharpest. She has prospered most when her adversities have been most severe. Hence the text *hints at victory*. The myrtle is the emblem of peace, and a significant token of *triumph*. The brows of conquerors were bound with myrtle and with laurel; and is not the Church ever victorious? Is not every Christian more than a conqueror through him that loved him? Living in peace, do not the saints fall asleep in the arms of victory?

SEPTEMBER 27

Happy art thou, O Israel;
who is like unto thee, O people saved by the Lord!
—*Deuteronomy 33:29*

HE who affirms that Christianity makes men miserable, is himself an utter stranger to it. It were strange indeed, if it made us wretched, for see *to what a position it exalts us!* It makes us sons of God. Suppose you that God will give all the happiness to his enemies, and reserve all the mourning for his own family? Shall his foes have mirth and joy, and shall his homeborn children inherit sorrow and wretchedness? Shall the sinner, who has no part in Christ, call himself rich in happiness, and shall we go mourning as if we were penniless beggars? No, we will rejoice in the Lord always, and glory in our inheritance, for we "have not received the spirit of bondage again to fear; but we have received the spirit of adoption, whereby we cry, 'Abba, Father.'" The rod of chastisement must rest upon us in our measure, but it worketh for us the comfortable fruits of righteousness; and therefore by the aid of the divine Comforter, we, the "people saved of the Lord," will joy in the God of our salvation. We are married unto Christ; and shall our great Bridegroom permit his spouse to linger in constant grief? Our hearts are knit unto him: we are his members, and though for awhile we may suffer as our Head once suffered, yet we are even now blessed with heavenly blessings in him. We have the earnest of our inheritance in the comforts of the Spirit, which are neither few nor small. Heritors of joy forever, we have foretastes of our portion. There are streaks of the light of joy to herald our eternal sunrising. Our riches are beyond the sea; our city with firm foundations lies on the other side the river; gleams of glory from the spiritworld cheer our hearts, and urge us onward. Truly is it said of us, "Happy art thou, O Israel; who is like unto thee, O people saved by the Lord?"

SEPTEMBER 28

The Lord looketh from heaven; he beholdeth all the sons of men.
—Psalm 33:13

ERHAPS no figure of speech represents God in a more gracious light than when he is spoken of as stooping from his throne, and coming down from heaven to attend to the wants and to behold the woes of mankind. We love him, who, when Sodom and Gomorrah were full of iniquity, would not destroy those cities until he had made a personal visitation of them. We cannot help pouring out our heart in affection for our Lord who inclines his ear from the highest glory, and puts it to the lip of the dying sinner, whose failing heart longs after reconciliation. How can we but love him when we know that he numbers the very hairs of our heads, marks our path, and orders our ways? Specially is this great truth brought near to our heart, when we recollect how attentive he is, not merely to the temporal interests of his creatures, but to their spiritual concerns. Though leagues of distance lie between the finite creature and the infinite Creator, yet there are links uniting both. When a tear is wept by thee, think not that God doth not behold; for, "Like as a father pitieth his children, so the Lord pitieth them that fear him." Thy sigh is able to move the heart of Jehovah; thy whisper can incline his ear unto thee; thy prayer can stay his hand; thy faith can move his arm. Think not that God sits on high taking no account of thee. Remember that however poor and needy thou art, yet the Lord thinketh upon thee. For the eyes of the Lord run to and fro throughout the whole earth, to show himself strong in the behalf of them whose heart is perfect towards him.

> Oh! then repeat the truth that never tires;
> No God is like the God my soul desires;
> He at whose voice heaven trembles, even he,
> *Great as he is, knows how to stoop to me.*

September 29

Behold, if the leprosy have covered all his flesh,
he shall pronounce him clean, that hath the plague.
—Leviticus 13:13

STRANGE enough this regulation appears, yet there was wisdom in it, for the throwing out of the disease proved that the constitution was sound. This morning it may be well for us to see the typical teaching of so singular a rule. We, too, are lepers, and may read the law of leper as applicable to ourselves. When a man sees himself to be altogether lost and ruined, covered all over with the defilement of sin, and no part free from pollution; when he disclaims all righteousness of his own, and pleads guilty before the Lord, then is he clean through the blood of Jesus, and the grace of God. Hidden, unfelt, unconfessed iniquity is the true leprosy, but when sin is seen and felt it has received its death blow, and the Lord looks with eyes of mercy upon the soul afflicted with it. Nothing is more deadly than self-righteousness, or more hopeful than contrition. We must confess that we are "nothing else but sin," for no confession short of this will be the whole truth, and if the Holy Spirit be at work with us, convincing us of sin, there will be no difficulty about making such an acknowledgment—it will spring spontaneously from our lips. What comfort does the text afford to those under a deep sense of sin! Sin mourned and confessed, however black and foul, shall never shut a man out from the Lord Jesus. Whosoever cometh unto him, he will in no wise cast out. Though dishonest as the thief, though unchaste as the woman who was a sinner, though fierce as Saul of Tarsus, though cruel as Manasseh, though rebellious as the prodigal, the great heart of love will look upon the man who feels himself to have no soundness in him, and will pronounce him clean, when he trusts in Jesus crucified. Come to him, then, poor heavy-laden sinner,

> Come needy, come guilty, come loathsome and bare;
> You can't come too filthy—come just as you are.

SEPTEMBER 30

Sing forth the honor of his name, make his praise glorious.
—Psalm 66:2

I T is not left to our own option whether we shall praise God or not. Praise is God's most righteous due, and every Christian, as the recipient of his grace, is bound to praise God from day to day. It is true we have no authoritative rubric for daily praise; we have no commandment prescribing certain hours of song and thanksgiving: but the law written upon the heart teaches us that it is right to praise God; and the unwritten mandate comes to us with as much force as if it had been recorded on the tables of stone, or handed to us from the top of thundering Sinai. Yes, it is the Christian's *duty* to praise God. It is not only a pleasurable exercise, but it is the absolute obligation of his life. Think not ye who are always mourning, that ye are guiltless in this respect, or imagine that ye can discharge your duty to your God without songs of praise. You are bound by the bonds of his love to bless his name so long as you live, and his praise should continually be in your mouth, for you are blessed, in order that you may bless him; "this people have I formed for myself, they shall show forth my praise;" and if you do not praise God, you are not bringing forth the fruit which he, as the Divine Husbandman, has a right to expect at your hands. Let not your harp then hang upon the willows, but take it down, and strive, with a grateful heart, to bring forth its loudest music. Arise and chant his praise. With every morning's dawn, lift up your notes of thanksgiving, and let every setting sun be followed with your song. Girdle the earth with your praises; surround it with an atmosphere of melody, and God himself will hearken from heaven and accept your music.

> E'en so I love thee, and will love,
> And in thy praise will sing,
> Because thou art my loving God,
> And my redeeming King.

OCTOBER 1

Pleasant fruits, new and old, which I have laid up for thee, O my beloved.
—*Song of Solomon 7:13*

HE spouse desires to give to Jesus all that she produces. Our heart has "all manner of pleasant fruits," both "old and new," and they are laid up for our Beloved. At this rich autumnal season of fruit, let us survey our stores. We have *new* fruits. We desire to feel new life, new joy, new gratitude; we wish to make new resolves and carry them out by new labors; our heart blossoms with new prayers, and our soul is pledging herself to new efforts. But we have some *old* fruits too. There is our first love: a choice fruit that! and Jesus delights in it. There is our first faith: that simple faith by which, having nothing, we became possessors of all things. There is our joy when first we knew the Lord: let us revive it. We have our old remembrances of the promises. How faithful has God been! In sickness, how softly did he make our bed! In deep waters, how placidly did he buoy us up! In the flaming furnace, how graciously did he deliver us. Old fruits, indeed! We have many of them, for his mercies have been more than the hairs of our head. Old sins we must regret, but then we have had repentances which he has given us, by which we have wept our way to the cross, and learned the merit of his blood. We have fruits, this morning, both new and old; but here is the point—*they are all laid up for Jesus.* Truly, those are the best and most acceptable services in which Jesus is the solitary aim of the soul, and his glory, without any admixture whatever, the end of all our efforts. Let our many fruits be laid up only for our Beloved; let us display them when he is with us, and not hold them up before the gaze of men. Jesus, we will turn the key in our garden door, and none shall enter to rob thee of one good fruit from the soil which thou hast watered with thy bloody sweat. Our all shall be thine, thine only, O Jesus, our Beloved!

OCTOBER 2

The hope which is laid up for you in heaven.
—*Colossians 1:5*

OUR hope in Christ for the future is the mainspring and the mainstay of our joy here. It will animate our hearts to think often of heaven, for all that we can desire is promised there. Here we are weary and toilworn, but yonder is the land of *rest* where the sweat of labor shall no more bedew the worker's brow, and fatigue shall be forever banished. To those who are weary and spent, the word "rest" is full of heaven. We are always in the field of battle; we are so tempted within, and so molested by foes without, that we have little or no peace; but in heaven we shall enjoy the *victory*, when the banner shall be waved aloft in triumph, and the sword shall be sheathed, and we shall hear our Captain say, "Well done, good and faithful servant." We have suffered bereavement after bereavement, but we are going to the land of the *immortal* where graves are unknown things. Here sin is a constant grief to us, but there we shall be perfectly *holy*, for there shall by no means enter into that kingdom anything which defileth. Hemlock springs not up in the furrows of celestial fields. Oh! is it not joy, that you are not to be in banishment forever, that you are not to dwell eternally in this wilderness, but shall soon inherit Canaan? Nevertheless let it never be said of us, that we are dreaming about the *future* and forgetting the *present*, let the future sanctify the present to highest uses. Through the Spirit of God the hope of heaven is the most potent force for the product of virtue; it is a fountain of joyous effort, it is the corner stone of cheerful holiness. The man who has this hope in him goes about his work with vigor, for the joy of the Lord is his strength. He fights against temptation with ardor, for the hope of the next world repels the fiery darts of the adversary. He can labor without present reward, for he looks for a reward in the world to come.

OCTOBER 3

Are they not all ministering spirits, sent forth to minister
for them who shall be heirs of salvation?
—Hebrews 1:14

NGELS are the unseen attendants of the saints of God; they bear us up in their hands, lest we dash our foot against a stone. Loyalty to their Lord leads them to take a deep interest in the children of his love; they rejoice over the return of the prodigal to his father's house below, and they welcome the advent of the believer to the King's palace above. In olden times the sons of God were favored with their visible appearance, and at this day, although unseen by us, heaven is still opened, and the angels of God ascend and descend upon the Son of man, that they may visit the heirs of salvation. Seraphim still fly with live coals from off the altar to touch the lips of men greatly beloved. If our eyes could be opened, we should see horses of fire and chariots of fire about the servants of the Lord; for we have come to an innumerable company of angels, who are all watchers and protectors of the seed-royal. Spenser's line is no poetic fiction, where he sings—

> How oft do they with golden pinions cleave
> The flitting skies, like flying pursuivant
> Against foul fiends to aid us militant!

To what dignity are the chosen elevated when the brilliant courtiers of heaven become their willing servitors! Into what communion are we raised since we have intercourse with spotless celestials! How well are we defended since all the twenty-thousand chariots of God are armed for our deliverance! To whom do we owe all this? Let the Lord Jesus Christ be forever endeared to us, for through him we are made to sit in heavenly places far above principalities and powers. He it is whose camp is round about them that fear him; he is the true Michael whose foot is upon the dragon. All hail, Jesus! thou Angel of Jehovah's presence, to thee this family offers its morning vows.

OCTOBER 4

At evening time it shall be light.
—Zechariah 14:7

FTENTIMES we look forward with forebodings to *the time of old age,* forgetful that at eventide it shall be light. To many saints, old age is the choicest season in their lives. A balmier air fans the mariner's cheek as he nears the shore of immortality, fewer waves ruffle his sea, quiet reigns, deep, still and solemn. From the altar of age the flashes of the fire of youth are gone, but the more real flame of earnest feeling remains. The pilgrims have reached the land Beulah, that happy country, whose days are as the days of heaven upon earth. Angels visit it, celestial gales blow over it, flowers of paradise grow in it, and the air is filled with seraphic music. Some dwell here for years, and others come to it but a few hours before their departure, but it is an Eden on earth. We may well long for the time when we shall recline in its shady groves and be satisfied with hope until the time of fruition comes. The setting sun seems larger than when aloft in the sky, and a splendor of glory tinges all the clouds which surround his going down. Pain breaks not the calm of the sweet twilight of age, for strength made perfect in weakness bears up with patience under it all. Ripe fruits of choice experience are gathered as the rare repast of life's evening, and the soul prepares itself for rest.

The Lord's people shall also enjoy light in *the hour of death.* Unbelief laments; the shadows fall, the night is coming, existence is ending. Ah no, crieth faith, the night is far spent, the true day is at hand. Light is come, the light of immortality, the light of a Father's countenance. Gather up thy feet in the bed, see the waiting bands of spirits! Angels waft thee away. Farewell, beloved one, thou art gone, thou wavest thine hand. Ah, now it is light. The pearly gates are open, the golden streets shine in the jasper light. We cover our eyes, but thou beholdest the unseen; adieu, brother, thou hast light at even-tide, such as we have not yet.

October 5

He arose, and did eat and drink,
and went in the strength of that meat forty days and forty nights.
—1 Kings 19:8

ALL the strength supplied to us by our gracious God is meant for service, not for wantonness or boasting. When the prophet Elijah found the cake baked on the coals, and the cruse of water placed at his head, as he lay under the juniper tree, he was no gentleman to be gratified with dainty fare that he might stretch himself at his ease; far otherwise, he was commissioned to go forty days and forty nights in the strength of it, journeying towards Horeb, the mount of God. When the Master invited the disciples to "Come and dine" with him, after the feast was concluded he said to Peter, "Feed my sheep;" further adding, "Follow me." Even thus it is with us; we eat the bread of heaven, that we may expend our strength in the Master's service. We come to the Passover, and eat of the paschal lamb with loins girt, and staff in hand, so as to start off at once when we have satisfied our hunger. Some Christians are for living *on* Christ, but are not so anxious to live *for* Christ. Earth should be a preparation for heaven; and heaven is the place where saints feast most and work most. They sit down at the table of our Lord, and they serve him day and night in his temple. They eat of heavenly food and render perfect service. Believer, in the strength you daily gain from Christ labor for him. Some of us have yet to learn much concerning the design of our Lord in giving us his grace. We are not to retain the precious grains of truth as the Egyptian mummy held the wheat for ages, without giving it an opportunity to grow: we must sow it and water it. Why does the Lord send down the rain upon the thirsty earth, and give the genial sunshine? Is it not that these may all help the fruits of the earth to yield food for man? Even so the Lord feeds and refreshes our souls that we may afterwards use our renewed strength in the promotion of his glory.

OCTOBER 6

Whosoever drinketh of the water that I shall give him shall never thirst.
—John 4:14

HE who is a believer in Jesus finds enough in his Lord to satisfy him now, and to content him forevermore. The believer is not the man whose days are weary for want of comfort, and whose nights are long from absence of heart-cheering thought, for he finds in religion such a spring of joy, such a fountain of consolation, that he is content and happy. Put him in a dungeon and he will find good company; place him in a barren wilderness, he will eat the bread of heaven; drive him away from friendship, he will meet the "friend that sticketh closer than a brother." Blast all his gourds, and he will find shadow beneath the Rock of Ages; sap the foundation of his earthly hopes, but his heart will still be fixed, trusting in the Lord. The heart is as insatiable as the grave till Jesus enters it, and then it is a cup full to overflowing. There is such a fullness in Christ that he alone is the believer's all. The true saint is so completely satisfied with the all-sufficiency of Jesus that he thirsts no more—except it be for deeper draughts of the living fountain. In that sweet manner, believer, shalt thou thirst; it shall not be a thirst of pain, but of loving desire; thou wilt find it a sweet thing to be panting after a fuller enjoyment of Jesus' love. One in days of yore said,

> I have been sinking my bucket down into the well full often, but now my thirst after Jesus has become so insatiable, that I long to put the well itself to my lips, and drink right on.

Is this the feeling of thine heart now, believer? Dost thou feel that all thy desires are satisfied in Jesus, and that thou hast no want now, but to know more of him, and to have closer fellowship with him? Then come continually to the fountain, and take of the water of life freely. Jesus will never think you take too much, but will ever welcome you, saying, "Drink, yea, drink abundantly, O beloved."

October 7

Wherefore hast thou afflicted thy servant?
—Numbers 11:11

UR heavenly Father sends us frequent troubles *to try our faith.* If our faith be worth anything, it will stand the test. Gilt is afraid of fire, but gold is not: the *paste* gem dreads to be touched by the diamond, but the true jewel fears no test. It is a poor faith which can only trust God when friends are true, the body full of health, and the business profitable; but that is true faith which holds by the Lord's faithfulness when friends are gone, when the body is sick, when spirits are depressed, and the light of our Father's countenance is hidden. A faith which can say, in the direst trouble, "Though he slay me, yet will I trust in him," is heaven-born faith. The Lord afflicts his servants *to glorify himself,* for he is greatly glorified in the graces of his people, which are his own handiwork. When "tribulation worketh patience; and patience, experience; and experience, hope," the Lord is honored by these growing virtues. We should never know the music of the harp if the strings were left untouched; nor enjoy the juice of the grape if it were not trodden in the winepress; nor discover the sweet perfume of cinnamon if it were not pressed and beaten; nor feel the warmth of fire if the coals were not utterly consumed. The wisdom and power of the great Workman are discovered by the trials through which his vessels of mercy are permitted to pass. Present afflictions *tend also to heighten future joy.* There must be shades in the picture to bring out the beauty of the lights. Could we be so supremely blessed in heaven, if we had not known the curse of sin and the sorrow of earth? Will not peace be sweeter after conflict, and rest more welcome after toil? Will not the recollection of past sufferings enhance the bliss of the glorified? There are many other comfortable answers to the question with which we opened our brief meditation, let us muse upon it all day long.

OCTOBER 8

Launch out into the deep, and let down your nets for a draught.
—Luke 5:4

WE learn from this narrative, the *necessity of human agency*. The draught of fishes was miraculous, yet neither the fisherman nor his boat, nor his fishing tackle were ignored; but all were used to take the fishes. So in the saving of souls, God worketh by means; and while the present economy of grace shall stand, God will be pleased by the foolishness of preaching to save them that believe. When God worketh without instruments, doubtless he is glorified; but he hath himself selected the plan of instrumentality as being that by which he is most magnified in the earth. *Means of themselves are utterly unavailing.* "Master, we have toiled all the night and have taken nothing." What was the reason of this? Were they not fishermen plying their special calling? Verily, they were no raw hands; they understood the work. Had they gone about the toil unskillfully? No. Had they lacked industry? No, they had toiled. Had they lacked perseverance? No, they had *toiled all the night.* Was there a deficiency of fish in the sea? Certainly not, for as soon as the Master came, they swam to the net in shoals. What, then, is the reason? Is it because there is no power in the means of themselves apart from the presence of Jesus? "Without him we can do nothing." But with Christ we can do all things. *Christ's presence confers success.* Jesus sat in Peter's boat, and his will, by a mysterious influence, drew the fish to the net. When Jesus is lifted up in his Church, his presence is the Church's power—the shout of a king is in the midst of her. "I, if I be lifted up, will draw all men unto me." Let us go out this morning on our work of soul fishing, looking up in faith, and around us in solemn anxiety. Let us toil till night comes, and we shall not labor in vain, for he who bids us let down the net, will fill it with fishes.

OCTOBER 9

Able to keep you from falling.
—Jude 24

IN some sense the path to heaven is very safe, but in other respects there is *no road so dangerous.* It is beset with difficulties. One false step (and how easy it is to take that if grace be absent), and down we go. What a slippery path is that which some of us have to tread! How many times have we to exclaim with the Psalmist, "My feet were almost gone, my steps had well nigh slipped." If we were strong, sure-footed mountaineers, this would not matter so much; but in ourselves, *how weak we are!* In the best roads *we soon falter,* in the smoothest paths we quickly stumble. These feeble knees of ours can scarcely support our tottering weight. A straw may throw us, and a pebble can wound us; we are mere children tremblingly taking our first steps in the walk of faith, our heavenly Father holds us by the arms or we should soon be down. Oh, if we are kept from falling, how must we bless the patient power which watches over us day by day! Think, how prone we are to sin, how apt to choose danger, how strong our tendency to cast ourselves down, and these reflections will make us sing more sweetly than we have ever done, "Glory be to him, who is able to keep us from falling." *We have many foes* who try to push us down. The road is rough and we are weak, but in addition to this, enemies lurk in ambush, who rush out when we least expect them, and labor to trip us up, or hurl us down the nearest precipice. Only an Almighty arm can preserve us from these unseen foes, who are seeking to destroy us. Such an arm is engaged for our defense. He is faithful that hath promised, and he is able to keep us from falling, so that with a deep sense of our utter weakness, we may cherish a firm belief in our perfect safety, and say, with joyful confidence,

> Against me earth and hell combine,
> But on my side is power divine;
> Jesus is all, and he is mine!

OCTOBER 10

Faultless before the presence of his glory.
—Jude 24

REVOLVE in your mind that wondrous word, *"faultless!"* We are far off from it now; but as our Lord never stops short of perfection in his work of love, we shall reach it one day. The Savior who will keep his people to the end, will also present them at last to himself, as "a glorious church, not having spot, or wrinkle, or any such thing, but holy and without blemish." All the jewels in the Savior's crown are of the first water and without a single flaw. All the maids of honor who attend the Lamb's wife are pure virgins without spot or stain. But how will Jesus make us faultless? He will wash us from our sins in his own blood until we are white and fair as God's purest angel; and we shall be clothed in his righteousness, that righteousness which makes the saint who wears it positively faultless; yea, perfect in the sight of God. We shall be unblameable and unreproveable even in his eyes. His law will not only have no charge against us, but it will be magnified in us. Moreover, the work of the Holy Spirit within us will be altogether complete. He will make us so perfectly holy, that we shall have no lingering tendency to sin. Judgment, memory, will—every power and passion shall be emancipated from the thralldom of evil. We shall be holy even as God is holy, and in his presence we shall dwell forever. Saints will not be out of place in heaven, their beauty will be as great as that of the place prepared for them. Oh the rapture of that hour when the everlasting doors shall be lifted up, and we, being made meet for the inheritance, shall dwell with the saints in light. Sin gone, Satan shut out, temptation past for ever, and ourselves "faultless" before God, this will be heaven indeed! Let us be joyful now as we rehearse the song of eternal praise so soon to roll forth in full chorus from all the bloodwashed host; let us copy David's exultings before the ark as a prelude to our ecstasies before the throne.

OCTOBER 11

Let us lift up our heart with our hands unto God in the heavens.
—Lamentations 3:41

THE act of prayer *teaches us our unworthiness,* which is a very salutary lesson for such proud beings as we are. If God gave us favors without constraining us to pray for them we should never know how poor we are, but a true prayer is an inventory of wants, a catalogue of necessities, a revelation of hidden poverty. While it is an application to divine wealth, it is a confession of human emptiness. The most healthy state of a Christian is to be always empty in self and constantly depending upon the Lord for supplies; to be always poor in self and rich in Jesus; weak as water personally, but mighty through God to do great exploits; and hence the use of prayer, because, while it adores God, it lays the creature where it should be, in the very dust. Prayer is in itself, apart from the answer which it brings, a great benefit to the Christian. As the runner gains strength for the race by daily exercise, so for the great race of life we acquire energy by the hallowed labor of prayer. Prayer plumes the wings of God's young eaglets, that they may learn to mount above the clouds. Prayer girds the loins of God's warriors, and sends them forth to combat with their sinews braced and their muscles firm. An earnest pleader cometh out of his closet, even as the sun ariseth from the chambers of the east, rejoicing like a strong man to run his race. Prayer is that uplifted hand of Moses which routs the Amalekites more than the sword of Joshua; it is the arrow shot from the chamber of the prophet foreboding defeat to the Syrians. Prayer girds human weakness with divine strength, turns human folly into heavenly wisdom, and gives to troubled mortals the peace of God. We know not what prayer cannot do! We thank thee, great God, for the mercy-seat, a choice proof of thy marvelous lovingkindness. Help us to use it aright throughout this day!

OCTOBER 12

I will meditate in thy precepts.
—Psalm 119:15

THERE are times when solitude is better than society, and silence is wiser than speech. We should be better Christians if we were more alone, waiting upon God, and gathering through meditation on his Word spiritual strength for labor in his service. We ought to muse *upon the things of God, because we thus get the real nutriment out of them.* Truth is something like the cluster of the vine: if we would have wine from it, we must bruise it; we must press and squeeze it many times. The bruiser's feet must come down joyfully upon the bunches, or else the juice will not flow; and they must well tread the grapes, or else much of the precious liquid will be wasted. So we must, by meditation, tread the clusters of truth, if we would get the wine of consolation therefrom. Our bodies are not supported by merely taking food into the mouth, but the process which really supplies the muscle, and the nerve, and the sinew, and the bone, is the process of digestion. It is by digestion that the outward food becomes assimilated with the inner life. Our souls are not nourished merely by listening awhile to this, and then to that, and then to the other part of divine truth. Hearing, reading, marking, and learning, all require inwardly digesting to complete their usefulness, and the inward digesting of the truth lies for the most part in meditating upon it. Why is it that some Christians, although they hear many sermons, make but slow advances in the divine life? Because they neglect their closets, and do not thoughtfully meditate on God's Word. They love the wheat, but they do not grind it; they would have the corn, but they will not go forth into the fields to gather it; the fruit hangs upon the tree, but they will not pluck it; the water flows at their feet, but they will not stoop to drink it. From such folly deliver us, O Lord, and be this our resolve this morning, "I will meditate in thy precepts."

OCTOBER 13

Godly sorrow worketh repentance.
—*2 Corinthians 7:10*

ENUINE, spiritual mourning for sin is *the work of the Spirit of God*. Repentance is too choice a flower to grow in nature's garden. Pearls grow naturally in oysters, but penitence never shows itself in sinners except divine grace works it in them. If thou hast one particle of real hatred for sin, God must have given it thee, for human nature's thorns never produced a single fig. "That which is born of the flesh is flesh."

True repentance *has a distinct reference to the Savior*. When we repent of sin, we must have one eye upon sin and another upon the cross, or it will be better still if we fix both our eyes upon Christ and see our transgressions only, in the light of his love.

True sorrow for sin is *eminently practical*. No man may say he hates sin, if he lives in it. Repentance makes us see the evil of sin, not merely as a theory, but experimentally—as a burnt child dreads fire. We shall be as much afraid of it, as a man who has lately been stopped and robbed is afraid of the thief upon the highway; and we shall shun it—shun it in everything—not in great things only, but in little things, as men shun little vipers as well as great snakes. True mourning for sin will make us very jealous over our tongue, lest it should say a wrong word; we shall be very watchful over our daily actions, lest in anything we offend, and each night we shall close the day with painful confessions of shortcoming, and each morning awaken with anxious prayers, that this day God would hold us up that we may not sin against him.

Sincere repentance is *continual*. Believers repent until their dying day. This dropping well is not intermittent. Every other sorrow yields to time, but this dear sorrow grows with our growth, and it is so sweet a bitter, that we thank God we are permitted to enjoy and to suffer it until we enter our eternal rest.

OCTOBER 14

*I count all things but loss
for the excellency of the knowledge of Christ Jesus my Lord.
—Philippians 3:8*

PIRITUAL knowledge of Christ will be a *personal* knowledge. I cannot know Jesus through another person's acquaintance with him. No, I must know him *myself;* I must know him on my own account. It will be an *intelligent* knowledge—I must know *him,* not as the visionary dreams of him, but as the Word reveals him. I must know his natures, divine and human. I must know his offices—his attributes—his works—his shame—his glory. I must meditate upon him until I,

> . . . comprehend with all saints what is the breadth, and length, and depth, and height; and know the love of Christ, which passeth knowledge.

It will be an *affectionate* knowledge of him; indeed, if I know him at all, I must love him. An ounce of heart knowledge is worth a ton of head learning. Our knowledge of him will be a *satisfying* knowledge. When I know my Savior, my mind will be full to the brim—I shall feel that I have that which my spirit panted after. "This is that bread whereof if a man eat he shall never hunger." At the same time it will be an *exciting* knowledge; the more I know of my Beloved, the more I shall want to know. The higher I climb the loftier will be the summits which invite my eager footsteps. I shall want the more as I get the more. Like the miser's treasure, my gold will make me covet more. To conclude; this knowledge of Christ Jesus will be a most *happy* one; in fact, so elevating, that sometimes it will completely bear me up above all trials, and doubts, and sorrows; and it will, while I enjoy it, make me something more than "Man that is born of woman, who is of few days, and full of trouble;" for it will fling about me the immortality of the everliving Savior, and gird me with the golden girdle of his eternal joy. Come, my soul, sit at Jesus' feet and learn of him all this day.

OCTOBER 15

But who may abide the day of His coming?
—Malachi 3:2

IS first coming was without external pomp or show of power, and yet in truth there were few who could abide its testing might. Herod and all Jerusalem with him were stirred at the news of the wondrous birth. Those who supposed themselves to be waiting for him, showed the fallacy of their professions by rejecting him when he came. His life on earth was a winnowing fan, which tried the great heap of religious profession, and few enough could abide the process. But what will his second advent be? What sinner can endure to think of it? "He shall smite the earth with the rod of his mouth, and with the breath of his lips shall he slay the wicked." When in his humiliation he did but say to the soldiers, "I am he," they fell backward; what will be the terror of his enemies when he shall more fully reveal himself as the "*I am*"? His death shook earth and darkened heaven, what shall be the dreadful splendor of that day in which as the living Savior, he shall summon the quick and dead before him? O that the terrors of the Lord would persuade men to forsake their sins and kiss the Son lest he be angry! Though a lamb, he is yet the lion of the tribe of Judah, rending the prey in pieces; and though he breaks not the bruised reed, yet will he break his enemies with a rod of iron, and dash them in pieces like a potter's vessel. None of his foes shall bear up before the tempest of his wrath, or hide themselves from the sweeping hail of his indignation; but his beloved bloodwashed people look for his appearing with joy, and hope to abide it without fear: to them he sits as a refiner even now, and when he has tried them they shall come forth as gold. Let us search ourselves this morning and make our calling and election sure, so that the coming of the Lord may cause no dark forebodings in our mind. O for grace to cast away all hypocrisy, and to be found of him sincere and without rebuke in the day of his appearing.

OCTOBER 16

Jesus saith unto them, "Come and dine."
—John 21:12

N these words the believer is invited to a holy *nearness to Jesus*. "Come and dine," implies the same table, the same meat; ay, and sometimes it means to sit side by side, and lean our head upon the Savior's bosom. It is being brought into the banqueting-house, where waves the banner of redeeming love. "Come and dine," gives us a vision of *union with Jesus*, because the only food that we can feast upon when we dine with Jesus is *himself*. Oh, what union is this! It is a depth which reason cannot fathom, that we thus feed upon Jesus. "He that eateth my flesh, and drinketh my blood, dwelleth in me, and I in him." It is also an invitation to enjoy *fellowship with the saints*. Christians may differ on a variety of points, but they have all one spiritual appetite; and if we cannot all *feel* alike, we can all *feed* alike on the bread of life sent down from heaven. At the table of fellowship with Jesus we are one bread and one cup. As the loving cup goes round we pledge one another heartily therein. Get nearer to Jesus, and you will find yourself linked more and more in spirit to all who are like yourself, supported by the same heavenly manna. If we were more near to Jesus we should be more near to one another. We likewise see in these words the *source of strength* for every Christian. To look at Christ is to live, but for strength to serve him you must "come and dine." We labor under much unnecessary weakness on account of neglecting this precept of the Master. We none of us need to put ourselves on low diet; on the contrary, we should fatten on the marrow and fatness of the gospel that we may accumulate strength therein, and urge every power to its full tension in the Master's service. Thus, then, if you would realize *nearness* to Jesus, *union* with Jesus, *love* to his people and *strength from Jesus*, "come and dine" with him by faith.

🌿

OCTOBER 17

And David said in his heart,
"I shall now perish one day by the hand of Saul."
—1 Samuel 27:1

HE thought of David's heart at this time was a *false* thought, because he certainly had no ground for thinking that God's anointing him by Samuel was intended to be left as an empty unmeaning act. On no one occasion had the Lord deserted his servant; he had been placed in perilous positions very often, but not one instance had occurred in which divine interposition had not delivered him. The trials to which he had been exposed had been varied; they had not assumed one form only, but many—yet in every case he who sent the trial had also graciously ordained a way of escape. David could not put his finger upon any entry in his diary, and say of it, "Here is evidence that the Lord will forsake me," for the entire tenor of his past life proved the very reverse. He should have argued from what God *had* done for him, that God would be his defender still. But is it not just in the same way that *we* doubt God's help? Is it not *mistrust without a cause?* Have we ever had the shadow of a reason to doubt our Father's goodness? Have not his lovingkindnesses been marvelous? Has he *once* failed to justify our trust? Ah, no! our God has not left us at any time. We have had dark nights, but the star of love has shone forth amid the blackness; we have been in stern conflicts, but over our head he has held aloft the shield of our defense. We have gone through many trials, but never to our detriment, always to our advantage; and the conclusion from our past experience is, that he who has been with us in six troubles, will not forsake us in the seventh. What we have known of our faithful God, proves that he will keep us to the end. Let us not, then, reason contrary to evidence. How can we ever be so ungenerous as to *doubt* our God? Lord, throw down the Jezebel of our unbelief, and let the dogs devour it.

OCTOBER 18

Thy paths drop fatness.
—Psalm 65:11

MANY are "the paths of the Lord" which "drop fatness," but an especial one is the *path of* prayer. No believer, who is much in the closet, will have need to cry, "My leanness, my leanness; woe unto me." Starving souls live at a distance from the mercy-seat, and become like the parched fields in times of drought. Prevalence with God in wrestling prayer is sure to make the believer strong—if not happy. The nearest place to the gate of heaven is the throne of the heavenly grace. Much alone, and you will have much assurance; little alone with Jesus, your religion will be shallow, polluted with many doubts and fears, and not sparkling with the joy of the Lord. Since the soulenriching path of prayer is open to the very weakest saint; since no high attainments are required; since you are not bidden to come because you are an advanced saint, but freely invited if you be a saint at all; see to it, dear reader, that you are often in the way of private devotion. Be much on your knees, for so Elijah drew the rain upon famished Israel's fields.

There is another especial path dropping with fatness to those who walk therein, it is the secret walk of *communion.* Oh! the delights of fellowship with Jesus! Earth hath no words which can set forth the holy calm of a soul leaning on Jesus' bosom. Few Christians understand it, they live in the lowlands and seldom climb to the top of Nebo: they live in the outer court, they enter not the holy place, they take not up the privilege of priesthood. At a distance they see the sacrifice, but they sit not down with the priest to eat thereof, and to enjoy the fat of the burnt offering. But, reader, sit thou ever under the shadow of Jesus; come up to that palm tree, and take hold of the branches thereof; let thy beloved be unto thee as the apple-tree among the trees of the wood, and thou shalt be satisfied as with marrow and fatness. O Jesus, visit us with thy salvation!

OCTOBER 19

Babes in Christ.
—1 Corinthians 3:1

RE you mourning, believer, because you are so weak in the divine life: because your faith is so little, your love so feeble? Cheer up, for you have cause for gratitude. Remember *that in some things you are equal to the greatest and most full-grown Christian.* You are as much bought with blood as he is. You are as much an adopted child of God as any other believer. An infant is as truly a child of its parents as is the full-grown man. You are as completely justified, for your justification is not a thing of degrees: your little faith has made you clean every whit. You have as much right to the precious things of the covenant as the most advanced believers, for your right to covenant mercies lies not in your growth, but in the covenant itself; and your faith in Jesus is not the measure, but the token of your inheritance in him. You are as rich as the richest, if not in enjoyment, yet in real possession. The smallest star that gleams is set in heaven; the faintest ray of light has affinity with the great orb of day. In the family register of glory the small and the great are written with the same pen. You are as dear to your Father's heart as the greatest in the family. Jesus is very tender over you. You are like the smoking flax; a rougher spirit would say, "put out that smoking flax, it fills the room with an offensive odor!" but the smoking flax *he* will not quench. You are like a bruised reed; and any less tender hand than that of the Chief Musician would tread upon you or throw you away, but he will never break the bruised reed. Instead of being downcast by reason of what you are, you should triumph in Christ. Am I but little in Israel? Yet in Christ I am made to sit in heavenly places. Am I poor in faith? Still in Jesus I am heir of all things. Though "less than nothing I can boast, and vanity confess," yet, if the root of the matter be in me I will rejoice in the Lord, and glory in the God of my salvation.

OCTOBER 20

Grow up into him in all things.
—Ephesians 4:15

ANY Christians remain stunted and dwarfed in spiritual things, so as to present the same appearance year after year. No up-springing of advanced and refined feeling is manifest in them. They *exist* but do not *"grow up into him in all things."* But should we rest content with being in the "green blade," when we might advance to "the ear," and eventually ripen into the "full corn in the ear"? Should we be satisfied to believe in Christ, and to say, "I am safe," without wishing to know in our own experience more of the fullness which is to be found in him. It should not be so; we should, as good traders in heaven's market, covet to be enriched in the knowledge of Jesus. It is all very well to keep other men's vineyards, but we must not neglect our own spiritual growth and ripening. Why should it always be winter time in our hearts? We must have our seed time, it is true, but O for a spring time—yea, a summer season, which shall give promise of an early harvest. If we would ripen in grace, we must live near to Jesus—in his presence—ripened by the sunshine of his smiles. We must hold sweet communion with him. We must leave the distant view of his face and come near, as John did, and pillow our head on his breast; then shall we find ourselves advancing in holiness, in love, in faith, in hope—yea, in every precious gift. As the sun rises first on mountain-tops and gilds them with his light, and presents one of the most charming sights to the eye of the traveler; so is it one of the most delightful contemplations in the world to mark the glow of the Spirit's light on the head of some saint, who has risen up in spiritual stature, like Saul, above his fellows, till, like a mighty Alp, snowcapped, he reflects first among the chosen, the beams of the Sun of Righteousness, and bears the sheen of his effulgence high aloft for all to see, and seeing it, to glorify his Father which is in heaven.

OCTOBER 21

The love of Christ constraineth us.
—2 Corinthians 5:14

OW much owest thou unto my Lord? Has he ever done anything for thee? Has he forgiven thy sins? Has he covered thee with a robe of righteousness? Has he set thy feet upon a rock? Has he established thy goings? Has he prepared heaven for thee? Has he prepared thee for heaven? Has he written thy name in his book of life? Has he given thee countless blessings? Has he laid up for thee a store of mercies, which eye hath not seen nor ear heard? Then do something for Jesus worthy of his love. Give not a mere wordy offering to a dying Redeemer. How will you feel when your Master comes, if you have to confess that you *did* nothing for him, but kept your love shut up, like a stagnant pool, neither flowing forth to his poor or to his work. Out on such love as that! What do men think of a love which never shows itself in action? Why, they say, "Open rebuke is better than secret love." Who will accept a love so weak that it does not actuate you to a single deed of self-denial, of generosity, of heroism, or zeal! Think how *he* has loved you, and given himself for you! Do you know the power of that love? Then let it be like a rushing mighty wind to your soul to sweep out the clouds of your worldliness, and clear away the mists of sin. "For Christ's sake" be this the tongue of fire that shall sit upon you: "for Christ's sake" be this the divine rapture, the heavenly afflatus to bear you aloft from earth, the divine spirit that shall make you bold as lions and swift as eagles in your Lord's service. Love should give wings to the feet of service, and strength to the arms of labor. Fixed on God with a constancy that is not to be shaken, resolute to honor him with a determination that is not to be turned aside, and pressing on with an ardor never to be wearied, let us manifest the constraints of love to Jesus. May the divine loadstone draw us heavenward towards itself!

OCTOBER 22

I will love them freely.
—Hosea 14:4

THIS sentence is a body of divinity in miniature. He who understands its meaning is a theologian, and he who can dive into its fullness is a true master in Israel. It is a condensation of the glorious message of salvation which was delivered to us in Christ Jesus our Redeemer. The sense hinges upon the word "freely." This is the glorious, the suitable, the divine way by which love streams from heaven to earth, a spontaneous love flowing forth to those who neither deserved it, purchased it, nor sought after it. It is, indeed, the only way in which God can love such as we are. The text is a death-blow to all sorts of fitness: "I will love them *freely*." Now, if there were any fitness necessary in us, then he would not love us freely, at least, this would be a mitigation and a drawback to the freeness of it. But it stands, "I will love you *freely*." We complain, "Lord, my heart is so hard." "I will love you freely." "But I do not feel my need of Christ as I could wish." "I will not love you because you feel your need; I will love you freely." "But I do not feel that softening of spirit which I could desire." Remember, the softening of spirit is not a condition, for there are no conditions; the covenant of grace has no conditionality whatever; so that we without any fitness may venture upon the promise of God which was made to us in Christ Jesus, when he said, "He that believeth on him is not condemned." It is blessed to know that the grace of God is free to us at all times, without preparation, without fitness, without money, and without price! "I will love them freely." These words *invite backsliders to return:* indeed, the text was specially written for such—"I will heal their backsliding; I will love them freely." Backslider! surely the generosity of the promise will at once break your heart, and you will return, and seek your injured Father's face.

October 23

Will ye also go away?
—John 6:67

MANY have forsaken Christ, and have walked no more with him; but *what reason have* YOU *to make a change?* Has there been any reason for it in the *past?* Has not Jesus proved himself all-sufficient? He appeals to you this morning—"Have I been a wilderness unto you?" When your soul has simply trusted Jesus, have you ever been confounded? Have you not up till now found your Lord to be a compassionate and generous friend to you, and has not simple faith in him given you all the peace your spirit could desire? Can you so much as dream of a better friend than he has been to you? Then change not the old and tried for new and false. As for *the present,* can that compel you to leave Christ? When we are hard beset with this world, or with the severer trials within the Church, we find it a most blessed thing to pillow our head upon the bosom of our Savior. This is the joy we have today that we are saved in him; and if this joy be satisfying, wherefore should we think of changing? Who barters gold for dross? We will not forswear the sun till we find a better light, nor leave our Lord until a brighter lover shall appear; and, since this can never be, we will hold him with a grasp immortal, and bind his name as a seal upon our arm. As for *the future,* can you suggest anything which can arise that shall render it necessary for you to mutiny, or desert the old flag to serve under another captain? We think not. If life be long—he changes not. If we are poor, what better than to have Christ who can make us rich? When we are sick, what more do we want than Jesus to make our bed in our sickness? When we die, is it not written that

> neither death, nor life, nor things present, nor things to come, shall
> be able to separate us from the love of God, which is in Christ Jesus
> our Lord!

We say with Peter, "Lord, to whom shall we go?"

OCTOBER 24

The trees of the Lord are full of sap.
—Psalm 104:16

WITHOUT sap the tree cannot flourish or even exist. *Vitality* is essential to a Christian. There must be *life*—a vital principle infused into us by God the Holy Ghost, or we cannot be trees of the Lord. The mere name of being a Christian is but a dead thing, we must be filled with the spirit of divine life. This life is *mysterious*. We do not understand the circulation of the sap, by what force it rises, and by what power it descends again. So the life within us is a sacred mystery. Regeneration is wrought by the Holy Ghost entering into man and becoming man's life; and this divine life in a believer afterwards feeds upon the flesh and blood of Christ and is thus sustained by divine food, but whence it cometh and whither it goeth who shall explain to us? What a *secret* thing the sap is! The roots go searching through the soil with their little spongioles, but we cannot see them suck out the various gases, or transmute the mineral into the vegetable; this work is done down in the dark. Our root is Christ Jesus, and our life is hid in him; this is the secret of the Lord. The radix of the Christian life is as secret as the life itself. How *permanently active* is the sap in the cedar! In the Christian the divine life is always full of energy—not always in fruit-bearing, but in inward operations. The believer's *graces*, are not every one of them in constant motion? but his life never ceases to palpitate within. He is not always working for God, but his heart is always living upon him. As the sap *manifests itself in producing the foliage and fruit of the tree,* so with a truly healthy Christian, his grace is externally manifested in his walk and conversation. If you talk with him, he cannot help speaking about Jesus. If you notice his actions you will see that he has been with Jesus. He has so much sap within, that it must fill his conduct and conversation with life.

OCTOBER 25

For the truth's sake, which dwelleth in us, and shall be with us forever.
—2 John 2

ONCE let the truth of God obtain an entrance into the human heart and subdue the whole man unto itself, no power human or infernal can dislodge it. We entertain it not as a guest but as the master of the house—this is a *Christian necessity*, he is no Christian who doth not thus believe. Those who feel the vital power of the gospel, and know the might of the Holy Ghost as he opens, applies, and seals the Lord's Word, would sooner be torn to pieces than be rent away from the gospel of their salvation. What a thousand mercies are wrapt up in the assurance that the truth will be with us forever; will be our living support, our dying comfort, our rising song, our eternal glory; this is *Christian privilege*, without it our faith were little worth. Some truths we outgrow and leave behind, for they are but rudiments and lessons for beginners, but we cannot thus deal with Divine truth, for though it is sweet food for babes, it is in the highest sense strong meat for men. The truth that we are sinners is painfully with us to humble and make us watchful; the more blessed truth that whosoever believeth on the Lord Jesus shall be saved, abides with us as our hope and joy. Experience, so far from loosening our hold of the doctrines of grace, has knit us to them more and more firmly; our grounds and motives for believing are now more strong, more numerous than ever, and we have reason to expect that it will be so till in death we clasp the Savior in our arms.

Wherever this abiding love of truth can be discovered, we are bound to exercise our love. No narrow circle can contain our gracious sympathies, wide as the election of grace must be our communion of heart. Much of error may be mingled with truth received, let us war with the error but still love the brother for the measure of truth which we see in him; above all let us love and spread the truth ourselves.

OCTOBER 26

"Ye looked for much, and, lo, it came to little; and when ye
brought it home, I did blow upon it. Why?" saith the Lord of hosts.
"Because of mine house, that is waste,
and ye run every man unto his own house."
—Haggai 1:9

CHURLISH souls stint their contributions to the ministry and missionary operations, and call such saving good economy; little do they dream that they are thus impoverishing themselves. Their excuse is that they must care for their own families, and they forget that to neglect the house of God is the sure way to bring ruin upon their own houses. Our God has a method in providence by which he can succeed our endeavors beyond our expectation, or can defeat our plans to our confusion and dismay; by a turn of his hand he can steer our vessel in a profitable channel, or run it aground in poverty and bankruptcy. It is the teaching of Scripture that the Lord enriches the liberal and leaves the miserly to find out that withholding tendeth to poverty. In a very wide sphere of observation, I have noticed that the most generous Christians of my acquaintance have been always the most happy, and almost invariably the most prosperous. I have seen the liberal giver rise to wealth of which he never dreamed; and I have as often seen the mean, ungenerous churl descend to poverty by the very parsimony by which he thought to rise. Men trust good stewards with larger and larger sums, and so it frequently is with the Lord; he gives by cartloads to those who give by bushels. Where wealth is not bestowed the Lord makes the little much by the contentment which the sanctified heart feels in a portion of which the tithe has been dedicated to the Lord. Selfishness looks first at home, but godliness seeks first the kingdom of God and his righteousness, yet in the long run selfishness is loss, and godliness is great gain. It needs faith to act towards our God with an open hand, but surely he deserves it of us; and all that we can do is a very poor acknowledgment of our amazing indebtedness to his goodness.

OCTOBER 27

It is a faithful saying.
—2 Timothy 2:11

AUL has four of these *"faithful sayings."* The first occurs in 1 Timothy 1:15, "This is a faithful saying, and worthy of all acceptation, that Christ Jesus came into the world to save sinners." The next is in 1 Timothy 4:8–9,

> Godliness is profitable unto all things, having the promise of the life that now is, and of that which is to come. This is a faithful saying, and worthy of all acceptation

The third is in 2 Timothy 2:12, "It is a faithful saying—If we suffer with him we shall also reign with him;" and the fourth is in Titus 3:8, "This is a faithful saying, that they which have believed in God might be careful to maintain good works." We may trace a connection between these faithful sayings. The first one lays the foundation of our eternal salvation in the free grace of God, as shown to us in the mission of the great Redeemer. The next affirms the double blessedness which we obtain through this salvation—the blessings of the upper and nether springs—of time and of eternity. The third shows one of the duties to which the chosen people are called; we are ordained to suffer for Christ with the promise that "if we suffer, we shall also reign with him." The last sets forth the active form of Christian service, bidding us diligently to maintain good works. Thus we have the root of salvation in free grace; next, the privileges of that salvation in the life which now is, and in that which is to come; and we have also the two great branches of suffering with Christ and serving with Christ, loaded with the fruits of the Spirit. Treasure up these faithful sayings. Let them be the guides of our life, our comfort, and our instruction. The apostle of the Gentiles proved them to be faithful, they are faithful still, not one word shall fall to the ground; they are worthy of all acceptation, let us accept them now, and prove their faithfulness. Let these four faithful sayings be written on the four corners of my house.

OCTOBER 28

I have chosen you out of the world.
—John 15:19

ERE is distinguishing grace and discriminating regard; for some are made the special objects of divine affection. Do not be afraid to dwell upon this high doctrine of election. When your mind is most heavy and depressed, you will find it to be a bottle of richest cordial. Those who doubt the doctrines of grace, or who cast them into the shade, miss the richest clusters of Eshcol; they lose the wines on the lees well refined, the fat things full of marrow. There is no balm in Gilead comparable to it. If the honey in Jonathan's wood when but touched enlightened *the eyes,* this is honey which will enlighten *your heart* to love and learn the mysteries of the kingdom of God. Eat, and fear not a surfeit; live upon this choice dainty, and fear not that it will be too delicate a diet. Meat from the King's table will hurt none of his courtiers. Desire to have your mind enlarged, that you may comprehend more and more the eternal, everlasting, discriminating love of God. When you have mounted as high as election, tarry on its sister mount, the covenant of grace. Covenant engagements are the munitions of stupendous rock behind which we lie entrenched; covenant engagements with the surety, Christ Jesus, are the quiet resting places of trembling spirits.

> His oath, his covenant, his blood,
> Support me in the raging flood;
> When every earthly prop gives way,
> This still is all my strength and stay.

If Jesus undertook to bring me to glory, and if the Father promised that he would give me to the Son to be a part of the infinite reward of the travail of his soul; then, my soul, till God himself shall be unfaithful, till Jesus shall cease to be the truth, thou art safe. When David danced before the ark, he told Michal that election made him do so. Come, my soul, exult before the God of grace and leap for joy of heart.

October 29

After this manner therefore pray ye:
"Our Father which art in heaven . . ."
—Matthew 6:9

THIS prayer begins where all true prayer must commence, with the spirit of *adoption*, "Our Father." There is no acceptable prayer until we can say, "I will arise, and go unto my Father." This child-like spirit soon perceives the grandeur of the Father "in heaven," and ascends to *devout adoration*, "Hallowed be thy name." The child lisping, "Abba, Father," grows into the cherub crying, "Holy, Holy, Holy." There is but a step from rapturous worship to the *glowing missionary spirit*, which is a sure outgrowth of filial love and reverent adoration—"Thy kingdom come, thy will be done on earth as it is in heaven." Next follows the heartfelt *expression of dependence* upon God:"Give us this day our daily bread." Being further illuminated by the Spirit, he discovers that he is not only dependent, but sinful, hence he *entreats for mercy*, "Forgive us our debts as we forgive our debtors:" and being pardoned, having the righteousness of Christ imputed, and knowing his acceptance with God, he humbly *supplicates for holy perseverance*, "Lead us not into temptation." The man who is really forgiven, is anxious not to offend again; the possession of justification leads to an anxious desire for sanctification. "Forgive us our debts," that is justification; "Lead us not into temptation, but deliver us from evil," that is sanctification in its negative and positive forms. As the result of all this, there follows a *triumphant ascription of praise*, "Thine is the kingdom, the power, and the glory, forever and ever, Amen." We rejoice that *our* King reigns in providence and shall reign in grace, from the river even to the ends of the earth, and of his dominion there shall be no end. Thus from a sense of adoption, up to fellowship with our reigning Lord, this short model of prayer conducts the soul. Lord, teach us thus to pray.

OCTOBER 30

I will praise thee, O Lord.
—Psalm 9:1

RAISE should always follow answered prayer; as the mist of earth's gratitude rises when the sun of heaven's love warms the ground. Hath the Lord been gracious to thee, and inclined his ear to the voice of thy supplication? Then praise him as long as thou livest. Let the ripe fruit drop upon the fertile soil from which it drew its life. Deny not a song to him who hath answered thy prayer and given thee the desire of thy heart. To be silent over God's mercies is to incur the guilt of ingratitude; it is to act as basely as the nine lepers, who after they had been cured of their leprosy, returned not to give thanks unto the healing Lord. To forget to praise God is to refuse to benefit ourselves; for praise, like prayer, is one great means of promoting the growth of the spiritual life. It helps to remove our burdens, to excite our hope, to increase our faith. It is a healthful and invigorating exercise which quickens the pulse of the believer, and nerves him for fresh enterprises in his Master's service. To bless God for mercies received is also the way to benefit our fellow-men; "the humble shall hear thereof and be glad." Others who have been in like circumstances shall take comfort if we can say, "Oh! magnify the Lord with me, and let us exalt his name together; this poor man cried, and the Lord heard him." Weak hearts will be strengthened, and drooping saints will be revived as they listen to our "songs of deliverance." Their doubts and fears will be rebuked, as we teach and admonish one another in psalms and hymns and spiritual songs. They too shall "sing in the ways of the Lord," when they hear us magnify his holy name. Praise is the most heavenly of Christian duties. The angels pray not, but they cease not to praise both day and night; and the redeemed, clothed in white robes, with palm-branches in their hands, are never weary of singing the new song, "Worthy is the Lamb."

OCTOBER 31

Renew a right spirit within me.
—Psalm 51:10

backslider, if there be a spark of life left in him will groan after restoration. In this renewal the same exercise of grace is required as at our conversion. We needed repentance then; we certainly need it now. We wanted faith that we might come to Christ at first; only the like grace can bring us to Jesus now. We wanted a word from the Most High, a word from the lip of the loving One, to end our fears then; we shall soon discover, when under a sense of present sin, that we need it now. No man can be renewed without as real and true a manifestation of the Holy Spirit's energy as he felt at first, because the work is as great, and flesh and blood are as much in the way now as ever they were. Let thy personal weakness, O Christian, be an argument to make thee pray earnestly to thy God for help. Remember, David when he felt himself to be powerless, did not fold his arms or close his lips, but he hastened to the mercy-seat with "renew a right spirit within me." Let not the doctrine that you, unaided, can do nothing, make you sleep; but let it be a goad in your side to drive you with an awful earnestness to Israel's strong Helper. O that you may have grace to plead with God, as though you pleaded for your very life—"Lord, renew a right spirit within me." He who *sincerely* prays to God to do this, will prove his honesty by using the means through which God works. Be much in prayer; live much upon the Word of God; kill the lusts which have driven your Lord from you; be careful to watch over the future uprisings of sin. The Lord has his own appointed ways; sit by the wayside and you will be ready when he passes by. Continue in all those blessed ordinances which will foster and nourish your dying graces; and, knowing that all the power must proceed from him, cease not to cry, "Renew a right spirit within me."

November 1

The Church in thy house.
—Philemon 2

S there a Church in this house? Are parents, children, friends, servants, all members of it? or are some still unconverted? Let us pause here and let the question go round—*Am I a member of the Church in this house?* How would father's heart leap for joy, and mother's eyes fill with holy tears if from the eldest to the youngest all were saved! Let us pray for this great mercy until the Lord shall grant it to us. Probably it had been the dearest object of Philemon's desires to have all his household saved; but it was not at first granted him in its fullness. He had a wicked servant, Onesimus, who, having wronged him, ran away from his service. His master's prayers followed him, and at last, as God would have it, Onesimus was led to hear Paul preach; his heart was touched, and he returned to Philemon, not only to be a faithful servant, but a brother beloved, adding another member to the Church in Philemon's house. Is there an unconverted servant or child absent this morning? Make special supplication that such may, on their return to their home, gladden all hearts with good news of what grace has done! Is there one present? Let him partake in the same earnest entreaty.

If there be such a Church in our house, let us order it well, and let all act as in the sight of God. Let us move in the common affairs of life with studied holiness, diligence, kindness, and integrity. More is expected of a Church than of an ordinary household; family worship must, in such a case, be more devout and hearty; internal love must be more warm and unbroken, and external conduct must be more sanctified and Christlike. We need not fear that the smallness of our number will put us out of the list of Churches, for the Holy Spirit has here enrolled a family-church in the inspired book of remembrance. As a Church let us now draw nigh to the great head of the one Church universal, and let us beseech him to give us grace to shine before men to the glory of his name.

NOVEMBER 2

I am the Lord, I change not.
—Malachi 3:6

IT is well for us that, amidst all the variableness of life, there is One whom change cannot affect; One whose heart can never alter, and on whose brow mutability can make no furrows. All things else have changed—all things are changing. The sun itself grows dim with age; the world is waxing old; the folding up of the wornout vesture has commenced; the heavens and earth must soon pass away; they shall perish, they shall wax old as doth a garment; but there is One who only hath immortality, of whose years there is no end, and in whose person there is no change. The delight which the mariner feels, when, after having been tossed about for many a day, he steps again upon the solid shore, is the satisfaction of a Christian when, amidst all the changes of this troublous life, he rests the foot of his faith upon this truth—*"I am the Lord, I change not."*

The stability which the anchor gives the ship when it has at last obtained a hold-fast, is like that which the Christian's hope affords him when it fixes itself upon this glorious truth. With God "is no variableness, neither shadow of turning." What ever his attributes were of old, they are now; his power, his wisdom, his justice, his truth, are alike unchanged. He has ever been the refuge of his people, their stronghold in the day of trouble, and he is their sure helper still. He is unchanged in his *love. He* has loved his people with "an everlasting love;" he loves them now as much as ever he did, and when all earthly things shall have melted in the last conflagration, his love will still wear the dew of its youth. Precious is the assurance that he changes not! The wheel of providence revolves, but its axle is eternal love.

> Death and change are busy ever,
> Man decays, and ages move;
> But his mercy waneth never;
> God is wisdom, God is love.

NOVEMBER 3

Behold, he prayeth.
—Acts 9:11

PRAYERS are instantly noticed in heaven. The moment Saul began to pray, the Lord heard him. Here is comfort for the distressed but praying soul. Oftentimes a poor brokenhearted one bends his knee, but can only utter his wailing in the language of sighs and tears; yet that groan has made all the harps of heaven thrill with music; that tear has been caught by God and treasured in the lachrymatory of heaven. "Thou puttest my tears into thy bottle," implies that they are caught as they flow. The suppliant, whose fears prevent his words, will be well understood by the Most High. He may only look up with misty eye; but "prayer is the falling of a tear." Tears are the diamonds of heaven; sighs are a part of the music of Jehovah's court, and are numbered with "the sublimest strains that reach the majesty on high." Think not that your prayer, however weak or trembling, will be unregarded. Jacob's ladder is lofty, but our prayers shall lean upon the Angel of the covenant and so climb its starry rounds. Our God not only *hears* prayer but also *loves* to hear it. "He forgetteth not the cry of the humble." True, he regards not high looks and lofty words; he cares not for the pomp and pageantry of kings; he listens not to the swell of martial music; he regards not the triumph and pride of man; but wherever there is a heart big with sorrow, or a lip quivering with agony, or a deep groan, or a penitential sigh, the heart of Jehovah is open; he marks it down in the registry of his memory; he puts our prayers, like rose leaves, between the pages of his book of remembrance, and when the volume is opened at last, there shall be a precious fragrance springing up therefrom.

> Faith asks no signal from the skies,
> To show that prayers accepted rise,
> Our Priest is in his holy place,
> And answers from the throne of grace.

November 4

For my strength is made perfect in weakness.
—2 Corinthians 12:9

primary qualification for serving God with any amount of success, and for doing God's work well and triumphantly, is a sense of our own weakness. When God's warrior marches forth to battle, strong in his own might, when he boasts, "I know that I shall conquer, my own right arm and my conquering sword shall get unto me the victory," defeat is not far distant. God will not go forth with that man who marches in his own strength. He who reckoneth on victory thus has reckoned wrongly, for "it is not by might, nor by power, but by my Spirit, saith the Lord of hosts." They who go forth to fight, boasting of their prowess, shall return with their gay banners trailed in the dust, and their armor stained with disgrace. Those who serve God must serve him in his own way, and in his strength, or he will never accept their service. That which man doth, unaided by divine strength, God can never own. The mere fruits of the earth he casteth away; he will only reap that corn, the seed of which was sown from heaven, watered by grace, and ripened by the sun of divine love. God will empty out all that thou hast before he will put his own into thee; he will first clean out thy granaries before he will fill them with the finest of the wheat. The river of God is full of water; but not one drop of it flows from earthly springs. God will have no strength used in his battles but the strength which he himself imparts. Are you mourning over your own weakness? Take courage, for there must be a consciousness of weakness before the Lord will give thee victory. Your emptiness is but the preparation for your being filled, and your casting down is but the making ready for your lifting up.

> When I am weak then am I strong,
> Grace is my shield and Christ my song.

NOVEMBER 5

No weapon that is formed against thee shall prosper.
—Isaiah 54:17

HIS day is notable in English history for two great deliverances wrought by God for us. On this day the plot of the Papists to destroy our Houses of Parliament was discovered, 1605.

> While for our princes they prepare
> In caverns deep a burning snare,
> He shot from heaven a piercing ray,
> And the dark treachery brought to day.

And secondly—today is the anniversary of the landing of King William III, at Torbay, by which the hope of Popish ascendancy was quashed, and religious liberty was secured, 1688.

This day ought to be celebrated, not by the saturnalia of striplings, but by the songs of saints. Our Puritan forefathers most devoutly made it a special time of thanksgiving. There is extant a record of the annual sermons preached by Matthew Henry on this day. Our Protestant feeling, and our love of liberty, should make us regard its anniversary with holy gratitude. Let our hearts and lips exclaim, "We have heard with our ears, and our fathers have told us the wondrous things which thou didst in their day, and in the old time before them." Thou hast made this nation the home of the gospel; and when the foe has risen against her, thou hast shielded her. Help us to offer repeated songs for repeated deliverances. Grant us more and more a hatred of Antichrist, and hasten on the day of her entire extinction. Till then and ever, we believe the promise, "No weapon that is formed against thee shall prosper." Should it not be laid upon the heart of every lover of the gospel of Jesus on this day to plead for the overturning of false doctrines and the extension of divine truth? Would it not be well to search our own hearts, and turn out any of the Popish lumber of self-righteousness which may lie concealed therein?

NOVEMBER 6

I will pour water upon him that is thirsty.
—Isaiah 44:3

WHEN a believer has fallen into a low, sad state of feeling, he often tries to lift himself out of it by chastening himself with dark and doleful fears. Such is not the way to rise from the dust, but to continue in it. As well chain the eagle's wing to make it mount, as doubt in order to increase our grace. It is not the law, but the gospel which saves the seeking soul at first; and it is not a legal bondage, but gospel liberty which can restore the fainting believer afterwards. Slavish fear brings not back the backslider to God, but the sweet wooings of love allure him to Jesus' bosom. Are you this morning thirsting for the living God, and unhappy because you cannot find him to the delight of your heart? Have you lost the joy of religion, and is this your prayer, "Restore unto me the joy of thy salvation"? Are you conscious also that you are barren, like the dry ground; that you are not bringing forth the fruit unto God which he has a right to expect of you; that you are not so useful in the Church, or in the world, as your heart desires to be? Then here is exactly the promise which you need, "I will pour water upon him that is thirsty." You shall receive the grace you so much require, and you shall have it to the utmost reach of your needs. Water refreshes the thirsty: you shall be refreshed; your desires shall be gratified. Water quickens sleeping vegetable life: your life shall be quickened by fresh grace. Water swells the buds and makes the fruits ripen; you shall have fructifying grace: you shall be made fruitful in the ways of God. Whatever good quality there is in divine grace, you shall enjoy it to the full. All the riches of divine grace you shall receive in plenty; you shall be as it were drenched with it: and as sometimes the meadows become flooded by the bursting rivers, and the fields are turned into pools, so shall you be—the thirsty land shall be springs of water.

NOVEMBER 7

Behold, I have graven thee upon the palms of my hands.
—*Isaiah 49:16*

O doubt a part of the wonder which is concentrated in the word *"Behold,"* is excited by the unbelieving lamentation of the preceding sentence. Zion said, "The Lord hath forsaken me, and my God hath forgotten me." How amazed the divine mind seems to be at this wicked unbelief! What can be more astounding than the unfounded doubts and fears of God's favored people? The Lord's loving word of rebuke should make us blush; he cries,

> How can I have forgotten thee, when I have graven thee upon the palms of my hands? How darest thou doubt my constant remembrance, when the memorial is set upon my very flesh?

O unbelief, how strange a marvel thou art! We know not which most to wonder at, the faithfulness of God or the unbelief of his people. He keeps his promise a thousand times, and yet the next trial makes us doubt him. He never faileth; he is never a dry well; he is never as a setting sun, a passing meteor, or a melting vapor; and yet we are as continually vexed with anxieties, molested with suspicions, and disturbed with fears, as if our God were the mirage of the desert. "Behold" *is a word intended to excite admiration.* Here, indeed, we have a theme for marveling. Heaven and earth may well be astonished that rebels should obtain so great a nearness to the heart of infinite love as to be written upon the palms of his hands. "I have graven *thee.*" It does not say, "thy name." The name is there, but that is not all: "I have graven *thee.*" See the fullness of this! I have graven thy person, thine image, thy case, thy circumstances, thy sins, thy temptations, thy weaknesses, thy wants, thy works; I have graven *thee,* everything about thee, all that concerns thee; I have put thee altogether there. Wilt thou ever say again that thy God hath forsaken thee when he has graven *thee* upon his own palms?

NOVEMBER 8

As ye have received Christ Jesus the Lord.
—Colossians 2:6

HE life of faith is represented as *receiving—an act which implies the very opposite of anything like merit.* It is simply the acceptance of a gift. As the earth drinks in the rain, as the sea receives the streams, as night accepts light from the stars, so we, giving nothing, partake freely of the grace of God. The saints are not, by nature, wells, or streams, they are but cisterns into which the living water flows; they are empty vessels into which God pours his salvation. The idea of receiving implies *a sense of realization,* making the matter a *reality.* One cannot very well receive a shadow; we receive that which is substantial: so is it in the life of faith, Christ becomes real to us. While we are without faith, Jesus is a mere name to us—a person who lived a long while ago, so long ago that his life is only a history to us now! By an act of faith Jesus becomes a real person in the consciousness of our heart. But receiving also means *grasping or getting possession of.* The thing which I receive becomes my own: I appropriate to myself that which is given. When I receive Jesus, he becomes my Savior, so mine that neither life nor death shall be able to rob me of him. All this is to receive Christ—to take him as God's free gift; to realize him in my heart, and to appropriate him as mine.

Salvation may be described as the blind receiving sight, the deaf receiving hearing, the dead receiving life; but we have not only received these blessings, we have received *Christ Jesus* himself. It is true that he gave us life from the dead. He gave us pardon of sin; he gave us imputed righteousness. These are all precious things, but we are not content with them; we have received *Christ himself.* The Son of God has been poured into us, and we have received him, and appropriated him. What a heart-full Jesus must be, for heaven itself cannot contain him!

NOVEMBER 9

So walk ye in him.
—*Colossians 2:6*

F we have received Christ himself in our inmost hearts, our new life will manifest its intimate acquaintance with him by a *walk of faith in him.* Walking implies *action.* Our religion is not to be confined to our closet; we must carry out into practical effect that which we believe. If a man walks in Christ, then he so acts as Christ would act; for Christ being in him, his hope, his love, his joy, his life, he is the reflex of the image of Jesus; and men say of that man, "He is like his Master; he lives like Jesus Christ." Walking signifies *progress.* "So walk ye in him;" proceed from grace to grace, run forward until you reach the uttermost degree of knowledge that a man can attain concerning our Beloved. Walking implies *continuance.* There must be a perpetual abiding in Christ. How many Christians think that in the morning and evening they ought to come into the company of Jesus, and may then give their hearts to the world all the day: but this is poor living; we should always be with him, treading in his steps and doing his will. Walking also implies *habit.* When we speak of a man's walk and conversation, we mean his habits, the constant tenor of his life. Now, if we sometimes enjoy Christ, and then forget him; sometimes call him ours, and anon lose our hold, that is not a habit; we do not *walk* in him. We must keep to him, cling to him, never let him go, but live and have our being in him. "As ye have received Christ Jesus the Lord, so walk ye in him;" persevere in the same way in which ye have begun, and, as at the first Christ Jesus was the trust of your faith, the source of your life, the principle of your action, and the joy of your spirit, so let him be the same till life's end; the same when you walk through the valley of the shadow of death, and enter into the joy and the rest which remain for the people of God. O Holy Spirit, enable us to obey this heavenly precept.

❦

November 10

The eternal God is thy refuge.
—Deuteronomy 33:27

HE word refuge may be translated "mansion," or "abiding-place," which gives the thought that *God is our abode, our home.* There is a fullness and sweetness in the metaphor, for dear to our hearts is our home, although it be the humblest cottage, or the scantiest garret; and dearer far is our blessed God, in whom we live, and move, and have our being. It is at home that we *feel safe:* we shut the world out and dwell in quiet security. So when we are with our God we "fear no evil." He is our shelter and retreat, our abiding refuge. At home, *we take our rest;* it is there we find repose after the fatigue and toil of the day. And so our hearts find rest in God, when, wearied with life's conflict, we turn to him, and our soul dwells at ease. At home, also, we *let our hearts loose;* we are not afraid of being misunderstood, nor of our words being misconstrued. So when we are with God we can commune freely with him, laying open all our hidden desires; for if the "secret of the Lord is with them that fear him," the secrets of them that fear him ought to be, and must be, with their Lord. Home, too, is the place of our *truest and purest happiness:* and it is in God that our hearts find their deepest delight. We have joy in him which far surpasses all other joy. *It is also for home that we work and labor.* The thought of it gives strength to bear the daily burden, and quickens the fingers to perform the task; and in this sense we may also say that God is our home. Love to him strengthens us. We think of him in the person of his dear Son; and a glimpse of the suffering face of the Redeemer constrains us to labor in his cause. We feel that we must work, for we have brethren yet to be saved, and we have our Father's heart to make glad by bringing home his wandering sons; we would fill with holy mirth the sacred family among whom we dwell. Happy are those who have thus the God of Jacob for their refuge!

315

NOVEMBER 11

Underneath are the everlasting arms.
—Deuteronomy 33:27

GOD—the eternal God—is himself *our support* at all times, and especially when we are sinking in deep trouble. There are seasons when the Christian *sinks very low in humiliation.* Under a deep sense of his great sinfulness, he is humbled before God till he scarcely knows how to pray, because he appears, in his own sight, so worthless. Well, child of God, remember that when thou art at thy worst and lowest, yet "underneath" thee "are everlasting arms." Sin may drag thee ever so low, but Christ's great atonement is still under all. You may have descended into the deeps, but you cannot have fallen so low as "the uttermost;" and to the uttermost he saves. Again, the Christian sometimes sinks very deeply in *sore trial from without.* Every earthly prop is cut away. What then? Still underneath him are "the everlasting arms." He cannot fall so deep in distress and affliction but what the covenant grace of an ever-faithful God will still encircle him. The Christian may be sinking under *trouble from within* through fierce conflict, but even then he cannot be brought so low as to be beyond the reach of the "everlasting arms"—they are underneath him; and, while thus sustained, all Satan's efforts to harm him avail nothing.

This assurance of support is a comfort to any *weary but earnest worker* in the service of God. It implies a promise of strength for each day, grace for each need, and power for each duty. And, further, *when death comes,* the promise shall still hold good. When we stand in the midst of Jordan, we shall be able to say with David, "I will fear no evil, for thou art with me." We shall descend into the grave, but we shall go no lower, for the eternal arms prevent our further fall. All through life, and at its close, we shall be upheld by the "everlasting arms"—arms that neither flag nor lose their strength, for "the everlasting God fainteth not, neither is weary."

NOVEMBER 12

The trial of your faith.
—1 Peter 1:7

FAITH untried may be true faith, but it is sure to be little faith, and it is likely to remain dwarfish so long as it is without trials. Faith never prospers so well as when all things are against her: tempests are her trainers, and lightnings are her illuminators. When a calm reigns on the sea, spread the sails as you will, the ship moves not to its harbor; for on a slumbering ocean the keel sleeps too. Let the winds rush howling forth, and let the waters lift up themselves, then, though the vessel may rock, and her deck may be washed with waves, and her mast may creak under the pressure of the full and swelling sail, it is then that she makes headway towards her desired haven. No flowers wear so lovely a blue as those which grow at the foot of the frozen glacier; no stars gleam so brightly as those which glisten in the polar sky; no water tastes so sweet as that which springs amid the desert sand; and no faith is so precious as that which lives and triumphs in adversity. Tried faith brings experience. You could not have believed your own weakness had you not been compelled to pass through the rivers; and you would never have known God's strength had you not been supported amid the waterfloods. Faith increases in solidity, assurance, and intensity, the more it is exercised with tribulation. Faith is precious, and its trial is precious too.

Let not this, however, discourage those who are young in faith. You will have trials enough without seeking them: the full portion will be measured out to you in due season. Meanwhile, if you cannot yet claim the result of long experience, thank God for what grace you have; praise him for that degree of holy confidence whereunto you have attained: walk according to that rule, and you shall yet have more and more of the blessing of God, till your faith shall remove mountains and conquer impossibilities.

NOVEMBER 13

The branch cannot bear fruit of itself.
—John 15:4

OW did you begin to bear fruit? It was when you came to Jesus and cast yourselves on his great atonement, and rested on his finished righteousness. Ah! what fruit you had then! Do you remember those early days? Then indeed the vine flourished, the tender grape appeared, the pomegranates budded forth, and the beds of spices gave forth their smell. Have you declined since then? If you have, we charge you to remember that time of love, and repent, and do thy first works. *Be most in those engagements which you have experimentally proved to draw you nearest to Christ,* because it is from him that all your fruits proceed. Any holy exercise which will bring you to him will help you to bear fruit. The sun is, no doubt, a great worker in fruit-creating among the trees of the orchard: and Jesus is still more so among the trees of his garden of grace. When have you been the most fruitless? Has not it been when you have lived farthest from the Lord Jesus Christ, when you have slackened in prayer, when you have departed from the simplicity of your faith, when your graces have engrossed your attention instead of your Lord, when you have said, "My mountain standeth firm, I shall never be moved;" and have forgotten where your strength dwells—has not it been *then* that your fruit has ceased? Some of us have been taught that we have nothing out of Christ, by terrible abasements of heart before the Lord; and when we have seen the utter barrenness and death of all creature power, we have cried in anguish, "From him all my fruit must be found, for no fruit can ever come from me." We are taught, by past experience, that the more simply we depend upon the grace of God in Christ, and wait upon the Holy Spirit, the more we shall bring forth fruit unto God. Oh! to trust Jesus for fruit as well as for life.

NOVEMBER 14

I will cut off them
that worship and that swear by the Lord
and that swear by Malcham.
—Zephaniah 1:5

UCH persons thought themselves safe because they were with both parties: they went with the followers of Jehovah, and bowed at the same time to Malcham. But duplicity is abominable with God, and hypocrisy his soul hateth. The idolater who distinctly gives himself to his false god, has one sin less than he who brings his polluted and detestable sacrifice unto the temple of the Lord, while his heart is with the world and the sins thereof. To hold with the hare and run with the hounds, is a dastard's policy. In the common matters of daily life, a double-minded man is despised, but in religion he is loathsome to the last degree. The penalty pronounced in the verse before us is terrible, but it is well deserved; for how should divine justice spare the sinner, who knows the right, approves it, and professes to follow it, and all the while loves the evil, and gives it dominion in his heart?

My soul, search thyself this morning, and see whether thou art guilty of double-dealing. thou professest to be a follower of Jesus—dost thou truly love him? Is thy heart right with God? Art thou of the family of old Father Honest, or art thou a relative of Mr. By-ends? A name to live is of little value if I be indeed dead in trespasses and sins. To have one foot on the land of truth, and another on the sea of falsehood, will involve a terrible fall and a total ruin. Christ will be all or nothing. God fills the whole universe, and hence there is no room for another god; if, then, he reigns in my heart, there will be no space for another reigning power. Do I rest alone on Jesus crucified, and live alone for him? Is it my desire to do so? Is my heart set upon so doing? If so, blessed be the mighty grace which has led me to salvation; and if not so, O Lord, pardon my sad offence, and unite my heart to fear thy name.

NOVEMBER 15

The Lord's portion is his people.
—Deuteronomy 32:9

OW are they his? By his own sovereign *choice. He* chose them, and set his love upon them. This he did altogether apart from any goodness in them at the time, or any goodness which he foresaw in them. He had mercy on whom he would have mercy, and ordained a chosen company unto eternal life; thus, therefore, are they his by his unconstrained election.

They are not only his by choice, but by *purchase. He* has bought and paid for them to the utmost farthing, hence about his title there can be no dispute. Not with corruptible things, as with silver and gold, but with the precious blood of the Lord Jesus Christ, the Lord's portion has been fully redeemed. There is no mortgage on his estate; no suits can be raised by opposing claimants, the price was paid in open court, and the Church is the Lord's freehold forever. See the blood-mark upon all the chosen, invisible to human eye, but known to Christ, for "the Lord knoweth them that are his;" he forgetteth none of those whom he has redeemed from among men; he counts the sheep for whom he laid down his life, and remembers well the Church for which he gave himself.

They are also his by *conquest.* What a battle he had in us before we would be won! How long he laid siege to our hearts! How often he sent us terms of capitulation! but we barred our gates, and fenced our walls against him. Do we not remember that glorious hour when he carried our hearts by storm? When he placed his cross against the wall, and scaled our ramparts, planting on our strongholds the blood-red flag of his omnipotent mercy? Yes, we are, indeed, the conquered captives of his omnipotent love. Thus chosen, purchased, and subdued, the rights of our divine possessor are inalienable: we rejoice that we never can be our own; and we desire, day by day, to do *his* will, and to show forth *his* glory.

NOVEMBER 16

"The Lord is my portion," saith my soul.
—Lamentations 3:24

I is not "The Lord is *partly* my portion," nor "The Lord is *in* my portion;" but he himself makes up the sum total of my soul's inheritance. Within the circumference of that circle lies all that we possess or desire. The *Lord* is my portion. Not his grace merely, nor his love, nor his covenant, but Jehovah himself. He has chosen us for his portion, and we have chosen him for ours. It is true that the Lord must first choose our inheritance for us, or else we shall never choose it for ourselves; but if we are really called according to the purpose of electing love, we can sing—

> Lov'd of my God for him again
> With love intense I burn;
> Chosen of him ere time began,
> I choose him in return.

The Lord is our *all-sufficient* portion. God fills himself; and if God is all-sufficient in himself, he must be allsufficient for us. It is not easy to satisfy man's desires. When he dreams that he is satisfied, anon he wakes to the perception that there is somewhat yet beyond, and straightway the horse-leech in his heart cries, "Give, give." But all that we can wish for is to be found in our divine portion, so that we ask, "Whom have I in heaven but thee? and there is none upon earth that I desire beside thee." Well may we "delight ourselves in the Lord" who makes us to drink of the river of his pleasures. Our faith stretches her wings and mounts like an eagle into the heaven of divine love as to her proper dwelling-place. "The lines have fallen to us in pleasant places; yea, we have a goodly heritage." Let us rejoice in the Lord always; let us show to the world that we are a happy and a blessed people, and thus induce them to exclaim, "We will go with you, for we have heard that God is with you."

NOVEMBER 17

To whom be glory forever. Amen.
—Romans 11:36

O whom be glory forever." This should be *the single* desire of the Christian. All other wishes must be subservient and tributary to this one. The Christian may wish for prosperity in his business, but only so far as it may help him to promote this—"To him be glory forever." He may desire to attain more gifts and more graces, but it should only be that "To him may be glory forever." You are not acting as you ought to do when you are moved by any other motive than a single eye to your Lord's glory. As a Christian, you are "of God, and through God," then live "to God." Let nothing ever set your heart beating so mightily as love to him. Let this ambition fire your soul; be this the foundation of every enterprise upon which you enter, and this your sustaining motive whenever your zeal would grow chill; make God your *only* object. Depend upon it, where self begins sorrow begins; but if God be my supreme delight and only object,

> To me 'tis equal whether love ordain
> My life or death—appoint me ease or pain.

Let your desire for God's glory be a *growing* desire. You blessed him in your youth, do not be content with such praises as you gave him then. Has God prospered you in business? Give him more as he has given you more. Has God given you experience? Praise him by stronger faith than you exercised at first. Does your knowledge grow? Then sing more sweetly. Do you enjoy happier times than you once had? Have you been restored from sickness, and has your sorrow been turned into peace and joy? Then give him more music; put more coals and more sweet frankincense into the censer of your praise. Practically in your life give him honor, putting the "Amen" to this doxology to your great and gracious Lord, by your own individual service and increasing holiness.

NOVEMBER 18

A spring shut up, a fountain sealed.
—Song of Solomon 4:12

I N this metaphor, which has reference to the inner life of a believer, we have very plainly the idea of *secrecy*. It is a spring *shut up*: just as there were springs in the East, over which an edifice was built, so that none could reach them save those who knew the secret entrance; so is the heart of a believer when it is renewed by grace: there is a mysterious life within which no human skill can touch. It is a secret which no other man knoweth; nay, which the very man who is the possessor of it cannot tell to his neighbor. The text includes not only secrecy, but *separation*. It is not the common spring, of which every passer-by may drink, it is one kept and preserved from all others; it is a fountain bearing a particular mark—a king's royal seal, so that all can perceive that it is not a common fountain, but a fountain owned by a proprietor, and placed specially by itself alone. So is it with the spiritual life. The chosen of God were separated in the eternal decree; they were separated by God in the day of redemption; and they are separated by the possession of a life which others have not; and it is impossible for them to feel at home with the world, or to delight in its pleasures. There is also the idea of *sacredness*. The spring shut up is preserved for the use of some special person: and such is the Christian's heart. It is a spring kept for Jesus. Every Christian should feel that he has God's seal upon him—and he should be able to say with Paul, "From henceforth let no man trouble me, for I bear in my body the marks of the Lord Jesus." Another idea is prominent—it is that of *security*. Oh! how sure and safe is the inner life of the believer! If all the powers of earth and hell could combine against it, that immortal principle must still exist, for he who gave it pledged his life for its preservation. And who "is he that shall harm you," when God is your protector?

NOVEMBER 19

Avoid foolish questions.
—Titus 3:9

OUR days are few, and are far better spent in doing good, than in disputing over matters which are, at best, of minor importance. The old schoolmen did a world of mischief by their incessant discussion of subjects of no practical importance; and our Churches suffer much from petty wars over abstruse points and unimportant questions. After everything has been said that can be said, neither party is any the wiser, and therefore the discussion no more promotes knowledge than love, and it is foolish to sow in so barren a field. Questions upon points wherein Scripture is silent; upon mysteries which belong to God alone; upon prophecies of doubtful interpretation; and upon mere modes of observing human ceremonials, are all foolish, and wise men avoid them. Our business is neither to ask nor answer foolish questions, but to avoid them altogether; and if we observe the apostle's precept (Titus 3:8) to be careful to maintain good works, we shall find ourselves far too much occupied with profitable business to take much interest in unworthy, contentious, and needless strivings.

There are, however, some questions which are the reverse of foolish, which we must not avoid, but fairly and honestly meet, such as these: Do I believe in the Lord Jesus Christ? Am I renewed in the spirit of my mind? Am I walking not after the flesh, but after the Spirit? Am I growing in grace? Does my conversation adorn the doctrine of God my Savior? Am I looking for the coming of the Lord, and watching as a servant should do who expects his master? What more can I do for Jesus? Such enquiries as these urgently demand our attention; and if we have been at all given to caviling, let us now turn our critical abilities to a service so much more profitable. Let us be peacemakers, and endeavor to lead others both by our precept and example, to "avoid foolish questions."

November 20

O Lord, thou hast pleaded the causes of my soul.
—*Lamentations 3:58*

OBSERVE how *positively* the prophet speaks. He doth not say, "I hope, I trust, I sometimes think, that God hath pleaded the causes of my soul;" but he speaks of it as a matter of fact not to be disputed. "Thou *hast* pleaded the causes of my soul." Let us, by the aid of the gracious Comforter, shake off those doubts and fears which so much mar our peace and comfort. Be this our prayer, that we may have done with the harsh croaking voice of surmise and suspicion, and may be able to speak with the clear, melodious voice of full assurance. Notice how *gratefully* the prophet speaks, ascribing all the glory to God alone! You perceive there is not a word concerning himself or his own pleadings. He doth not ascribe his deliverance in any measure to any man, much less to his own merit; but it is *"thou"*—"O Lord, thou hast pleaded the causes of my soul; *thou* hast redeemed my life." A grateful spirit should ever be cultivated by the Christian; and especially after deliverances we should prepare a song for our God. Earth should be a temple filled with the songs of grateful saints, and every day should be a censor smoking with the sweet incense of thanksgiving. How *joyful* Jeremiah seems to be while he records the Lord's mercy. How triumphantly he lifts up the strain! He has been in the low dungeon, and is even now no other than the weeping prophet; and yet in the very book which is called "Lamentations," clear as the song of Miriam when she dashed her fingers against the tabor, shrill as the note of Deborah when she met Barak with shouts of victory, we hear the voice of Jeremy going up to heaven—"Thou hast pleaded the causes of my soul; thou hast redeemed my life." O children of God, seek after a vital experience of the Lord's lovingkindness, and when you have it, speak positively of it; sing gratefully; shout triumphantly.

NOVEMBER 21

Grieve not the Holy Spirit.
—Ephesians 4:30

LL that the believer has must come from Christ, but it comes solely through the channel of the Spirit of grace. Moreover, as all blessings thus flow to you through the Holy Spirit, so also no good thing can come out of you in holy thought, devout worship, or gracious act, apart from the sanctifying operation of the same Spirit. Even if the good seed be sown in you, yet it lies dormant except he worketh in you to will and to do of his own good pleasure. Do you desire to speak for Jesus—how can you unless the Holy Ghost touch your tongue? Do you desire to pray? Alas! what dull work it is unless the Spirit maketh intercession for you! Do you desire to subdue sin? Would you be holy? Would you imitate your Master? Do you desire to rise to superlative heights of spirituality? Are you wanting to be made like the angels of God, full of zeal and ardor for the Master's cause? You cannot without the Spirit—"Without me ye can do nothing." O branch of the vine, thou canst have no fruit without the sap! O child of God, thou hast no life within thee apart from the life which God gives thee through his Spirit! Then let us not grieve him or provoke him to anger by our sin. Let us not quench him in one of his faintest motions in our soul; let us foster every suggestion, and be ready to obey every prompting. If the Holy Spirit be indeed so mighty, let us attempt nothing without him; let us begin no project, and carry on no enterprise, and conclude no transaction, without imploring his blessing. Let us do him the due homage of feeling our entire weakness apart from him, and then depending alone upon him, having this for our prayer,

> Open thou my heart and my whole being to thine incoming, and uphold me with thy free Spirit when I shall have received that Spirit in my inward parts.

November 22

Israel served for a wife, and for a wife he kept sheep.
—Hosea 12:12

JACOB, while expostulating with Laban, thus describes his own toil,

> This twenty years have I been with thee. That which was torn of beasts I brought not unto thee: I bare the loss of it; of my hand didst thou require it, whether stolen by day, or stolen by night. Thus I was; in the day the drought consumed me, and the frost by night; and my sleep departed from mine eyes.

Even more toilsome than this was the life of our Savior here below. He watched over all his sheep till he gave in as his last account, "Of all those whom thou hast given me I have lost none." His hair was wet with dew, and his locks with the drops of the night. Sleep departed from his eyes, for all night he was in prayer wrestling for his people. One night Peter must be pleaded for; anon, another claims his tearful intercession. No shepherd sitting beneath the cold skies, looking up to the stars, could ever utter such complaints because of the hardness of his toil as Jesus Christ might have brought, if he had chosen to do so, because of the sternness of his service in order to procure his spouse—

> Cold mountains and the midnight air,
> Witnessed the fervor of his prayer;
> The desert his temptations knew,
> His conflict and his victory too.

It is sweet to dwell upon the spiritual parallel of Laban having required all the sheep at Jacob's hand. If they were torn of beasts, Jacob must make it good; if any of them died, he must stand as surety for the whole. Was not the toil of Jesus for his Church the toil of one who was under suretiship obligations to bring every believing one safe to the hand of him who had committed them to his charge? Look upon toiling Jacob, and you see a representation of him of whom we read, "He shall feed his flock like a shepherd."

NOVEMBER 23

Fellowship with him.
—1 John 1:6

WHEN we were united by faith to Christ, we were brought into such complete fellowship with him, that we were made one with him, and his interests and ours became mutual and identical. We have fellowship with Christ in his *love.* What he loves we love. He loves the saints—so do we. He loves sinners—so do we. He loves the poor perishing race of man, and pants to see earth's deserts transformed into the garden of the Lord—so do we. We have fellowship with him in his *desires.* He desires the glory of God—we also labor for the same. He desires that the saints may be with him where he is—we desire to be with him there too. He desires to drive out sin—behold we fight under his banner. He desires that his Father's name may be loved and adored by all his creatures—we pray daily, "Let thy kingdom come and thy will be done on earth, even as it is in heaven." We have fellowship with Christ in his *sufferings.* We are not nailed to the cross, nor do we die a cruel death, but when he is reproached, we are reproached; and a very sweet thing it is to be blamed for his sake, to be despised for following the Master, to have the world against us. The disciple should not be above his Lord. In our measure we commune with him in his *labors,* ministering to men by the word of truth and by deeds of love. Our meat and our drink, like his, is to do the will of him who hath sent us and to finish his work. We have also fellowship with Christ in his *joys.* We are happy in his happiness, we rejoice in his exaltation. Have you ever tasted that joy, believer? There is no purer or more thrilling delight to be known this side of heaven than that of having Christ's joy fulfilled in us, that our joy may be full. His *glory* awaits us to complete our fellowship, for his Church shall sit with him upon his throne, as his well-beloved bride and queen.

NOVEMBER 24

The glorious Lord will be unto us
a place of broad rivers and streams.
—Isaiah 33:21

BROAD rivers and streams produce fertility, and abundance in the land. Places near broad rivers are remarkable for the variety of their plants and their plentiful harvests. God is all this to his Church. Having God she has *abundance*. What can she ask for that he will not give her? What want can she mention which he will not supply? "In this mountain shall the Lord of Hosts make unto all people a feast of fat things." Want ye the bread of life? It drops like manna from the sky. Want ye refreshing streams? The rock follows you, and that Rock is Christ. If you suffer any want it is your own fault; if you are straitened you are not straitened in him, but in your own bowels. Broad rivers and streams also point to *commerce*. Our glorious Lord is to us a place of heavenly merchandize. Through our Redeemer we have commerce with the past; the wealth of Calvary, the treasures of the covenant, the riches of the ancient days of election, the stores of eternity, all come to us down the broad stream of our gracious Lord. We have commerce, too, with the future. What galleys, laden to the water's edge, come to us from the millennium! What visions we have of the days of heaven upon earth! Through our glorious Lord we have commerce with angels; communion with the bright spirits washed in blood, who sing before the throne; nay, better still, we have fellowship with the Infinite One. Broad rivers and streams are specially intended to set forth the idea of *security*. Rivers were of old a defense. Oh! beloved, what a defense is God to his Church! The devil cannot cross this broad river of God. How he wishes he could turn the current, but fear not, for God abideth immutably the same. Satan may worry, but he cannot destroy us; no galley with oars shall invade our river, neither shall gallant ship pass thereby.

NOVEMBER 25

To preach deliverance to the captives.
—Luke 4:18

NONE but Jesus can give deliverance to captives. Real liberty cometh from him only. It is a liberty *righteously bestowed;* for the Son, who is Heir of all things, has a right to make men free. The saints honor the justice of God, which now secures their salvation. It is a liberty which has been *dearly purchased.* Christ speaks it by his power, but he bought it by his blood. He makes thee free, but it is by his own bonds. Thou goest clear, because he bare thy burden for thee: thou art set at liberty, because he has suffered in thy stead. But, though dearly purchased, *he freely gives it.* Jesus asks nothing of us as a preparation for this liberty. He finds us sitting in sackcloth and ashes, and bids us put on the beautiful array of freedom; he saves us just as we are, and all without our help or merit. When Jesus sets free, the liberty is *perpetually entailed;* no chains can bind again. Let the Master say to me, "Captive, I have delivered thee," and it is done forever. Satan may plot to enslave us, but if the Lord be on our side, whom shall we fear? The world, with its temptations, may seek to ensnare us, but mightier is he who is for us than all they who be against us. The machinations of our own deceitful hearts may harass and annoy us, but he who hath begun the good work in us will carry it on and perfect it to the end. The foes of God and the enemies of man may gather their hosts together, and come with concentrated fury against us, but if God acquitteth, who is he that condemneth? Not more free is the eagle which mounts to his rocky eerie, and afterwards outsoars the clouds, than the soul which Christ hath delivered. If we are no more under the law, but free from its curse, let our liberty be *practically exhibited* in our serving God with gratitude and delight. "I am thy servant, and the son of thine handmaid: thou hast loosed my bonds." "Lord, what wilt thou have me to do?"

NOVEMBER 26

Whatsoever thy hand findeth to do, do it with thy might.
—Ecclesiastes 9:10

WHATSOEVER thy hand findeth to do," refers to works that are *possible*. There are many things which our *heart* findeth to do which we never shall do. It is well it is in our heart; but if we would be eminently useful, we must not be content with forming schemes in our heart, and talking of them; we must practically carry out *"whatsoever our hand findeth to do."* One good deed is more worth than a thousand brilliant theories. Let us not wait for large opportunities, or for a different kind of work, but do just the things we "find to do" day by day. We have no other time in which to live. The past is gone; the future has not arrived; we never shall have any time but time *present*. Then do not wait until your experience has ripened into maturity before you attempt to serve God. Endeavor now to bring forth fruit. Serve God now, but be careful as to the way in which you perform what you find to do—*"do it with thy might."* Do it *promptly*; do not fritter away your life in thinking of what you intend to do tomorrow as if that could recompense for the idleness of today. No man ever served God by doing things tomorrow. If we honor Christ and are blessed, it is by the things which we do *today*. Whatever you do for Christ throw your whole soul into it. Do not give Christ a little slurred labor, done as a matter of course now and then; but when you do serve him, do it with heart, and soul, and strength.

But where is the might of a Christian? It is not in himself, for he is perfect weakness. His might lieth in the Lord of Hosts. Then let us seek his help; let us proceed with prayer and faith, and when we have done what our "hand findeth to do," let us wait upon the Lord for his blessing. What we do thus will be well done, and will not fail in its effect.

331

NOVEMBER 27

Joshua the high priest, standing before the angel of the Lord.
—Zechariah 3:1

IN Joshua *the high priest* we see a picture of each and every child of God, who has been made nigh by the blood of Christ, and has been taught to minister in holy things, and enter into that which is within the veil. Jesus has made us priests and kings unto God, and even here upon earth we exercise the priesthood of consecrated living and hallowed service. But this high priest is said to be "*standing* before the angel of the Lord," that is, standing to minister. This should be the perpetual position of every true believer. Every place is now God's temple, and his people can as truly serve him in their daily employments as in his house. They are to be always "ministering," offering the spiritual sacrifice of prayer and praise, and presenting themselves a "living sacrifice." But notice where it is that Joshua stands to minister, it is *before the angel* of Jehovah. It is only through a mediator that we poor defiled ones can ever become priests unto God. I present what I have before the messenger, the angel of the covenant, the Lord Jesus; and through him my prayers find acceptance wrapped up in *his* prayers; my praises become sweet as they are bound up with bundles of myrrh, and aloes, and cassia from Christ's own garden. If I can bring him nothing but my tears, he will put them with his own tears in his own bottle for he once wept; if I can bring him nothing but my groans and sighs, he will accept these as an acceptable sacrifice, for he once was broken in heart, and sighed heavily in spirit. I myself, standing in him, am accepted in the Beloved; and all my polluted works, though in themselves only objects of divine abhorrence, are so received, that God smelleth a sweet savor. He is content and I am blessed. See, then, the position of the Christian—"a priest, *standing* before the angel of the Lord."

NOVEMBER 28

*For I rejoiced greatly, when the brethren came and testified of the truth
that is in thee, even as thou walkest in the truth.*
—3 John 3

HE truth was in Gaius, and Gaius walked in the truth. If the first had not been the case, the second could never have occurred; and if the second could not be said of him the first would have been a mere pretence. Truth must enter into the soul, penetrate and saturate it, or else it is of no value. Doctrines held as a matter of creed are like bread in the hand, which ministers no nourishment to the frame; but doctrine accepted by the heart, is as food digested, which, by assimilation, sustains and builds up the body. In us truth must be a living force, an active energy, an indwelling reality, a part of the woof and warp of our being. If it be *in us*, we cannot henceforth part with it. A man may lose his garments or his limbs, but his inward parts are vital, and cannot be torn away without absolute loss of life. A Christian can die, but he cannot deny the truth. Now it is a rule of nature that the inward affects the outward, as light shines from the center of the lantern through the glass: when, therefore, the truth is kindled within, its brightness soon beams forth in the outward life and conversation. It is said that the food of certain worms colors the cocoons of silk which they spin: and just so the nutriment upon which a man's inward nature lives gives a tinge to every word and deed proceeding from him. To walk in the truth, imports a life of integrity, holiness, faithfulness, and simplicity—the natural product of those principles of truth which the gospel teaches, and which the Spirit of God enables us to receive. We may judge of the secrets of the soul by their manifestation in the man's conversation. Be it ours today, O gracious Spirit, to be ruled and governed by thy divine authority, so that nothing false or sinful may reign in our hearts, lest it extend its malignant influence to our daily walk among men.

NOVEMBER 29

Thou shalt not go up and down as a talebearer among thy people . . .
Thou shalt in any wise rebuke thy neighbor, and not suffer sin upon him.
—*Leviticus 19:16–17*

ALE-BEARING emits a threefold poison; for it injures the teller, the hearer, and the person concerning whom the tale is told. Whether the report be true or false, we are by this precept of God's Word forbidden to spread it. The reputations of the Lord's people should be very precious in our sight, and we should count it shame to help the devil to dishonor the Church and the name of the Lord. Some tongues need a bridle rather than a spur. Many glory in pulling down their brethren, as if thereby they raised themselves. Noah's wise sons cast a mantle over their father, and he who exposed him earned a fearful curse. We may ourselves one of these dark days need forbearance and silence from our brethren, let us render it cheerfully to those who require it now. Be this our family rule, and our personal bond—*speak evil of no man.*

The Holy Spirit, however, permits us to censure sin, and prescribes the way in which we are to do it. It must be done by rebuking our brother to his face, not by railing behind his back. This course is manly, brotherly, Christlike, and under God's blessing will be useful. Does the flesh shrink from it? Then we must lay the greater stress upon our conscience, and keep ourselves to the work, lest by suffering sin upon our friend we become ourselves partakers of it. Hundreds have been saved from gross sins by the timely, wise, affectionate warnings of faithful ministers and brethren. Our Lord Jesus has set us a gracious example of how to deal with erring friends in his warning given to Peter, the prayer with which he preceded it, and the gentle way in which he bore with Peter's boastful denial that he needed such a caution.

NOVEMBER 30

*And Amaziah said to the man of God, "But what shall we do
for the hundred talents which I have given to the army of Israel?"
And the man of God answered, "The Lord is able to give thee
much more than this."—2 Chronicles 25:9*

 very important question this seemed to be to the king of Judah, and possibly it is of even more weight with the tried and tempted Christian. To lose money is at no times pleasant, and when principle involves it, the flesh is not always ready to make the sacrifice.

Why lose that which may be so usefully employed? May not the truth itself be bought too dear? What shall we do without it? Remember the children, and our small income!

All these things and a thousand more would tempt the Christian to put forth his hand to unrighteous gain, or stay himself from carrying out his conscientious convictions, when they involve serious loss. All men cannot view these matters in the light of faith; and even with the followers of Jesus, the doctrine of "we must live" has quite sufficient weight.

"The Lord is able to give thee much more than this" is a very satisfactory answer to the anxious question. Our Father holds the purse-strings, and what we lose for his sake he can repay a thousand-fold. It is ours to obey his will, and we may rest assured that he will provide for us. The Lord will be no man's debtor at the last. Saints know that a grain of heart's-ease is of more value than a ton of gold. He who wraps a threadbare coat about a good conscience has gained a spiritual wealth far more desirable than any he has lost. God's smile and a dungeon are enough for a true heart; his frown and a palace would be hell to a gracious spirit. Let the worst come to the worst, let all the talents go, we have not lost our treasure, for that is above, where Christ sitteth at the right hand of God. Meanwhile, even now, the Lord maketh the meek to inherit the earth, and no good thing doth he withhold from them that walk uprightly.

DECEMBER 1

Thou hast made summer and winter.
—Psalm 74:17

Y soul, begin this wintry month with thy God. The cold snows and the piercing winds all remind thee that he keeps his covenant with day and night, and tend to assure thee that he will also keep that glorious covenant which he has made with thee in the person of Christ Jesus. He who is true to his Word in the revolutions of the seasons of this poor sin-polluted world, will not prove unfaithful in his dealings with his own well beloved Son.

Winter in the soul is by no means a comfortable season, and if it be upon thee just now it will be very painful to thee: but there is this comfort, namely, that *the Lord* makes it. He sends the sharp blasts of adversity to nip the buds of expectation: he scattereth the hoarfrost like ashes over the once verdant meadows of our joy: he casteth forth his ice like morsels freezing the streams of our delight. He does it all, he is the great Winter King, and rules in the realms of frost, and therefore thou canst not murmur. Losses, crosses, heaviness, sickness, poverty, and a thousand other ills, are of the Lord's sending, and come to us with wise design. Frosts kill noxious insects, and put a bound to raging diseases; they break up the clods, and sweeten the soul. O that such good results would always follow our winters of affliction!

How we prize the fire just now! how pleasant is its cheerful glow! Let us in the same manner prize our Lord, who is the constant source of warmth and comfort in every time of trouble. Let us draw nigh to him, and in him find joy and peace in believing. Let us wrap ourselves in the warm garments of his promises, and go forth to labors which befit the season, for it were ill to be as the sluggard who will not plough by reason of the cold; for he shall beg in summer and have nothing.

DECEMBER 2

Thou art all fair, my love.
—Song of Solomon 4:7

HE Lord's admiration of his Church is very wonderful, and his description of her beauty is very glowing. She is not merely *fair*, but *"all* fair." He views her in himself, washed in his sin-atoning blood and clothed in his meritorious righteousness, and he considers her to be full of comeliness and beauty. No wonder that such is the case, since it is but his own perfect excellency that he admires; for the holiness, glory, and perfection of his Church are his own glorious garments on the back of his own well-beloved spouse. She is not simply pure, or well-proportioned; she is positively lovely and fair! She has actual merit! Her deformities of sin are removed; but more, she has through her Lord obtained a meritorious righteousness by which an actual beauty is conferred upon her. Believers have a positive righteousness given to them when they become "accepted in the beloved" (Eph. 1:6). Nor is the Church barely lovely, she is *superlatively so. Her* Lord styles her "Thou fairest among women." She has a real worth and excellence which cannot be rivaled by all the nobility and royalty of the world. If Jesus could exchange his elect bride for all the queens and empresses of earth, or even for the angels in heaven, he would not, for he puts her first and foremost—"fairest among women." Like the moon she far outshines the stars. Nor is this an opinion which he is ashamed of, for he invites all men to hear it. He sets a "behold" before it, a special note of exclamation, inviting and arresting attention. *"Behold,* thou art fair, my love; *behold,* thou art fair" (Song of Sol. 4:1). His opinion he publishes abroad even now, and one day from the throne of his glory he will avow the truth of it before the assembled universe. "Come, ye blessed of my Father" (Matt. 25:34), will be his solemn affirmation of the loveliness of his elect.

337

DECEMBER 3

There is no spot in thee.
—Song of Solomon 4:7

AVING pronounced his Church positively full of beauty, our Lord confirms his praise by a precious negative, "There is no spot in thee." As if the thought occurred to the Bridegroom that the carping world would insinuate that he had only mentioned her comely parts, and had purposely omitted those features which were deformed or defiled, he sums up all by declaring her universally and entirely fair, and utterly devoid of stain. A spot may soon be removed, and is the very least thing that can disfigure beauty, but even from this little blemish the believer is delivered in his Lord's sight. If he had said there is no hideous scar, no horrible deformity, no deadly ulcer, we might even then have marveled; but when he testifies that she is free from the slightest spot, all these other forms of defilement are included, and the depth of wonder is increased. If he had but promised to remove all spots by-and-by, we should have had eternal reason for joy; but when he speaks of it as already done, who can restrain the most intense emotions of satisfaction and delight? O my soul, here is marrow and fatness for thee; eat thy full, and be satisfied with royal dainties.

Christ Jesus has no quarrel with his spouse. She often wanders from him, and grieves his Holy Spirit, but he does not allow her faults to affect his love. He sometimes chides, but it is always in the tenderest manner, with the kindest intentions: it is "my love" even then. There is no remembrance of our follies, he does not cherish ill thoughts of us, but he pardons and loves as well after the offence as before it. It is well for us it is so, for if Jesus were as mindful of injuries as we are, how could he commune with us? Many a time a believer will put himself out of humor with the Lord for some slight turn in providence, but our precious Husband knows our silly hearts too well to take any offence at our ill manners.

DECEMBER 4

I have much people in this city.
—Acts 18:10

THIS should be a great encouragement to try to do good, since God has among the vilest of the vile, the most reprobate, the most debauched and drunken, an elect people who *must* be saved. When you take the Word to them, you do so because God has ordained you to be the messenger of life to their souls, and *they must* receive it, for so the decree of predestination runs. They are as much redeemed by blood as the saints before the eternal throne. They are Christ's property, and yet perhaps they are lovers of the ale-house, and haters of holiness; but if Jesus Christ purchased them he will have them. God is not unfaithful to forget the price which his Son has paid. He will not suffer his substitution to be in any case an ineffectual, dead thing. Tens of thousands of redeemed ones are not regenerated yet, but regenerated they must be; and this is our comfort when we go forth to them with the quickening Word of God.

Nay, more, these ungodly ones are prayed for by Christ before the throne. "Neither pray I for these alone," saith the great Intercessor, "but for *them also which shall believe* on me through their word." Poor, ignorant souls, they know nothing about prayer for themselves, but Jesus prays for them. Their names are on his breastplate, and ere long they must bow their stubborn knee, breathing the penitential sigh before the throne of grace. "The time of figs is not yet." The predestinated moment has not struck; but, when it comes, *they shall obey,* for God will have his own; *they must,* for the Spirit is not to be withstood when he cometh forth with fullness of power—*they must* become the willing servants of the living God. "My people shall be willing in the day of my power." "He shall justify many." "He shall see of the travail of his soul." "I will divide him a portion with the great, and he shall divide the spoil with the strong."

339

DECEMBER 5

Ask, and it shall be given you.
—Matthew 7:7

E know of a place in England still existing, where a dole of bread is served to every passerby who chooses to ask for it. Whoever the traveler may be, he has but to knock at the door of St. Cross Hospital, and there is the dole of bread for him. Jesus Christ so loveth sinners that he has built a St. Cross Hospital, so that whenever a sinner is hungry, he has but to knock and have his wants supplied. Nay, he has done better; he has attached to this Hospital of the Cross a bath; and whenever a soul is black and filthy, it has but to go there and be washed. The fountain is always full, always efficacious. No sinner ever went into it and found that it could not wash away his stains. Sins which were scarlet and crimson have all disappeared, and the sinner has been whiter than snow. As if this were not enough, there is attached to this Hospital of the Cross a wardrobe, and a sinner making application simply as a sinner, may be clothed from head to foot; and if he wishes to be a soldier, he may not merely have a garment for ordinary wear, but armor which shall cover him from the sole of his foot to the crown of his head. If he asks for a sword, he shall have that given to him, and a shield too. Nothing that is good for him shall be denied him. He shall have spending-money so long as he lives, and he shall have an eternal heritage of glorious treasure when he enters into the joy of his Lord.

If all these things are to be had by merely knocking at mercy's door, O my soul, knock hard this morning, and ask large things of thy generous Lord. Leave not the throne of grace till all thy wants have been spread before the Lord, and until by faith thou hast a comfortable prospect that they shall be all supplied. No bashfulness need retard when Jesus invites. No unbelief should hinder when Jesus promises. No cold-heartedness should restrain when such blessings are to be obtained.

December 6

As is the heavenly, such are they also that are heavenly.
—1 Corinthians 15:48

 HE head and members are of one nature, and not like that monstrous image which Nebuchadnezzar saw in his dream. The head was of fine gold, but the belly and thighs were of brass, the legs of iron, and the feet, part of iron and part of clay. Christ's mystical body is no absurd combination of opposites; the members were mortal, and therefore Jesus died; the glorified head is immortal, and therefore the body is immortal too, for thus the record stands, "Because I live, ye shall live also." As is our loving Head, such is the body, and every member in particular. A chosen Head and chosen members; an accepted Head, and accepted members; a living Head, and living members. If the head be pure gold, all the parts of the body are of pure gold also. Thus is there a double union of nature as a basis for the closest communion. Pause here, devout reader, and see if thou canst without ecstatic amazement, contemplate the infinite condescension of the Son of God in thus exalting thy wretchedness into blessed union with his glory. Thou art so mean that in remembrance of thy mortality, thou mayest say to corruption, "Thou art my father," and to the worm, "Thou art my sister;" and yet in Christ thou art so honored that thou canst say to the Almighty, "Abba, Father," and to the Incarnate God, "Thou art my brother and my husband." Surely if relationships to ancient and noble families make men think highly of themselves, *we* have whereof to glory over the heads of them all. Let the poorest and most despised believer lay hold upon this privilege; let not a senseless indolence make him negligent to trace his pedigree, and let him suffer no foolish attachment to present vanities to occupy his thoughts to the exclusion of this glorious, this heavenly honor of union with Christ.

DECEMBER 7

Base things of the world hath God chosen.
—1 Corinthians 1:28

ALK the streets by moonlight, if you dare, and you will see sinners then. Watch when the night is dark, and the wind is howling, and the picklock is grating in the door, and you will see sinners then. Go to yon jail, and walk through the wards, and mark the men with heavy over-hanging brows, men whom you would not like to meet at night, and there are sinners there. Go to the Reformatories, and note those who have betrayed a rampant juvenile depravity, and you will see sinners there. Go across the seas to the place where a man will gnaw a bone upon which is reeking human flesh, and there is a sinner there. Go where you will, you need not ransack earth to find sinners, for they are common enough; you may find them in every lane and street of every city, and town, and village, and hamlet. It is for such that Jesus died. If you will select me the grossest specimen of humanity, if he be but born of woman, I will have hope of him yet, because Jesus Christ is come to seek and to save *sinners*. Electing love has selected some of the worst to be made the best. Pebbles of the brook grace turns into jewels for the crown royal. Worthless dross he transforms into pure gold. Redeeming love has set apart many of the worst of mankind to be the reward of the Savior's passion. Effectual grace calls forth many of the vilest of the vile to sit at the table of mercy, and therefore let none despair.

Reader, by that love looking out of Jesus' tearful eyes, by that love streaming from those bleeding wounds, by that faithful love, that strong love, that pure, disinterested, and abiding love; by the heart and by the bowels of the Savior's compassion, we conjure you turn not away as though it were nothing to you; but believe on him and you shall be saved. Trust your soul with him and he will bring you to his Father's right hand in glory everlasting.

DECEMBER 8

Thou hast a few names
even in Sardis which have not defiled their garments;
and they shall walk with me in white: for they are worthy.
—Revelation 3:4

E may understand this to refer to *justification*. "They shall walk in white;" that is, they shall enjoy a constant sense of their own justification by faith; they shall understand that the righteousness of Christ is imputed to them, that they have all been washed and made whiter than the newly-fallen snow.

Again, it refers to *joy and gladness:* for white robes were holiday dresses among the Jews. They who have not defiled their garments shall have their faces always bright; they shall understand what Solomon meant when he said,

> Go thy way, eat thy bread with joy, and drink thy wine with a merry heart. Let thy garments be always white, for God hath accepted thy works.

He who is accepted of God shall wear white garments of joy and gladness, while he walks in sweet communion with the Lord Jesus. Whence so many doubts, so much misery, and mourning? It is because so many believers defile their garments with sin and error, and hence they lose the joy of their salvation, and the comfortable fellowship of the Lord Jesus, they do not here below walk in white.

The promise also refers to *walking in white before the throne of God.* Those who have not defiled their garments here shall most certainly walk in white up yonder, where the white-robed hosts sing perpetual hallelujahs to the Most High. They shall possess joys inconceivable, happiness beyond a dream, bliss which imagination knoweth not, blessedness which even the stretch of desire hath not reached. The "undefiled in the way" shall have all this—not of merit, nor of works, but of grace. They shall walk with Christ in white, for he has made them "worthy." In his sweet company they shall drink of the living fountains of waters.

DECEMBER 9

Therefore will the Lord wait that he may be gracious unto you.
—Isaiah 30:18

GOD often *delays in answering prayer.* We have several instances of this in sacred Scripture. Jacob did not get the blessing from the angel until near the dawn of day—he had to wrestle all night for it. The poor woman of Syrophenicia was answered not a word for a long while. Paul besought the Lord *thrice* that "the thorn in the flesh" might be taken from him, and he received no assurance that it should be taken away, but instead thereof a promise that God's grace should be sufficient for him. If thou hast been knocking at the gate of mercy, and hast received no answer, shall I tell thee why the mighty Maker hath not opened the door and let thee in? Our Father has reasons peculiar to himself for thus keeping us waiting. Sometimes it is to show his power and his sovereignty, that men may know that Jehovah has a right to give or to withhold. More frequently the delay is for our profit. Thou art perhaps kept waiting in order that thy desires may be more fervent. God knows that delay will quicken and increase desire, and that if he keeps thee waiting thou wilt see thy necessity more clearly, and wilt seek more earnestly; and that thou wilt prize the mercy all the more for its long tarrying. There may also be something wrong in thee which has need to be removed, before the joy of the Lord is given. Perhaps thy views of the Gospel plan are confused, or thou mayest be placing some little reliance on thyself, instead of trusting simply and entirely to the Lord Jesus. Or, God makes thee tarry awhile that he may the more fully display the riches of his grace to thee at last. Thy prayers are all filed in heaven, and if not immediately answered they are certainly not forgotten, but in a little while shall be fulfilled to thy delight and satisfaction. Let not despair make thee silent, but continue instant in earnest supplication.

December 10

So shall we ever be with the Lord.—1 Thessalonians 4:17

EVEN the sweetest visits from Christ, how short they are—and how transitory! One moment our eyes see him, and we rejoice with joy unspeakable and full of glory, but again a little time and we do not see him, for our beloved withdraws himself from us; like a roe or a young hart he leaps over the mountains of division; he is gone to the land of spices, and feeds no more among the lilies.

> If today he deigns to bless us
> With a sense of pardoned sin,
> He tomorrow may distress us,
> Make us feel the plague within.

Oh, how sweet the prospect of the time when we shall not behold him at a distance, but see him face to face: when he shall not be as a wayfaring man tarrying but for a night, but shall eternally enfold us in the bosom of his glory. We shall not see him for a little season, but

> Millions of years our wondering eyes,
> Shall o'er our Savior's beauties rove;
> And myriad ages we'll adore,
> The wonders of his love.

In heaven there shall be no interruptions from care or sin; no weeping shall dim our eyes; no earthly business shall distract our happy thoughts; we shall have nothing to hinder us from gazing forever on the Sun of Righteousness with unwearied eyes. Oh, if it be so sweet to see him now and then, how sweet to gaze on that blessed face for aye, and never have a cloud rolling between, and never have to turn one's eyes away to look on a world of weariness and woe! Blest day, when wilt thou dawn? Rise, O unsetting sun! The joys of sense may leave us as soon as they will, for this shall make glorious amends. If to die is but to enter into uninterrupted communion with Jesus, then death is indeed gain, and the black drop is swallowed up in a sea of victory.

DECEMBER 11

Faithful is he that calleth you, who also will do it.
—1 Thessalonians 5:24

HEAVEN is a place where we shall never sin; where we shall cease our constant watch against an indefatigable enemy, because there will be no tempter to ensnare our feet. There the wicked cease from troubling, and the weary are at rest. Heaven is the "undefiled inheritance;" it is the land of perfect holiness, and therefore of complete security. But do not the saints even on earth sometimes taste the joys of blissful security? The doctrine of God's word is, that all who are in union with the Lamb are safe; that all the righteous shall hold on their way; that those who have committed their souls to the keeping of Christ shall find him a faithful and immutable preserver. Sustained by such a doctrine we can enjoy security even on earth; not that high and glorious security which renders us free from every slip, but that holy security which arises from the sure promise of Jesus that none who believe in him shall ever perish, but shall be with him where he is. Believer, let us often reflect with joy on the doctrine of the perseverance of the saints, and honor the faithfulness of our God by a holy confidence in him.

May our God bring home to you a sense of your safety in Christ Jesus! May he assure you that your name is graven on his hand; and whisper in your ear the promise, "Fear not, I am with thee." Look upon him, the great Surety of the covenant, as faithful and true, and, therefore, bound and engaged to present you, the weakest of the family, with all the chosen race, before the throne of God; and in such a sweet contemplation you will drink the juice of the spiced wine of the Lord's pomegranate, and taste the dainty fruits of Paradise. You will have an antepast of the enjoyments which ravish the souls of the perfect saints above, if you can believe with unstaggering faith that "faithful is he that calleth you, who also will do it."

DECEMBER 12

His ways are everlasting.
—Habakkuk 3:6

WHAT he hath done at one time, he will do yet again. Man's ways are variable, but God's ways are everlasting. There are many reasons for this most comforting truth: among them are the following—the Lord's ways are *the* result of wise deliberation; he ordereth all things according to the counsel of his own will. Human action is frequently the hasty result of passion, or fear, and is followed by regret and alteration; but nothing can take the Almighty by surprise, or happen otherwise than he has foreseen. His ways are *the outgrowth of an immutable character*, and in them the fixed and settled attributes of God are clearly to be seen. Unless the Eternal One himself can undergo change, his ways, which are himself in action, must remain forever the same. Is he eternally just, gracious, faithful, wise, tender?—then his ways must ever be distinguished for the same excellences. Beings act according to their nature: when those natures change, their conduct varies also; but since God cannot know the shadow of a turning, his ways will abide everlastingly the same. Moreover there is no reason from without which could reverse the divine ways, since they are *the embodiment of irresistible might*. The earth is said, by the prophet, to be cleft with rivers, mountains tremble, the deep lifts up its hands, and sun and moon stand still, when Jehovah marches forth for the salvation of his people. Who can stay his hand, or say unto him, What doest thou? But it is not might alone which gives stability; God's ways are *the manifestation of the eternal principles of right*, and therefore can never pass away. Wrong breeds decay and involves ruin, but the true and the good have about them a vitality which ages cannot diminish.

This morning let us go to our heavenly Father with confidence, remembering that Jesus Christ is the same yesterday, today, and forever, and in him the Lord is ever gracious to his people.

DECEMBER 13

Salt without prescribing how much.
—*Ezra 7:22*

 ALT was used in every offering made by fire unto the Lord, and from its preserving and purifying properties it was the grateful emblem of divine grace in the soul. It is worthy of our attentive regard that, when Artaxerxes gave salt to Ezra the priest, he set no limit to the quantity, and we may be quite certain that when the King of kings distributes grace among his royal priesthood, the supply is not cut short by *him*. Often are we straitened in ourselves, but never in the Lord. He who chooses to gather much manna will find that he may have as much as he desires. There is no such famine in Jerusalem that the citizens should eat their bread by weight and drink their water by measure. Some things in the economy of grace are measured; for instance our vinegar and gall are given us with such exactness that we never have a single drop too much, but of the salt of grace no stint is made, "Ask what thou wilt and it shall be given unto thee." Parents need to lock up the fruit cupboard, and the sweet jars, but there is no need to keep the salt-box under lock and key, for few children will eat too greedily from that. A man may have too much money, or too much honor, but he cannot have too much grace. When Jeshurun waxed fat in the flesh, he kicked against God, but there is no fear of a man's becoming too full of grace: a *plethora* of grace is impossible. More wealth brings more care, but more grace brings more joy. Increased wisdom is increased sorrow, but abundance of the Spirit is fullness of joy. Believer, go to the throne for a large supply of heavenly salt. It will season thine afflictions, which are unsavory without salt; it will preserve thy heart which corrupts if salt be absent, and it will kill thy sins even as salt kills reptiles. Thou needest much; seek much, and have much.

DECEMBER 14

They go from strength to strength.
—Psalm 84:7

HEY go *from strength to strength.* There are various renderings of these words, but all of them contain the idea of progress. Our own good translation of the authorized version is enough for us this morning. "They go from strength to strength." That is, they grow stronger and stronger. Usually, if we are walking, we go from strength to weakness; we start fresh and in good order for our journey, but by-and-by the road is rough, and the sun is hot, we sit down by the wayside, and then again painfully pursue our weary way. But the Christian pilgrim having obtained fresh supplies of grace, is as vigorous after years of toilsome travel and struggle as when he first set out. He may not be quite so elate and buoyant, nor perhaps quite so hot and hasty in his zeal as he once was, but he is much stronger in all that constitutes real power, and travels, if more slowly, far more surely. Some gray-haired veterans have been as firm in their grasp of truth, and as zealous in diffusing it, as they were in their younger days; but, alas, it must be confessed it is often otherwise, for the love of many waxes cold and iniquity abounds, but this is their own sin and not the fault of the promise which still holds good:

> The youths shall faint and be weary, and the young men shall utterly fall, but they that wait upon the Lord shall renew their strength; they shall mount up with wings as eagles, they shall run and not be weary, and they shall walk and not faint.

Fretful spirits sit down and trouble themselves about the future. "Alas!" say they, "we go from affliction to affliction." Very true, O thou of little faith, but then thou goest from strength to strength also. Thou shalt never find a bundle of affliction which has not bound up in the midst of it sufficient grace. God will give the strength of ripe manhood with the burden allotted to full-grown shoulders.

DECEMBER 15

Orpah kissed her mother-in-law; but Ruth clave unto her.
—Ruth 1:14

BOTH of them had an affection for Naomi, and therefore set out with her upon her return to the land of Judah. But the hour of test came; Naomi most unselfishly set before each of them the trials which awaited them, and bade them if they cared for ease and comfort to return to their Moabitish friends. At first both of them declared that they would cast in their lot with the Lord's people; but upon still further consideration Orpah with much grief and a respectful kiss left her mother in law, and her people, and her God, and went back to her idolatrous friends, while Ruth with all her heart gave herself up to the God of her mother in law. It is one thing to love the ways of the Lord when all is fair, and quite another to cleave to them under all discouragements and difficulties. The kiss of outward profession is very cheap and easy, but the practical cleaving to the Lord, which must show itself in holy decision for truth and holiness, is not so small a matter. How stands the case with us, is our heart fixed upon Jesus, is the sacrifice bound with cords to the horns of the altar? Have we counted the cost, and are we solemnly ready to suffer all worldly loss for the Master's sake? The after gain will be an abundant recompense, for Egypt's treasures are not to be compared with the glory to be revealed. Orpah is heard of no more; in glorious ease and idolatrous pleasure her life melts into the gloom of death; but Ruth lives in history and in heaven, for grace has placed her in the noble line whence sprung the King of kings. Blessed among women shall those be who for Christ's sake can renounce all; but forgotten and worse than forgotten shall those be who in the hour of temptation do violence to conscience and turn back unto the world. O that this morning we may not be content with the form of devotion, which may be no better than Orpah's kiss, but may the Holy Spirit work in us a cleaving of our whole heart to our Lord Jesus.

December 16

Come unto me—Matthew 11:28

THE cry of the Christian religion is the gentle word, "Come." The Jewish law harshly said,

> Go, take heed unto thy steps as to the path in which thou shalt walk. Break the commandments, and thou shalt perish; keep them, and thou shalt live.

The law was a dispensation of terror, which drove men before it as with a scourge; the gospel draws with bands of love. Jesus is the good Shepherd going before his sheep, bidding them follow him, and ever leading them onwards with the sweet word, "Come." The law repels, the gospel attracts. The law shows the distance which there is between God and man; the gospel bridges that awful chasm, and brings the sinner across it.

From the first moment of your spiritual life until you are ushered into glory, the language of Christ to you will be, *"Come, come* unto me." As a mother puts out her finger to her little child and woos it to walk by saying, *"Come,"* even so does Jesus. He will always be ahead of you, bidding you follow him as the soldier follows his captain. He will always go before you to pave your way, and clear your path, and you shall hear his animating voice calling you after him all through life; while in the solemn hour of death, his sweet words with which he shall usher you into the heavenly world shall be—"Come, ye blessed of my Father."

Nay, further, this is not only Christ's cry to you, but, if you be a believer, this is your cry to Christ—"Come! come!" You will be longing for his second advent; you will be saying, "Come quickly, even so come Lord Jesus." You will be panting for nearer and closer communion with him. As his voice to you is "Come," your response to him will be,

> Come, Lord, and abide with me. Come, and occupy alone the throne of my heart; reign there without a rival, and consecrate me entirely to thy service.

DECEMBER 17

I remember thee.
—Jeremiah 2:2

ET us note that Christ delights to think upon his Church, and to look upon her beauty. As the bird returneth often to its nest, and as the wayfarer hastens to his home, so doth the mind continually pursue the object of its choice. We cannot look too often upon that face which we love; we desire always to have our precious things in our sight. It is even so with our Lord Jesus. From all eternity "his delights were with the sons of men;" his thoughts rolled onward to the time when his elect should be born into the world; he viewed them in the mirror of his foreknowledge. "In thy book," he says, "all my members were written, which in continuance were fashioned, when as yet there was none of them" (Ps. 139:16). When the world was set upon its pillars, he was there, and he set the bounds of the people according to the number of the children of Israel. Many a time before his incarnation, he descended to this lower earth in the similitude of a man; on the plains of Mamre (Gen. 18), by the brook of Jabbok (Gen. 32:24–30), beneath the walls of Jericho (Josh. 5:13), and in the fiery furnace of Babylon (Dan. 3:19, 25), the Son of Man visited his people. Because his soul delighted in them, he could not rest away from them, for his heart longed after them. Never were they absent from his heart, for he had written their names upon his hands, and graven them upon his side. As the breastplate containing the names of the tribes of Israel was the most brilliant ornament worn by the high priest, so the names of Christ's elect were his most precious jewels, and glittered on his heart. We may often forget to meditate upon the perfections of our Lord, but he never ceases to remember us. Let us chide ourselves for past forgetfulness, and pray for grace ever to bear him in fondest remembrance. Lord, paint upon the eyeballs of my soul the image of thy Son.

December 18

Rend your heart, and not your garments.
—Joel 2:13

ARMENT-RENDING and other outward signs of religious emotion, are *easily manifested* and are *frequently hypocritical;* but to feel true repentance is far more difficult, and consequently far less common. Men will attend to the most multiplied and minute ceremonial regulations—for such things are *pleasing to the flesh*—but true religion is too humbling, too heart-searching, too thorough for the tastes of the carnal men; they prefer something more ostentatious, flimsy, and worldly. Outward observances are *temporarily comfortable;* eye and ear are pleased; self-conceit is fed, and self-righteousness is puffed up: but they are *ultimately delusive,* for in the article of death, and at the day of judgment, the soul needs something more substantial than ceremonies and rituals to lean upon. Apart from vital godliness all religion is *utterly vain;* offered without a sincere heart, every form of worship is a solemn sham and an impudent mockery of the majesty of heaven.

Heart-rending is *divinely wrought and solemnly felt.* It is a secret grief which is *personally experienced,* not in mere form, but as a deep, soul-moving work of the Holy Spirit upon the inmost heart of each believer. It is not a matter to be merely talked of and believed in, but keenly and sensitively felt in every living child of the living God. It is *powerfully humiliating,* and *completely sin-purging;* but then it is *sweetly preparative* for those gracious consolations which proud unhumbled spirits are unable to receive; and it is *distinctly discriminating,* for it belongs to the elect of God, and to them alone.

The text commands us to rend our hearts, but they are naturally hard as marble: how, then, can this be done? We must take them to Calvary: a dying Savior's voice rent the rocks once, and it is as powerful now. O blessed Spirit, let us hear the death-cries of Jesus, and our hearts shall be rent even as men rend their vestures in the day of lamentation.

DECEMBER 19

*The lot is cast into the lap,
but the whole disposing thereof is of the Lord.*
—Proverbs 16:33

IF the disposal of the lot is the Lord's, whose is the arrangement of our whole life? If the simple casting of a lot is guided by him, how much more the events of our entire life—especially when we are told by our blessed Savior: "The very hairs of your head are all numbered: not a sparrow falleth to the ground without your Father." It would bring a holy calm over your mind, dear friend, if you were always to remember this. It would so relieve your mind from anxiety, that you would be the better able to walk in patience, quiet, and cheerfulness as a Christian should. When a man is anxious he cannot pray with faith; when he is troubled about the world, he cannot serve his Master, his thoughts are serving himself. If you would "seek first the kingdom of God and his righteousness," all things would then be added unto you. You are meddling with Christ's business, and neglecting your own when you fret about your lot and circumstances. You have been trying "providing" work and forgetting that it is yours to obey. Be wise and attend to the obeying, and let Christ manage the providing. Come and survey your Father's storehouse, and ask whether he will let you starve while he has laid up so great an abundance in his garner? Look at his heart of mercy; see if that can ever prove unkind! Look at his inscrutable wisdom; see if that will ever be at fault. Above all, look up to Jesus Christ your Intercessor, and ask yourself, while he pleads, can your Father deal ungraciously with you? If he remembers even sparrows, will he forget one of the least of his poor children? "Cast thy burden upon the Lord, and he will sustain thee. He will never suffer the righteous to be moved."

> My soul, rest happy in thy low estate,
> Nor hope nor wish to be esteem'd or great;
> To take the impress of the Will Divine,
> Be that thy glory, and those riches thine.

DECEMBER 20

Yea, I have loved thee with an everlasting love.
—Jeremiah 31:3

OMETIMES the Lord Jesus *tells* his Church his love thoughts.

He does not think it enough behind her back to tell it, but in her very presence he says, "Thou art all fair, my love." It is true, this is not his ordinary method; he is a wise lover, and knows when to keep back the intimation of love and when to let it out; but there are times when he will make no secret of it; times when he will put it beyond all dispute in the souls of his people.

—R. Erskine's Sermons

The Holy Spirit is often pleased, in a most gracious manner, to witness with our spirits of the love of Jesus. He takes of the things of Christ and reveals them unto us. No voice is heard from the clouds, and no vision is seen in the night, but we have a testimony more sure than either of these. If an angel should fly from heaven and inform the saint personally of the Savior's love to him, the evidence would not be one whit more satisfactory than that which is borne in the heart by the Holy Ghost. Ask those of the Lord's people who have lived the nearest to the gates of heaven, and they will tell you that they have had seasons when the love of Christ towards them has been a fact so clear and sure, that they could no more doubt it than they could question their own existence. Yes, beloved believer, you and I have had times of refreshing from the presence of the Lord, and then our faith has mounted to the topmost heights of assurance. We have had confidence to lean our heads upon the bosom of our Lord, and we have no more questioned our Master's affection to us than John did when in that blessed posture; nay, nor so much: for the dark question, "Lord, is it I that shall betray thee?" has been put far from us. He has kissed us with the kisses of his mouth, and killed our doubts by the closeness of his embrace. His love has been sweeter than wine to our souls.

DECEMBER 21

Yet he hath made with me an everlasting covenant.
—2 Samuel 23:5

THIS covenant is *divine in its origin.* "*He* hath made with me an everlasting covenant." Oh that great word *he!* Stop, my soul. God, the everlasting Father, has positively made a covenant with thee; yes, that God who spake the world into existence by a word; he, stooping from his majesty, takes hold of thy hand and makes a covenant with thee. Is it not a deed, the stupendous condescension of which might ravish our hearts forever if we could really understand it? "HE hath made with me a covenant." A king has not made a covenant with me—that were somewhat; but the Prince of the kings of the earth, Shaddai, the Lord All-sufficient, the Jehovah of ages, the everlasting Elohim, "He hath made with me an everlasting covenant." But notice, *it is particular in its application.* "Yet hath he made with ME an everlasting covenant." Here lies the sweetness of it to each believer. It is naught for me that he made peace for the world; I want to know whether he made peace for *me!* It is little that he hath made a covenant, I want to know whether he has made a covenant *with me.* Blessed is the assurance that he hath made a covenant with me! If God the Holy Ghost gives me assurance of this, then his salvation is mine, his heart is mine, he himself is mine—*he is my God.*

This covenant is *everlasting in its duration.* An everlasting covenant means a covenant which had no beginning, and which shall never, never end. How sweet amidst all the uncertainties of life, to know that "the foundation of the Lord standeth sure," and to have God's own promise, "My covenant will I not break, nor alter the thing that is gone out of my lips." Like dying David, I will sing of this, even though my house be not so with God as my heart desireth.

December 22

I will strengthen thee.
—Isaiah 41:10

OD has a strong reserve with which to discharge this engagement; for he is able to do all things. Believer, till thou canst drain dry the ocean of omnipotence, till thou canst break into pieces the towering mountains of almighty strength, thou never needest to fear. Think not that the strength of man shall ever be able to overcome the power of God. Whilst the earth's huge pillars stand, thou hast enough reason to abide firm in thy faith. The same God who directs the earth in its orbit, who feeds the burning furnace of the sun, and trims the lamps of heaven, has promised to supply thee with daily strength. While he is able to uphold the universe, dream not that he will prove unable to fulfill his own promises. Remember what he did in the days of old, in the former generations. Remember how he spake and it was done; how he commanded, and it stood fast. Shall he that created the world grow weary? He hangeth the world upon nothing; shall he who doth this be unable to support his children? Shall he be unfaithful to his word for want of power? Who is it that restrains the tempest? Doth not he ride upon the wings of the wind, and make the clouds his chariots, and hold the ocean in the hollow of his hand? How can he fail thee? When he has put such a faithful promise as this on record, wilt thou for a moment indulge the thought that he has outpromised himself, and gone beyond his power to fulfill? Ah, no! Thou canst doubt no longer.

O thou who art my God and my strength, I can believe that this promise shall be fulfilled, for the boundless reservoir of thy grace can never be exhausted, and the overflowing storehouse of thy strength can never be emptied by thy friends or rifled by thine enemies.

Now let the feeble all be strong,
And make Jehovah's arm their song.

DECEMBER 23

Friend, go up higher.—Luke 14:10

HEN first the life of grace begins in the soul, we do indeed draw near to God, but it is with great fear and trembling. The soul conscious of guilt, and humbled thereby, is overawed with the solemnity of its position; it is cast to the earth by a sense of the grandeur of Jehovah, in whose presence it stands. With unfeigned bashfulness it takes the lowest room.

But, in after life, as the Christian grows in grace, although he will never forget the solemnity of his position, and will never lose that holy awe which must encompass a gracious man when he is in the presence of the God who can create or can destroy; yet his fear has all its terror taken out of it; it becomes a holy reverence, and no more an overshadowing dread. He is called up higher, to greater access to God in Christ Jesus. Then the man of God, walking amid the splendors of Deity, and veiling his face like the glorious cherubim, with those twin wings, the blood and righteousness of Jesus Christ, will, reverent and bowed in spirit, approach the throne; and seeing there a God of love, of goodness, and of mercy, he will realize rather the covenant character of God than his absolute Deity. He will see in God rather his goodness than his greatness, and more of his love than of his majesty. Then will the soul, bowing still as humbly as aforetime, enjoy a more sacred liberty of intercession; for while prostrate before the glory of the Infinite God, it will be sustained by the refreshing consciousness of being in the presence of boundless mercy and infinite love, and by the realization of acceptance "in the Beloved." Thus the believer is bidden to come up higher, and is enabled to exercise the privilege of rejoicing in God, and drawing near to him in holy confidence, saying, "Abba, Father."

> So may we go from strength to strength,
> And daily grow in grace,
> Till in thine image raised at length,
> We see thee face to face.

❦

December 24

For your sakes he became poor.
—2 Corinthians 8:9

THE Lord Jesus Christ was eternally *rich*, glorious, and exalted; but "though *he was rich*, yet for your sakes he became poor." As the rich saint cannot be true in his communion with his poor brethren unless of his substance he ministers to their necessities, so (the same rule holding with the head as between the members), it is impossible that our Divine Lord could have had fellowship with us unless he had imparted to us of his own abounding wealth, and had become poor to make us rich. Had he remained upon his throne of glory, and had we continued in the ruins of the fall without receiving his salvation, communion would have been impossible on both sides. Our position by the fall, apart from the covenant of grace, made it as impossible for fallen man to communicate with God as it is for Belial to be in concord with Christ. In order, therefore, that communion might be compassed, it was necessary that the rich kinsman should bestow his estate upon his poor relatives, that the righteous Savior should give to his sinning brethren of his own perfection, and that we, the poor and guilty, should receive of his fullness grace for grace; that thus in giving and receiving, the One might descend from the heights, and the other ascend from the depths, and so be able to embrace each other in true and hearty fellowship. Poverty must be enriched by him in whom are infinite treasures before it can venture to commune; and guilt must lose itself in imputed and imparted righteousness ere the soul can walk in fellowship with purity. Jesus must clothe his people in his own garments, or he cannot admit them into his palace of glory; and he must wash them in his own blood, or else they will be too defiled for the embrace of his fellowship.

O believer, herein is love! For *your sake* the Lord Jesus "became poor" that he might lift you up into communion with himself.

DECEMBER 25

Behold, a virgin shall conceive, and bear a son,
and shall call his name Immanuel.
—Isaiah 7:14

LET us today go down to Bethlehem, and in company with wondering shepherds and adoring Magi, let us see him who was born King of the Jews, for we by faith can claim an interest in him, and can sing, "*Unto us* a child is born, *unto us* a son is given." Jesus is Jehovah incarnate, our Lord and our God, and yet our brother and friend; let us adore and admire. Let us notice at the very first glance *his miraculous conception.* It was a thing unheard of before, and unparalleled since, that a virgin should conceive and bear a Son. The first promise ran thus, "*The seed of the woman,*" not the offspring of the man. Since venturous woman led the way in the sin which brought forth Paradise lost, she, and she alone, ushers in the Regainer of Paradise. Our Savior, although truly man, was as to his human nature the Holy One of God. Let us reverently bow before the holy Child whose innocence restores to manhood its ancient glory; and let us pray that he may be formed in us, the hope of glory. Fail not to note *his humble parentage.* His mother has been described simply as "a virgin," not a princess, or prophetess, nor a matron of large estate. True, the blood of kings ran in her veins; nor was her mind a weak and untaught one, for she could sing most sweetly a song of praise; but yet how humble her position, how poor the man to whom she stood affianced, and how miserable the accommodation afforded to the new-born King!

Immanuel, God with us in our nature, in our sorrow, in our lifework, in our punishment, in our grave, and now with us, or rather we with him, in resurrection, ascension, triumph, and Second Advent splendor.

DECEMBER 26

The last Adam.
—1 Corinthians 15:45

JESUS is the federal head of his elect. As in Adam, every heir of flesh and blood has a personal interest, because he is the covenant head and representative of the race as considered under the law of works; so under the law of grace, every redeemed soul is one with the Lord from heaven, since he is the Second Adam, the Sponsor and Substitute of the elect in the new covenant of love. The apostle Paul declares that Levi was in the loins of Abraham when Melchizedek met him: it is a certain truth that the believer was in the loins of Jesus Christ, the Mediator, when in old eternity the covenant settlements of grace were decreed, ratified, and made sure forever. Thus, whatever Christ hath done, he hath wrought for the whole body of his Church. We were crucified in him and buried with him (read Col. 2:10–13), and to make it still more wonderful, we are risen with him and even ascended with him to the seats on high (Eph. 2:6). It is thus that the Church has fulfilled the law, and is "accepted in *the beloved.*" It is thus that she is regarded with complacency by the just Jehovah, for he views her in Jesus, and does not look upon her as separate from her covenant head. As the Anointed Redeemer of Israel, Christ Jesus has nothing distinct from his Church, but all that he has, he holds for her. Adam's righteousness was ours so long as he maintained it, and his sin was ours the moment that he committed it; and in the same manner, all that the Second Adam is or does, is ours as well as his, seeing that he is our representative. Here is the foundation of the covenant of grace. This gracious system of representation and substitution, which moved Justin Martyr to cry out, "O blessed change, O sweet permutation!" this is the very groundwork of the gospel of our salvation, and is to be received with strong faith and rapturous joy.

DECEMBER 27

Can the rush grow up without mire?
—Job 8:11

 HE rush is spongy and hollow, and even so is a hypocrite; there is no substance or stability in him. It is shaken to and fro in every wind just as formalists yield to every influence; for this reason the rush is not broken by the tempest, neither are hypocrites troubled with persecution. I would not willingly be a deceiver or be deceived; perhaps the text for this day may help me to try myself whether I be a hypocrite or no. The rush by nature lives in water, and owes its very existence to the mire and moisture wherein it has taken root; let the mire become dry, and the rush withers very quickly. Its greenness is absolutely dependent upon circumstances, a present abundance of water makes it flourish, and a drought destroys it at once. Is this my case? Do I only serve God when I am in good company, or when religion is profitable and respectable? Do I love the Lord only when temporal comforts are received from his hands? If so I am a base hypocrite, and like the withering rush, I shall perish when death deprives me of outward joys. But can I honestly assert that when bodily comforts have been few, and my surroundings have been rather adverse to grace than at all helpful to it, I have still held fast my integrity? then have I hope that there is genuine vital godliness in me. The rush cannot grow without mire, but plants of the Lord's right hand planting can and do flourish even in the year of drought. A godly man often grows best when his worldly circumstances decay. He who follows Christ for his bag is a Judas; they who follow for loaves and fishes are children of the devil; but they who attend him out of love to himself are his own beloved ones. Lord, let me find my life in *thee,* and not in the mire of this world's favor or gain.

DECEMBER 28

The life which I now live in the flesh,
I live by the faith of the Son of God.
—Galatians 2:20

HEN the Lord in mercy passed by and saw us in our blood, he first of all said, "Live;" and this he did *first*, because life is one of the absolutely essential things in spiritual matters, and until it be bestowed we are incapable of partaking in the things of the kingdom. Now the life which grace confers upon the saints at the moment of their quickening is none other than the life of Christ, which, like the sap from the stem, runs into us, the branches, and establishes a living connection between our souls and Jesus. Faith is the grace which perceives this union, having proceeded from it as its first fruit. It is the neck which joins the body of the Church to its all-glorious Head.

> Oh Faith! thou bond of union with the Lord,
> Is not this office thine? and thy fit name,
> In the economy of gospel types,
> And symbols apposite—the Church's *neck;*
> Identifying her in will and work
> With him ascended?

Faith lays hold upon the Lord Jesus with a firm and determined grasp. She knows his excellence and worth, and no temptation can induce her to repose her trust elsewhere; and Christ Jesus is so delighted with this heavenly grace, that he never ceases to strengthen and sustain her by the loving embrace and all-sufficient support of his eternal arms. Here, then, is established a living, sensible, and delightful union which casts forth streams of love, confidence, sympathy, complacency, and joy, whereof both the bride and bridegroom love to drink. When the soul can evidently perceive this oneness between itself and Christ, the pulse may be felt as beating for both, and the one blood as flowing through the veins of each. Then is the heart as near heaven as it can be on earth, and is prepared for the enjoyment of the most sublime and spiritual kind of fellowship.

DECEMBER 29

Hitherto hath the Lord helped us.
—1 Samuel 7:12

HE word "hitherto" seems like a hand pointing in the direction of the *past.* Twenty years or seventy, and yet, "hitherto the Lord hath helped!" Through poverty, through wealth, through sickness, through health, at home, abroad, on the land, on the sea, in honor, in dishonor, in perplexity, in joy, in trial, in triumph, in prayer, in temptation, "hitherto hath the Lord helped us!"

We delight to look down a long avenue of trees. It is delightful to gaze from end to end of the long vista, a sort of verdant temple, with its branching pillars and its arches of leaves; even so look down the long aisles of your years, at the green boughs of mercy overhead, and the strong pillars of lovingkindness and faithfulness which bear up your joys. Are there no birds in yonder branches singing? Surely there must be many, and they all sing of mercy received "hitherto."

But the word also points *forward.* For when a man gets up to a certain mark and writes "hitherto," he is not yet at the end, there is still a distance to be traversed. More trials, more joys; more temptations, more triumphs; more prayers, more answers; more toils, more strength; more fights, more victories; and then come sickness, old age, disease, death. Is it over now? No! there is more yet—awakening in Jesus' likeness, thrones, harps, songs, psalms, white raiment, the face of Jesus, the society of saints, the glory of God, the fullness of eternity, the infinity of bliss. O be of good courage, believer, and with grateful confidence raise thy "Ebenezer," for—

> He who hath helped thee hitherto
> Will help thee all thy journey through.

When read in heaven's light, how glorious and marvelous a prospect will thy "hitherto" unfold to thy grateful eye!

DECEMBER 30

Better is the end of a thing than the beginning thereof.
—Ecclesiastes 7:8

LOOK at David's Lord and Master; see his beginning. He was despised and rejected of men; a man of sorrows and acquainted with grief. Would you see the end? He sits at his Father's right hand, expecting until his enemies be made his footstool. "As he is, so are we also in this world." You must bear the cross, or you shall never wear the crown; you must wade through the mire, or you shall never walk the golden pavement. Cheer up, then, poor Christian. "Better is the end of a thing than the beginning thereof." See that creeping worm, how contemptible its appearance! It is the beginning of a thing. Mark that insect with gorgeous wings, playing in the sunbeams, sipping at the flower bells, full of happiness and life; that is the end thereof. That caterpillar is yourself, until you are wrapped up in the chrysalis of death; but when Christ shall appear you shall be like him, for you shall see him as he is. Be content to be like him, a worm and no man, that like him you may be satisfied when you wake up in his likeness. That rough-looking diamond is put upon the wheel of the lapidary. He cuts it on all sides. It loses much—much that seemed costly to itself. The king is crowned; the diadem is put upon the monarch's head with trumpet's joyful sound. A glittering ray flashes from that coronet, and it beams from that very diamond which was just now so sorely vexed by the lapidary. You may venture to compare yourself to such a diamond, for you are one of God's people; and this is the time of the cutting process. Let faith and patience have their perfect work, for in the day when the crown shall be set upon the head of the King, Eternal, Immortal, Invisible, one ray of glory shall stream from you. "They shall be mine," saith the Lord, "in the day when I make up my jewels." "Better is the end of a thing than the beginning thereof."

DECEMBER 31

*In the last day, that great day of the feast, Jesus stood and cried,
saying, "If any man thirst, let him come unto me and drink."*
—John 7:37

PATIENCE had her perfect work in the Lord Jesus, and until
the last day of the feast he pleaded with the Jews, even as on
this last day of the year he pleads with us, and waits to be
gracious to us. Admirable indeed is the longsuffering of the
Savior in bearing with some of us year after year, notwithstanding our provocations, rebellions, and resistance of his Holy Spirit.
Wonder of wonders that we are still in the land of mercy!

Pity expressed herself most plainly, for Jesus *cried,* which implies not only
the loudness of his voice, but the tenderness of his tones. He entreats us to
be reconciled. "We *pray* you," says the Apostle, "as though God did *beseech*
you by us." What earnest, pathetic terms are these! How deep must be the
love which makes the Lord weep over sinners, and like a mother woo his
children to his bosom! Surely at the call of such a cry our willing hearts will
come.

Provision is made most plenteously; all is provided that man can need to
quench his soul's thirst. To his conscience the atonement brings peace; to
his understanding the gospel brings the richest instruction; to his heart the
person of Jesus is the noblest object of affection; to the whole man the
truth as it is in Jesus supplies the purest nutriment. Thirst is terrible, but
Jesus can remove it. Though the soul were utterly famished, Jesus could restore it.

Proclamation is made most freely, that every thirsty one is welcome. No
other distinction is made but that of thirst. Whether it be the thirst of avarice, ambition, pleasure, knowledge, or rest, he who suffers from it is invited. The thirst may be bad in itself, and be no sign of grace, but rather a

mark of inordinate sin longing to be gratified with deeper draughts of lust; but it is not goodness in the creature which brings him the invitation, the Lord Jesus sends it freely, and without respect of persons.

Personality is declared most fully. The sinner must come to *Jesus*, not to works, ordinances, or doctrines, but to a personal Redeemer, who his own self bare our sins in his own body on the tree. The bleeding, dying, rising Savior, is the only star of hope to a sinner. Oh for grace to come now and drink, ere the sun sets upon the year's last day!

No waiting or preparation is so much as hinted at. Drinking represents a reception for which no fitness is required. A fool, a thief, a harlot can drink; and so sinfulness of character is no bar to the invitation to believe in Jesus. We want no golden cup, no bejeweled chalice, in which to convey the water to the thirsty; the mouth of poverty is welcome to stoop down and quaff the flowing flood. Blistered, leprous, filthy lips may touch the stream of divine love; they cannot pollute it, but shall themselves be purified. Jesus is the fount of hope. Dear reader, hear the dear Redeemer's loving voice as he cries to each of us,

If any man thirst,
let him
come unto me
and drink.

Subject Index

details of our lives, Dec. 19; *sovereign, control,* Aug. 12; over our lives, Dec. 19; *plan,* Aug. 2; *strength,* Feb. 22; *in trials,* Dec. 14; *our comfort,* Nov. 11; *our supply for service,* Oct. 5; *perfected in our weakness,* Nov. 4; *voice, hearing,* May 12; *will, confidence in,* May 23; *seeking,* Feb. 9; *Word; benefits of,* Feb. 21; *meditation on,* Oct. 12; *memorizing,* Feb. 21; *sanctified by,* July 4; *testing us,* June 12 (see also Scriptures; Truth); *wrath,* Feb. 25, Apr. 8, Oct. 15

Godliness, July 26 (see also Christlikeness; Holiness; Sanctification); *faith and holiness,* Sept. 18

Golgotha (see Calvary)

Good works, *diligence in,* Nov. 26; *faith and,* Sept. 18

Goodness, recalling God's, July 9

Gospel, Mar. 13; *human wisdom corrupts,* July 14

Gospel invitation, Apr. 8, May 6, June 6, 13, July 17, Dec. 31

Gossip, don't spread, Nov. 29

Grace, Feb. 24, Mar. 4; *abundant,* May 16, 20, Dec. 13; *ask and receive,* Dec. 13; *continual need for,* Aug. 28; *daily need for,* Feb. 14, July 16; *fullness of,* Jan. 27; *growing in,* Jan. 4; *growth in,* Dec. 23; *irresistible,* Dec. 4, 7; *law superseded by,* Sept. 4; *proven means of,* Nov. 13; *refreshing,* July 1, Sept. 13; *strengthening for service,* Oct. 5; *strong in,* Mar. 15; *sustaining,* June 16

Gratitude, Apr. 24

Grief, *end of,* Aug. 23; *over Christ's suffering,* Mar. 31, Apr. 9

Growth, Oct. 20

Grumbling, Apr. 30

Guidance, Sept. 1

Guilt, *absolved,* May 15; *cleansed by Christ's blood,* Apr. 17, 18; *remedy for,* Feb. 2

Hate, for evil, June 7

Healing, *Christ's power for,* May 7; *spiritual,* May 7, June 2

Heart, Dec. 18; *sanctified,* Nov. 18

Heaven, *assurance of,* Jan. 10; *benefits of,* July 10; *Christ's presence is,* Jan. 17; *citizens of,* July 10; *foretaste of,* July 20; *inheritance awaiting us,* Jan. 10; *longing for,* Jan. 1; *perfect communion in,* Dec. 10; *perfection of,* Aug. 9; *rest in,* Jan. 18; *unbroken fellowship in,* Dec. 19

Holiness, Apr. 6, Sept. 11; *combine with faith,* Sept. 18; *confirming genuine faith,* Dec. 15; *desiring,* June 25; *false show of,* June 23; *hope of future perfection,* Oct. 27; *perfection in,* Oct. 10; *rejoicing in,* June 14 (see also Sanctification)

Holy Spirit, *comforting,* June 19; *dependance on,* Nov. 21; *filling,* June 19; *focuses us on Christ,* June 28; *foretaste of heaven,* July 20; *grieving,* Nov. 21; *illuminating,* June 19; *in step with,* Sept. 18; *inner witness of,* Sept. 3; *repentance prompted by,* Dec. 18; *purging sin,* June 19; *regenerating,* Mar. 6, June 19; *sanctifying,* June 19

Home, God's presence in, Sept. 2

Honor, Apr. 22

Hope, *consolation in,* Jan. 29; *in God,* Jan. 9, Feb. 28; *of glory,* Feb. 28; *of heaven,* Jan. 1, Oct. 2; *rejoicing in,* May 13; *strengthened by remembrance,* Dec. 29

Human agency, Sept. 20, Oct. 8

Humility, Jan. 22, Aug. 16, 29; *growing in,* Jan. 4; *in service,* July 18; *outcome of,* May 19

Hypocrisy, June 23, 26, Aug. 8, Dec. 27; *God hates,* Nov. 14

Idleness, Nov. 26

Idolatry, avoiding, May 4

Imitation of Christ, May 17, Aug. 10

Immanuel, Dec. 25

Immortality, Jan. 18

Imputation, Apr. 3, 4, Dec. 26

Incarnation, Dec. 24, 25

Inheritance, July 20; *in Christ,* May 14, June 30; *rejoicing in our,* Sept. 27 (see also Union; Position; Standing; Calling)

Integrity, Nov. 30

Intermediate state, Apr. 20, June 29

Introspection, dangers in, June 28

Irresistible grace, Dec. 4 (see also Effectual Calling; Grace, irresistible)

Jesus, *fullness,* June 21; *precious,* June 21; *precious name,* Feb. 8 (see also Christ)

Joy, *rejoicing in the Lord,* Jan. 9; *despite trials,* June 9; *heaven's perfect,* Aug. 23; *laughing for,* June 15 (see also Rejoice)

Judgment, *final,* Apr. 8; *of the Lost,* Feb. 25; *self,* June 12

Justification, Feb. 3, May 15, Sept. 23, 25, Dec. 8, 26; *God's work complete,* July 14; *glorification follows,* May 28 (see also Imputation; Perfection)

Scripture Index

Morning by Morning

The text of this book is set in Goudy Old Style and Goudy Small Caps with Woodtype Ornaments.

Typeset in Corel Ventura Publisher.

Publisher's Preface by Patricia Klein.

Page layout, interior design, and production by Publication Resources, Inc., of Ipswich, MA.
www.pubresources.com